THE GROWTH OF LONE PARENTHOOD

THE GROWTH OF LONE PARENTHOOD

Diversity and dynamics

Karen Rowlingson and Stephen McKay

Policy Studies Institute
LONDON

PUBLISHING

The publishing imprint of the independent
POLICY STUDIES INSTITUTE
100 Park Village East, London NW1 3SR
Tel. 0171 468 0468   Fax. 0171 388 0914

ISBN 0 85374 735 0
PSI Report 850

A CIP catalogue record of this book is available from the British Library.

PSI publications are available from: Grantham Book Services Ltd,
Isaac Newton Way, Alma Park Industrial Estate, Grantham NG31 9SD

Orders: (tel) 01476 541080   (fax) 01476 541061

Books will normally be dispatched within 24 hours. Cheques should be made payable to Grantham Book Services Ltd.

Booktrade representation (UK and Eire): Broadcast Books,
24 De Montfort Road, London SW16 1LZ Tel. 0181 677 5129

PSI subscriptions are available from PSI's subscription agent:
Carfax Publishing Company Ltd, P O Box 25, Abingdon, Oxford OX14 3UE

Typeset by Policy Studies Institute
Printed in Great Britain by Page Bros, Norwich

Policy Studies Institute (PSI) is one of Europe's leading research organisations undertaking studies of economic, industrial and social policy and the workings of political institutions. The Institute is a registered charity and is not associated with any political party, pressure group or commercial interest.

PSI is a wholly owned subsidiary of the University of Westminster.

Contents

Acknowledgements

The Policy Studies Institute (PSI) was funded by the Economic and Social Research Council (ESRC) to conduct both qualitative and quantitative analysis under the ESRC Population and Household Change Programme (Award number L315253002).

The project, 'Explaining the growth of lone parenthood' was carried out by Karen Rowlingson and Stephen McKay who were responsible for the qualitative and quantitative elements respectively. The project was led by Richard Berthoud who made a substantial contribution at all stages. All three researchers were at PSI when the proposal was originally submitted to the ESRC but all subsequently moved to the university sector. Karen Rowlingson is now a Senior Lecturer in Sociology at the University of Derby and Stephen McKay is now a Research Fellow at the Centre for Research in Social Policy at Loughborough University. Richard Berthoud is now a Professor in Social Policy at the University of Essex.

We would like to thank the qualitative interviewers on this study, Louise Brown, Sarah Harkcom and Marie Kennedy. All three worked extremely hard to complete their assignments and produced data of the highest quality. The Department of Social Security also helped with the qualitative research by giving us permission to use a sample of lone parents from their records to find some of the respondents for this study.

At PSI, Reuben Ford helped at a number of key stages of the study and Sue Johnson provided, as always, an invaluable library service.

We would also like to acknowledge the comments made by Reuben Ford and Susan McRae on an early draft of this report.

Chapter 1

Background to the growth of lone parenthood

Since the 1960s, there have been significant increases in both the number and proportion of families headed by a lone mother. This trend has been accompanied by other demographic changes such as increasing cohabitation outside marriage and increasing rates of divorce. At the time of the Finer inquiry, in the early 1970s, there were fewer than 600,000 one parent families (Haskey, 1994). This number had risen to around 1.4 million in 1992 and is now over one and a half million. The incidence of lone parent households is now higher than at any time in the last two centuries and is high in comparison with most other European countries (Ermisch, 1991).

A vast array of studies have investigated different aspects of lone parenthood: some have documented the circumstances faced by lone parents and their children (Bradshaw and Millar, 1991; McKay and Marsh, 1994; Haskey, 1994; Ford and others, 1995; Marsh and others, 1997 forthcoming); others have considered the effect on children of living in a lone parent family (Burghes, 1994; Cockett and Tripp, 1994); and others have looked at the employment prospects and barriers to work facing this group (Ford, 1996; McKay and Marsh, 1994; Bryson and others, 1997). This book looks beyond the current circumstances faced by lone parents and their children to investigate the growth of lone parenthood over the last 20 or so years. Based on quantitative and qualitative research, funded by the ESRC, we document and analyse the increase in lone motherhood in Britain.

This introduction is in four parts: the first charts the growth of lone parenthood using official statistics; the second discusses some of the key themes and issues surrounding this growth; the third gives details of the quantitative and qualitative research methods used for

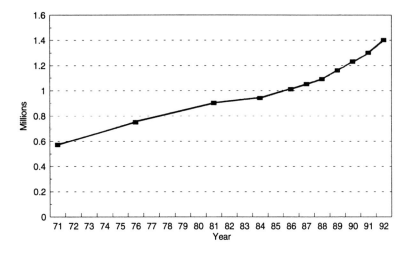

Source: Haskey, 1994

Figure 1.1 Growth in number of lone parents

this study; and the final part discusses the difficulties in defining lone parenthood as a whole and in distinguishing between different types of lone parent.

CHARTING THE GROWTH OF LONE PARENTHOOD

Starting from a very low base in the 1950s and 1960s, there has been a rapid increase in the number of lone parent families in the last 20 years (Haskey, 1994). Figure 1.1 shows that in 1971 there were 570,000 lone parents. Ten years later, this number had grown steadily to about 900,000. The rate of growth then slowed slightly over the next few years only to cross the one million mark by 1986. The rate of growth then picked up again to reach 1.4 million by 1992.

Official statistics also show that lone parenthood grew faster than the overall growth in the number of households or of the number of families[1] with children. For example, in 1971, 3 per cent of all households were lone parent households, according to the General Household Survey. By 1994, this figure had risen to 7 per cent (see Figure 1.2). Among families with dependent children, lone parents

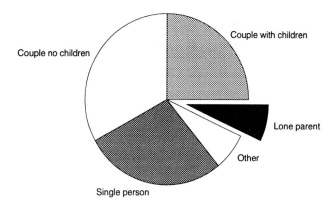

Source: GHS, 1994

Figure 1.2   Households in Britain (percentages)

accounted for 8 per cent in 1971. This figure almost tripled by 1994 so that almost a quarter (23 per cent) of all families with children in 1994 were headed by a lone parent. This means that a very significant proportion of children live in lone parent families. In 1972, 6 per cent of children lived in a lone parent family. By 1994–5, this had increased to 20 per cent (Central Statistical Office, 1996). This is smaller than the percentage of families who are lone parents because couples tend to have more children than lone parents. These figures represent the stock of lone parent families but given that family change is a dynamic process, an even larger proportion of children will experience one or more periods of living in a lone parent family.

Whilst lone parenthood is often discussed as though it were a uniform phenomenon, there are actually several different types of lone parent. Throughout the 1970s, 1980s and 1990s, about nine lone parents in ten have been women. Lone fatherhood is not a very widespread phenomenon and has become a smaller component of lone parenthood in the last 20 years. In 1971, there were 70,000 lone fathers – 13 per cent of all lone parents (Haskey, 1994). By 1991, there were 100,000 – 9 per cent of all lone parents. Lone fathers tend to be widowers or separated/divorced. By definition, they are unable

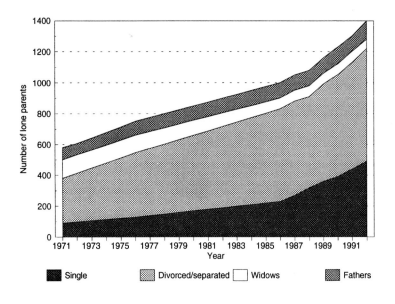

Figure 1.3 Growth of different types of lone parenthood

to become lone parents by having a baby while single, although if a partner were to die in childbirth or a couple to separate soon after a birth, then a man might find himself in similar circumstances to a single mother.

The majority of lone mothers in the 1970s, 1980s and 1990s had separated or divorced from their spouse. A smaller, though increasing group, were single, never-married women with children. It is important to note, however, that official statistics rely heavily on marital status to define lone mothers and this means that women who have had children with a cohabiting partner and then separate from him are classified as single, never-married lone mothers, along with single women who have never cohabited but have a baby. As we shall see in the rest of this report, the growth of cohabitation in the last 20 or so years therefore exaggerates the growth in the number of single women who have babies outside a steady partnership. Alongside divorced, separated and single lone mothers, a small, and shrinking, percentage over this period were women who had become lone parents through widowhood.

Figure 1.3 shows that in the 1970s, the proportion of lone parents who had separated or divorced from their spouses rose faster than other groups. In the early 1980s, separated/divorced women continued to be an increasingly important component of lone parenthood but in the late 1980s and early 1990s, the proportion of 'separated' lone parents tailed off slightly, giving way to a rapid growth in the proportion of lone parents who were 'single' never-married mothers. But, as we shall discuss later in this book, some of these never-married mothers would have been living with the father of their child(ren) in the past.

Table 1.1 summarises the annual percentage increase in the different types of lone parenthood. It shows that the largest increase between 1971 and 1986 was in the proportion of divorced mothers (up 16 per cent), but that between 1987 and 1992 the proportion of single mothers increased by 16 per cent. The table also illustrates a further complexity in that the growth of lone parenthood which was due to marital separation or divorce, was mainly due to an increase in divorces during 1971–1986, but which had almost completely reversed to being due to marital separations in 1987–1992. Clearly, in many cases, the description as divorced or separated is one of timing. Perhaps in the earlier period people divorced soon after separation and remarried a long time after whereas now they separate but delay divorce until they want to remarry.

Table 1.1   Annual average percentage increase in numbers of different types of lone parent

	1971–1986	1987–1992
Single mothers	+10	+16
Separated women	+1	+10
Divorced women	+16	+1
Widows	-2	-3
Lone fathers	+3	+4
All	+5	+7

Source: Haskey, 1994

The reasons for the growth in 'separated/divorced' lone parenthood in the 1970s and early 1980s may be different from the reasons for the growth of 'single' lone parenthood in the late 1980s and early 1990s. It

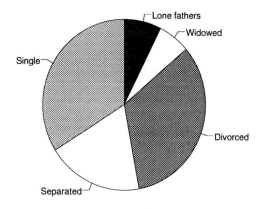

Source: Haskey, 1994

Figure 1.4   Types of lone parent families in 1992 (percentages)

is therefore important to analyse these groups separately while accepting that they belong to the same overall category of lone parent.

The number of widowed lone parents has declined since the 1970s. In 1971, there were 120,000 widowed lone parents (Haskey, 1994). By 1976, this number had fallen slightly to 115,000 and by 1986, this number had fallen more substantially to about 70,000, where it has remained, more or less, ever since (Haskey, 1994). Widowed lone parents tend to be older and have older children than other lone parents. Given that there are relatively few of them and their numbers have declined, the rest of this book concentrates on single lone mothers and separated/divorced lone mothers. Figure 1.4 summarises the different types of lone parent family in 1992.

THEMES AND ISSUES

There has been much debate about the growth of lone parenthood in terms of its implications for many aspects of social policy such as childcare, employment, housing and social security (see Bradshaw, 1989; Brown, 1988; Bryson and others, 1997; Ford, 1996; McKay and

Marsh, 1994; McKendrick, 1995; Millar, 1997; Whiteford and Bradshaw, 1994; Wilson, 1994). There has also been debate about the poverty and hardship experienced by lone parents and their children, as well as the cost to the taxpayer of funding benefits for this group (George, 1975; Millar, 1987; 1989). But, with very few exceptions (such as Ermisch, 1991), much of this debate has taken place in the absence of a fundamental understanding of the nature of that growth. This book seeks to fill that gap.

Diversity and dynamics

A number of themes and issues are raised when we map the growth of lone parenthood. This book focuses in particular on two: dynamics and diversity. We have already mentioned that it is important to look at the issue of dynamics both to see how long people remain as lone parents and also whether this length of time changes year on year. There is, however, another important dimension to the issue of dynamics, which is that lone parenthood is a process that involves a number of different stages. At each of these stages, people face different degrees of choice and constraint as to their actions.

Alongside the issue of dynamics is that of diversity, and in this book we consider the different types of lone parent that exist and how the composition of lone parenthood has been changing. As mentioned above, most lone parents are women who have separated or divorced from their spouses; but in the period since the mid to late 1980s, the number of lone parents who are single, never-married women with children, while still the minority, has increased greatly. Most of the growth in lone parenthood has involved lone mothers rather than lone fathers and more than nine in ten lone parents are women. This report therefore focuses on the growth of different types of lone motherhood.

In charting the increase in the number of lone mothers, and more particularly in seeking to explain it, we must therefore be aware of the following points:

- Lone parenthood is a diverse family type; lone parents who have separated from a partner may be very different from single women who become mothers.
- Any change in the number of lone parents may be attributed to one or both of the following:
  - more people becoming lone parents;
  - people staying as lone parents for longer.

If there are systematic reasons for the increase in the number of lone parents, these may be different for different routes into lone parenthood. External factors – such as the level of unemployment – may impact differently on how many people become single or separated lone parents. Similarly, factors which affect the duration of lone parenthood may impact differently on different types of lone parent.

Epistemological perspectives

This book aims to go beyond simple descriptions which chart the rise of lone parenthood to provide an analysis of the factors associated with this rise. In conducting research into the underlying causes of family change there are a number of different epistemological perspectives which can be applied. First, one might argue that decisions about families are the result of so many individual circumstances as to be not readily amenable to social scientific analysis. When qualitative researchers have investigated the reasons for (say) increased divorce, divorcees often mention very personal factors – such as the effects of alcohol, violence, or extra-marital affairs – rather than more general social trends such as changing levels of unemployment or female labour force participation. However, the changes in family formation that have been observed are common to so many countries that this seems an overly simplistic view. For example, simple aggregate analysis suggests strong correlation between rates of divorce and the proportion of women in employment, and between fertility rates and women's pay (Ermisch, 1995), which may be taken as at least initial evidence of some over-arching structural forces at work.

Second, people may put forward a range of rather ad hoc theories, suggesting that behavioural changes result from changes in 'attitudes', or from changes in the legal framework governing family life. It is commonly argued that divorce, lone parenthood, premarital childbearing and so on were socially stigmatised in past decades, but that changing social attitudes have made them acceptable today. Such an explanation implies that if further changes in social attitudes were to take place, this might halt or even reverse trends in family structures. This explanation may be partly helpful, but suffers from a number of flaws. It must first be explained why attitudes have moved in similar directions in many countries, although at different rates. Moreover it is not inconceivable that changes in attitudes come after changes in behaviour, and that is indeed what American research tends to suggest. In the United States it seems that attitudes towards divorce only 'softened' some time after divorce rates had climbed (Cherlin, 1992).

Alongside various ad hoc theories, there are also others encompassing theoretically-based explanations of family change. Economists, in particular, have found inspiration in the work of Nobel Laureate Gary Becker, an approach (the 'economics of the family') which applies the tools of micro-economic analysis to decisions about family formation and dissolution. It is hypothesised that people are rational, informed individuals who take steps to maximise their level of satisfaction. It is further assumed that marriage becomes more likely the greater the gains from it, which in Becker's particular formulation has much to do with the degree of complementarity between the two partners – men having a comparative advantage in production outside the home, women for production inside the home. The gains to being in a couple are reduced to the extent that men are unable to fulfil such a role, or women can be as well-off in individual units. This type of model has been applied to British data on family formation (Ermisch, 1991). Of course such a model has several critics (for example, Leibenstein, 1974) and may seem to ignore the importance of social norms and instead impose somewhat stereotypical pictures. The same type of predictions could also be consistent with alternative models. For instance there is considerable overlap with the 'social exchange' theory of marital breakdown which analyses the gains traded between marriage partners (Price and McKenry, 1988).

In the absence of a universally accepted theoretical framework, UK analysts therefore draw on a range of resources and hypotheses in a multi-dimensional approach. We review some of the key hypotheses and themes in the next section.

The role of economic and social change

Explanations for the growth of lone parenthood have revolved around a number of key economic and social changes which have occurred from about the 1970s onwards. These include:

- changes in the overall and relative employment prospects of men and women;
- changes in the availability of social security and housing;
- changes in divorce legislation and attitudes to divorce;

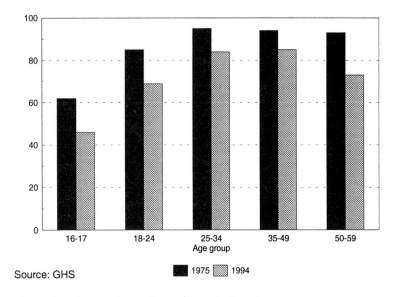

Source: GHS

Figure 1.5   Percentage of men in work, by age

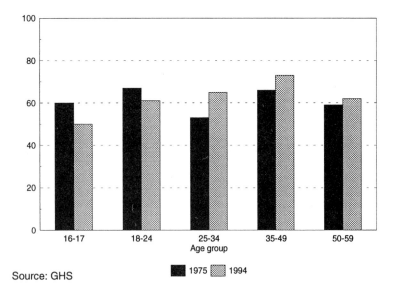

Source: GHS

Figure 1.6   Percentage of women in work, by age

- changes in sexual attitudes and behaviour, including changes in availability of contraception and abortion;
- changes in attitudes to 'the family' and the individual.

Each of these changes could have an effect on:

- the number of single women who have children;
- the number of women with children who separate from partners;
- the length of time women remain as lone parents.

We briefly review some of the current evidence for these explanations.

Employment prospects of men and women

Since the 1960s, there has been a rise in the proportion of women who are in paid employment, particularly those in the middle of their working lives. Over a similar period, there has been a dramatic decline in male employment, particularly among men at both ends of the age distribution (see Figures 1.5 and 1.6). According to the General Household Survey (Central Statistical Office, 1996), 79 per cent of men were in work in 1975 compared with 64 per cent in 1994, and the decline is much more significant for men in their teenage years and early twenties. Among women, the figures are 47 per cent in work in 1979 and 50 per cent in 1994. This is a relatively small increase given all that is claimed about increasing female labour market participation, but if we focus on women in particular age groups – in this case their late twenties and early thirties – the changes are much more pronounced. And the main changes for women have occurred among those who are married and, even more so, among those who are married and have young children. In 1977–79 only about a quarter (27 per cent) of married women with children under 5 were in paid work. By 1992–94 the proportion had risen to a half (51 per cent). Most of these women are working part-time but about a third of them are working full-time. So there have been considerable changes in the relative labour market experiences of men and women, especially in relation to family formation issues. American researchers have argued:

> The evidence suggests that the major factor underlying this growth [in lone parenthood] is the shift in the relative earnings opportunities of men and women. The roots of the shift differ by race. For whites, the shift is

traceable primarily to the dramatic increase in labour force participation of women, which accelerated after World War II and has continued ever since. By working and earning more, women have achieved greater economic independence, which has reduced the costs of being single and increased the likelihood of experiencing marital disruption. For blacks, the decline in male employment opportunities... appears to be the critical factor. Male unemployment not only reduces the economic gains from marriage; it also undermines the role of the husband as breadwinner. Hence it increases marital disruption and reduces the likelihood that formerly married mothers (or unwed pregnant teenagers) will marry. (Garfinkel and McLanahan, 1986, p167)

Changes in the labour market and in the relative economic prospects of young men and women could have various effects on the growth of lone parenthood. For example, they could:

- increase conflict within marriage as traditional gender roles break down (for example, because women are less keen to do (all the) unpaid work in the home after a day in their paid job);
- enable women in unhappy relationships to feel they have enough economic independence to leave their partners;
- increase the opportunities for both men and women to find alternative partners (at work) or to have extra-marital affairs which could lead to relationship breakdown;
- enable women in well-paid jobs to afford to have a baby without a partner;
- reduce the attraction of young single men as potential breadwinners and therefore encourage young single women to have children without cohabiting with the fathers;
- enable lone parents to support their families through employment thus reducing the need to find a partner who is a breadwinner.

This book considers each of these.

The availability of social security and housing

It has become widely believed, even among lone parents themselves, that some women become lone mothers because they know that they will receive social security and a council flat from the state for simply being a lone parent. However, there have been social security benefits for lone parents ever since the Second World War and so the existence of social security and social housing, in themselves, have not led to the growth of lone parenthood. Marsden (1969), however, has argued that although social security benefits were available to lone parents in the 1960s, there was a 'conspiracy of silence' surrounding information about their availability. There is certainly no such conspiracy today. But, regardless of levels of knowledge, what may have changed is the acceptability of claiming benefit as a lone parent and the increasing scarcity of local authority accommodation.

Although lone parents have been able to claim benefits for many years, there have been some changes in recent years which may have made a difference. For example, the 1988 Fowler reforms generally targeted benefits towards families with children and so could be seen as encouraging (lone) parenthood. Also, 16–17 year olds are only entitled to benefits in certain circumstances, one of which is being a lone parent. So lone parenthood may be one of the few options for economic independence for young teenage women.

There is also some concern in government that social security benefits for lone parents are more generous than those for couples. This apparent incentive to be a lone parent is now being addressed by reforming One Parent Benefit and the Lone Parent Premium within Income Support and other means-tested benefits. Such a view is not supported, however, by research which suggests that couples can live as cheaply (if not more cheaply) than single people (Berthoud and Ford, 1996).

As mentioned above, social housing is becoming increasingly scarce and one way of being a priority on a housing list is to have children – whether with a partner or not (although there have been some moves to change this). If we put all these changes together then lone parenthood may be a relatively attractive option for teenage women from poor backgrounds.

Comparative research (Whiteford and Bradshaw, 1994) suggests that social security systems do not affect behaviour in a way which will provide either incentives or disincentives to become a lone parent. For example, the United States has one of the highest levels of lone parenthood in the developed world and yet also has very low levels of benefits after housing costs. Whiteford and Bradshaw also suggest caution when moving from correlation to causation. They argue that the correlation between generous levels of benefits and high levels of lone parenthood in some countries does not necessarily imply that generous benefits lead to lone parenthood. It is probably more likely to be the case that countries with high levels of lone parenthood then reform their social security systems to relieve the poverty experienced by a growing group.

Hoynes (1996) reviews a number of studies in the US and concludes that: 'the evidence suggests that family structure decisions are not sensitive to financial incentives'. She makes the important point that there has been a dramatic decline in the value of Aid to Families with Dependent Children (AFDC) benefits since the 1960s – the very period during which the number of lone parent families increased and the number of births to single women increased.

Divorce law

Every time there are proposals to change (usually liberalise) divorce legislation, there is concern that this might lead to an increase in separations. The evidence shows that there was an increase in divorces in the 1970s soon after the Divorce Act came into effect in 1971. However, there had been increases in divorce in the late 1960s which led to the introduction of the Act. So increase in divorces probably led to the Act rather than vice versa. It is probably true that the Act made it easier for people who wanted to to divorce and so the number of divorces probably did also increase as a result of the law. But it is more difficult to argue that the Act would have encouraged people to separate.

In America, more than half of all the states had enacted some form of no-fault divorce legislation in the 1970s (beginning with California in 1970). Divorce statistics show, however, that the rates of divorce were no higher in these states than would be expected from the trend in states which had not reformed their laws (Wright and Stetson, 1978). So the introduction of no-fault divorce should be seen as a reaction to changing attitudes and behaviour rather than a cause of such changes.

Sexual attitudes and behaviour

There have been significant changes in sexual attitudes and behaviour over the last 20 to 30 years which may have led to an increase in lone parenthood. For example, people are starting to have sexual intercourse at younger ages and this may increase the chances that a single woman will get pregnant. However, the increasing availability of the pill from the late 1960s onwards was supposed to free women from the fear of unwanted pregnancy, so the wider incidence of premarital sex on its own cannot account for the growth in single lone parenthood. The availability of contraceptive technology, however, is not sufficient on its own to guarantee its successful use. In a similar way, the lack of contraceptive technology on its own does not necessarily lead to high fertility rates. For example, during the 1930s depression in America, birth rates plunged, despite a lack of modern contraceptive technology (Blake and Das Gupta, 1975). We can conclude, therefore, that economic conditions, social attitudes and motivations to either conceive or avoid conception, play an equally important role as the availability of contraception. A similar case can be made about the availability of abortion which became legal in 1968. As we shall see, rates of abortion are fairly high, but availability is only the first step on the road to having an abortion – social attitudes will also play a major part.

Attitudes to 'the family' and individual happiness

It has been argued that the growth of individualism can account for both the growth of the nuclear family in the 1950s and its decline in later parts of the 20th century. It is argued that the 19th century extended family was progressively destroyed by the growth of individualism which led, in the 1950s, to the promotion of a smaller family unit – the nuclear family. But the spread of the individualistic ethos did not stop there and has progressed to destroy the nuclear family, this time in favour of lone parent families and people living on their own. Individual happiness is now promoted rather than the good of the community, the extended family, or the nuclear family. Such arguments often lack a gender dimension since it was often the woman who subsumed her happiness for the good of others. The growth of individualism may therefore have combined with the development of the women's movement to shatter traditional concepts of the family.

Attitudes to lone parenthood have certainly changed over the last 50 years. But it is difficult to know whether such attitudinal changes were the cause or effect of changes in behaviour. Studies have tended to show that attitudes to the family have followed rather than led to changes in behaviour (Cherlin, 1992): for example, opinion poll data in the US have shown that attitudes to divorce did not begin to change noticeably until about 1970, whereas the increase in divorce rates began in the mid to late 1960s. But although these changes in attitude were not the initial driving force for changes in behaviour, they may have fed back into a second round, or second generation, of behavioural changes (Cherlin, 1992), which has led to a spiralling of changes.

Further evidence of the relationship between attitudes and behaviour comes from an American panel study which involved interviews with 900 young, white mothers. These women were interviewed between 1962 and 1977. Those who had originally agreed with the statement: 'when there are children in the family, parents should stay together even if they don't get along', were only slightly less likely to be separated or divorced by the end of the study period than those who had disagreed with it. So their attitudes to the family appear to have had little impact on their behaviour. However, their behaviour then had an impact on their attitudes – those who had separated or divorced by the end of the study period were much less likely to agree with the statement subsequently (Thornton, 1985).

Changing families

The main theme of this book is that the last 20 years have witnessed major changes in family structures and demographic forms. Lone parenthood must be seen in the context of more general demographic change. People are cohabiting rather than, or in advance of, getting married. They are getting married and having children at later ages than in the 1950s and 1960s. They are having fewer children and more are not having any children at all. They are also more likely to get divorced and remarry, leading to a rise in the number of stepfamilies. People are also more likely than before to live on their own, particularly if they are older people, due to the lengthening of lifespans, but there has also been a rise in the number of younger people who are single and live alone. Many of these changes have been investigated by researchers working on the ESRC's Population and Household Change Programme, of which our research was also a part (see McRae, 1998 forthcoming).

Although the main focus of this book is on the last 20 years, a longer historical perspective is informative. Some of the trends in family structures just mentioned, such as increasing age at marriage, decreasing fertility and increasing rates of separation and divorce, have been occurring since the mid-19th century (Cherlin, 1992). These trends were reversed in the 1950s, perhaps as a response to

World War II and the boom in the economy which followed it. The 1950s saw the heyday of the nuclear family with early marriage and a low rate of divorce. The growth in lone parenthood in the 1970s and 1980s therefore began from a very low historical base in the 1950s. But it soon outstripped what might have been expected even if the reversal in the trend had not occurred in the 1950s. And the growth in single lone parenthood was certainly a new historical development. We therefore need to recognise that the growth of lone parenthood was partly a continuation of longer-term trends but was also a particular phenomenon of the 1970s onwards.

Changes in family structures, accompanied by social and economic change, have led to changes in relationships within the family – between women and men, between parents and children, and between adults and their parents. The 'breadwinner/housewife' model which reached its peak in the 1950s is far less common today. This is due partly to the rise of lone parenthood but, even among couples with children, the woman is quite likely to be in employment, at least part-time. The increase in numbers of absent fathers and of stepfamilies has changed the relationships between parents and children such that biological ties have been loosened from social ties, even if organisations such as the Child Support Agency are trying to enforce obligations based on past biological associations rather than current personal and/or socio-economic associations. As we shall see in this book, the growth of lone parenthood has, in some cases, encouraged closer ties between adults and their parents (particularly women and their mothers). Ties between adults and their parents have also been changing due to the ageing of the population. People in middle age are increasingly confronting decisions about the care of their parents.

Changes in family structures and relationships have led to changes in social norms. Cohabitation was once, and not too long ago, deemed to be 'living in sin'. Divorce was seen as shameful, so too was illegitimacy. Such conventions have largely (but not wholly) changed, probably as a result of changes in behaviour rather than vice versa, but there may, again, be some feedback mechanism by which changes in behaviour lead to changes in social norms which then feed back into changes in behaviour.

Changes in family structures, relationships and norms may have major implications for the relationship between the individual, the family and the state. This is certainly true for lone parenthood. Most lone parents are living on social security and are thus financially dependent on the state. Prior to the growth of lone parenthood, most women in couples were financially dependent on the male breadwinner in their family or, if the man was unemployed, on the male benefit claimant. Thus the direct dependence of women on men (who may themselves be dependent on the state) has been replaced by a more direct dependence of women on the state. This is what concerns many commentators about the growth of lone parenthood (alongside concerns about the poverty of these women and their children). As we shall see in this book, lone parents tend to feel more independent than they had while in a couple. This is because direct dependence on the state is experienced as less oppressive than direct dependence on a man. The state may not pay much money but at least it is regular money with few conditions attached in terms of required behaviour. The theme of dependence and independence from men, parents and the state frequently recurs in this book.

The final theme to mention, which links in with the previous one, is that of individualism. We shall see, in this book, that women felt that they had both the right and the ability to make decisions based on what they saw as being best for themselves (and their children). They did not feel constrained by social norms and economic necessity to become martyrs to the ideal of a nuclear family. This was partly, as we have argued, because such norms had become fairly weak, but it was also because these women now had the opportunity to embark on life as a lone parent due to the availability and (relative) acceptability of state support and, in some cases, their own employment opportunities.

RESEARCHING LONE PARENTHOOD

We have employed a combination of both quantitative and qualitative methods to investigate the growth of lone parenthood. Such a combination of methods has enabled us both to measure the importance of various factors to the growth of lone parenthood (through the quantitative research) and to explain the mechanism by which these factors relate to the growth of lone parenthood (mainly through the qualitative research).

The use of different methods therefore allows us to explore the relationship between structural and agency factors. For example, one hypothesis is that separation and divorce is more likely if the male partner in a couple is unemployed. We have carried out quantitative analysis to see whether such a hypothesis is supported or rejected at the micro level. Our qualitative research then explored how such a factor actually affected an individual's actions.

The quantitative research considered movement in and out of lone parenthood as events, with people moving from one state to another. But these movements are experienced more as processes than events. Qualitative depth interviews therefore explored the stages people went through when becoming a lone parent and leaving lone parenthood. How much choice did people have or exercise over these changes? Who made the decisions? Which factors influenced them at each stage and how?

The qualitative research also investigated what it means to be a lone parent, as the boundaries around lone parenthood may not be clear in practice. Official definitions may differ from people's own identities (Crow and Hardey, 1992). And yet people's own identities may affect decisions about family change.

Quantitative research

Information about lone parenthood is available from a number of quantitative surveys, including the General Household Survey and the Labour Force Survey. However the most comprehensive and specific information comes from three cross-section surveys of lone parents conducted in 1989, 1991 and 1993 (respectively Bradshaw and Millar, 1991; McKay and Marsh, 1994; Ford and others, 1995). Further research continues at the Policy Studies Institute, where lone parents in the initial cross-section surveys are being followed up from time to time to investigate changes in circumstances. Whilst informative, these studies cannot be used to look at what affects routes into lone parenthood, because for that we need information on people who do not become lone parents, even though they might face similar circumstances. Furthermore, looking at a cross-section of current lone parents will have fewer short-term lone parents and more who have been lone parents for a long time, compared with a cohort of people who become lone parents at a point in time.[2] Finally, data on those currently lone parents cannot, by definition, tell us about those most likely to leave lone parenthood and the circumstances in which they might do so. The PSI research does, however, increasingly make use of follow-up data.

Alongside these bespoke cross-section surveys, there has been some analysis of more general datasets, such as the life history data from the Women and Employment Survey (WES) (Ermisch, 1991) and the British Household Panel Survey (BHPS) (Ermisch 1995). While this research is also useful, the data from WES do not provide important information about cohabitation and are now rather out-of-date, having been collected in 1980. BHPS data are far more up-to-date, but did not contain life history data in the first wave and have so far not been used to analyse duration of lone parenthood. Data from the Family and Working Lives Survey (FAWLS) would be ideal for carrying out further analysis but have only just become publicly available.

Analysis of inflow and duration is vital to understanding the increase in number of lone parents. The inflow comprises separation among couples with children (of which divorce is the major component), and births to single adults. The rate of outflow is mainly determined by the marriage and remarriage rates of this group (or gaining new non-marital partners), and by children leaving the household or growing older. For the analysis to be useful, each of a number of hypotheses must be operationalised into predictions concerning transition rates. For example, easier access to divorce may increase the inflow to lone parenthood, but has less clear implications for outflow.

The quantitative data being analysed in this report are from the Social Change and Economic Life Initiative (SCELI). The SCELI dataset consists of around 1,000 interviews carried out in each of six towns among respondents who were aged between 16 and 60 at time of interview. The questionnaire covered a range of employment and personal areas including movement in and out of paid work, dates of marriage, having children, and changes of living arrangements. Complete life and work histories were collected – to the nearest month in most cases – for the period from age 16 to date of interview. As a result, the data can be used to analyse flows into and out of different family types, including lone parenthood.

The study was based in six areas, defined by Travel-To-Work Areas.[3] This means that information about the local labour market can be included in the analysis to consider what effect the state of the labour market might have on the decision to have children, get married, or split from a partner. This has been identified as a key factor in American academic work. The attraction of this design is therefore that respondents face, in each locality, a relatively contained set of economic circumstances, which differs across the localities. More information on SCELI is contained in Appendix 2.

The main disadvantage of this dataset is its age. The data were collected in 1986. This is a strong limitation on what can be said about the recent increase in single women having children, but is less of an issue when looking at the longer-term increase in divorce and separation that has been documented.

We have analysed the SCELI data using 'event history analysis' which is a series of techniques that are used to look at the length of time it takes for something to happen. This could be the length of time before a machine fails, or the length of time that a person lives. This study is concerned with how long people spend in one family type or another, before moving into another family type. A simple guide to the technique is given in Appendix 1.

To undertake this quantitative analysis, it has to be assumed that people are in well-defined family types, that can be distinguished from all other relevant family types. The accuracy of this assumption has been explored in the qualitative work and has already been discussed in this introduction.

Qualitative research

The qualitative research involved depth interviews with 44 women who were, or had recently been, lone parents. As with the quantitative analysis, lone fathers were excluded from this research as they form a relatively small group who probably differ from lone mothers in quite systematic ways (for example, they are much more likely than women to have become lone parents through the death of a spouse). Lone fathers are certainly an interesting group but the scope of this research could not be extended to them. Widows were also excluded from the qualitative project since they are also a relatively small group of lone mothers who (usually) play no active role in becoming a lone parent. We know, from other research, that widows wait longer than separated women to re-partner. This is partly due to norms about what is considered to be a respectable period to wait before doing so but also partly due to the different social, economic and demographic profile of widowed lone parents.

The 44 depth interviews were categorised according to two criteria. The first criterion was whether a woman had become a lone parent by having her first baby while single or by separating from a partner (either a husband or a cohabiting partner) with whom she already had children. The second criterion was the current status of the interviewee. This broke down into three sub-groups. The first sub-group comprised current lone parents who had been lone parents for less than two years. These were labelled 'recent' lone parents and were included in the study because their recall of the events leading to becoming a lone parent would be fresh in their minds. The most 'recent' lone parent we interviewed was a single woman who had given birth only six weeks before, but it was much more common for these women to have become lone parents between one and two years ago.

We also interviewed some long-term lone parents: women who had been lone parents for more than two years. This group were interesting because they could tell us about how they became lone parents and also why they were still lone parents. The longest 'long-term' lone parent had been on her own for 15 years and had never lived with anyone, but it was more common for the women to have been lone parents for about 5 years. Some of the 'long-term' lone parents had been in relationships since first becoming a lone parent but, when interviewed, were on their own once again.

The final sub-group were former lone parents: women who had been lone parents in the past but had found a partner in the last two years and were now living in a couple. These women could tell us about becoming a lone parent as well as about the process of leaving lone motherhood

The respondents were found using a number of methods. The Department of Social Security agreed that we could approach a sample of lone parents who had been interviewed as part of a large-scale survey at the end of 1994. All of these women had been asked if they would be prepared to take part in further research and we selected only those who had said that they were. We knew from the analysis of this survey which respondents were single lone parents and which were separated lone parents. We then selected those in the appropriate areas (Midlands, South West and London) and sent them a letter about the study. Interviewers then approached them and found out whether they were still lone parents (and therefore long-term lone parents) or were now in a couple (and therefore former lone parents). We could not find any recent lone parents via this sample and so we had to employ a combination of methods to find this particular group.

Some snowballing was allowed so that if a respondent knew a recent lone parent the interviewer would follow up the recommendation (but only one further interview was allowed for each respondent, to avoid groups of friends being interviewed who might be very similar to each other). As well as snowballing, interviewers wrote to childcare groups and put up posters about the study in community centres and other venues where lone parents might be found.

By the end of the fieldwork, which took place in 1996, we had achieved the following interviews:

Table 1.2   Breakdown of depth interviews carried out

	Single	Separated	Total
Recent	6	6	12
Long-term	9	7	16
Former	7	9	16
Total	22	22	44

The interviews took an average of about 1.5 hours but interviews of two hours duration were not uncommon and the longest interview took five hours. The length of interview was due to the nature of the topic guide (see Appendix 4) which, more or less, amounted to a qualitative life history, covering changes of circumstances in great detail. Further information about the qualitative methods is contained in Appendix 3.

DEFINING LONE PARENTHOOD

When lone parents are discussed in the media or elsewhere, the term may seem fairly clear. But, as has been argued elsewhere (Crow and Hardey, 1992), the boundaries around lone parenthood are vague and there are several different types of lone parent.

The boundaries around lone parenthood

Lone parents are generally defined as people who are not living with a partner but are living with dependent children. This raises two main definitional questions: how do we define 'living with a partner'? And how do we define a child as being 'dependent'?

In the past, analysis of lone parenthood has relied on marital status to define lone parents. An unmarried woman with a child would therefore be classified as a lone parent even if she was living with a man. With the rise of cohabitation, such definitions became questioned and living arrangements rather than marital status became more important. Today, a single woman with a child who is 'living as married' with a man would not be considered a lone parent and a married woman with a child who is living alone would be considered a lone parent. But there is still an issue about whether cohabiting couples should be equated with married couples, as cohabitation can take a variety of forms and may mean very different things to the couple. Thus two further questions arise: how should cohabitation be defined? And how should it be treated in analysis?

A number of official guidelines have been developed to determine whether or not two people are cohabiting. According to the guidelines used by the Department of Social Security, to be deemed to be cohabiting a couple should be members of the opposite sex who are members of the same household and may be in a stable relationship. They may also have joint financial arrangements or share responsibilities for childcare. The couple may be having a sexual relationship and if a man and woman are publicly acknowledged to be 'a couple' this is likely to be taken as an indication that they are taking on the conventions of marriage. No single factor in the guidelines can be taken as conclusive proof that cohabitation is taking place (although it is impossible for a homosexual couple to be defined as a couple for benefit purposes even if they fulfil all other criteria). Each aspect of the criteria is weighed up before a final decision is reached. Similarly, the fact that a couple does not fulfil any of these criteria does not prove that they are not cohabiting. These are the official guidelines for the purposes of social security. Other official guidelines may differ, for example, some may recognise that two people of the same sex could be living as a couple.

But individuals may not agree with official guidelines for defining cohabitation and even if they do agree with them, their lives may not neatly fit into one category or another. Most survey data on lone parenthood are now based on asking someone a single question about their living arrangements. If someone who is living with a dependent child says that they are not living with a partner, then they will be categorised as a lone parent. They may say, moreover, that they are not living with a partner even if, by some of the more objective criteria shown above, they would be classified as doing so. The growth in lone parenthood, as reflected in official figures, could therefore be partly a result of people increasingly defining themselves as living without a partner even though, on more objective criteria, they may appear to have a partner.

The definition of 'dependent children' may seem unproblematic at first but there are a number of difficulties with it. At what age do children stop being dependent? Are we talking about financial dependence only or other types, such as emotional dependence? If care of a child is shared, which parent is that child dependent on? For example, if a couple split up and both have access to the child, do both parents become lone parents? Or is custody of a child more important than access? The Child Support Agency rules reflect the complexity of defining 'dependent' children (see the Child Poverty Action Group's handbook on the Child Support Agency (1996) for further information on this).

The difficulties in defining lone parenthood are, perhaps, most acute at the beginning and the end of a spell. For example, if a man leaves his wife and children, does the wife immediately become a lone parent? If he returns the next day, the woman may not consider herself to have experienced lone parenthood. Then again, if she did not know whether he would return or not, she may have begun to consider her options and to see herself in a new way. Equally, there are difficulties defining the end of lone parenthood. If a lone parent has a boyfriend who stays over with her some nights, at what point do they become a couple? This report will explore these issues in detail.

It is worth pointing out that becoming part of a couple is only one way of leaving lone parenthood. Figure 1.7 shows some of the alternatives, such as the children growing up or leaving the lone parent's home (perhaps to live with the absent parent), or the death of the lone parent. Our analysis focuses on the issue of lone parents who become part of a couple since this requires an element of choice which is mostly lacking from other exits.

Different types of lone parent

As argued earlier in this chapter, one of the main distinctions made between different types of lone parent relates to the way in which they become lone parents, such as:

- through the death of a spouse (widows/widowers);
- through separation or divorce from a partner;
- through giving birth to a baby while not living with a partner.

This is also illustrated in Figure 1.7.

Our research involved both quantitative and qualitative elements, with the latter giving much more detail about the nature of different types of lone parenthood. The SCELI survey obscured any ambiguities in people's relationships as the interviewers could only code whether a respondent said they were living with someone or they were not. Where there was any doubt, the respondent would have had to make a decision about which side of the cohabitation line they were on. This survey therefore gives the impression that cohabitation is a phenomenon with clear boundaries.

Our qualitative research tells a different story. We interviewed 44 lone parents in depth, half of whom were chosen because they had become lone parents through separation from a partner (separated lone mothers), and half of whom were chosen because they had become lone parents through having a baby while single (single lone mothers). In our classification, separated lone parents included women

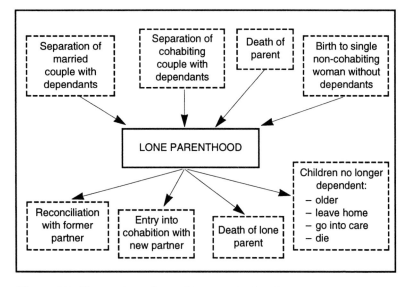

Figure 1.7 Routes in and out of lone parenthood

who had separated from a cohabiting partner as well as women who had separated (and, in some cases, divorced) from a husband.

Our distinction between separated and single lone mothers may seem fairly clear but in some cases it was not easy to decide which of these categories a lone mother should be placed into. For example, among the 22 single lone parents, eight had never lived with a man but had had regular boyfriends, including one 19 year-old woman who had been going out with her boyfriend for two years before she got pregnant. She was still living at home with her mother but her boyfriend stayed over occasionally. They continued seeing each other for some time after the birth but then separated. She was classified as 'single' even though there had been a regular man in her life. Should she have been classified as a separated lone parent? We decided not, because she had not formally lived with her boyfriend at the time she had her baby. Our definition of single lone mothers therefore depends on the woman's situation at the time she has a baby.

A further six of the 22 single lone parents had previously lived with a partner at some point in their lives. Three had lived with someone in the past but were not living with a partner at the time they conceived their baby. The other three had been living with the father of their child at the time they conceived, but then split up before the child was born and so were technically 'single' lone mothers (by our definition) because they had a baby while not living with a partner.

Table 1.3 shows the different types of single mother who took part in the depth interviews:

Table 1.3   Types of single mother interviewed

Had never cohabited	16
Had cohabited at some point previous to having their baby	6
Total	22
Had casual or no boyfriend	8
Had regular boyfriend	8
Stopped cohabiting before conceiving	3
Separated while pregnant	3
Total	22

Among the 22 separated lone mothers, there were also differences depending on the nature of the relationships they had been in. Most

(16) had been married to the partner from whom they had separated. The remaining six had been living with someone before separating and becoming a lone parent (see Table 1.4). In some of these cases, the relationships had been fairly brief and casual and so these women may have had more in common with some of the single lone mothers than some of the women who had been married many years and then separated. For example, one woman had been with her boyfriend 'on and off' before she got pregnant at the age of 19. He moved in with her at this time and was with her when she had their child, but he left soon afterwards only to return and leave a number of times before the relationship ended for the last time when she was 25. Another woman moved in with her boyfriend when she was pregnant and was with him when she had the baby, but then they separated permanently when the baby was three months old. Another woman had split up from her partner when the baby was a month old, and although her partner had been living with her he had also had a place of his own which he then moved back to. Some of the women who had separated from a cohabiting relationship had, however, been in that relationship for a number of years; three for at least four years. Perhaps the length of a relationship is a more important factor than its legal status.

Table 1.4   Types of separated lone mother interviewed

Had separated from a marriage	16
Had separated from a cohabitation	6
Total	22

In some ways, the single women who had had regular boyfriends or had separated from a cohabitation before the birth of a child were more similar to those who had separated from a cohabitation after the birth, than they were to other single mothers. For example, if we look at the average age of the women when they became lone parents there are some striking, if fairly predictable, differences (see Table 1.5). We know from previous research that single, never-married lone mothers are younger, on average, than women who separate or divorce from a husband (Ford and others, 1995). Among our in-depth interviewees, the average age of the single lone mothers was 22 years. But there was quite a difference between the ages of those who had never had a partner and those who had cohabited, at some point, in the past (19 years compared with 25 years). The average age of separated lone mothers was 29 years, far higher than that for single lone mothers. However, within this category, those who had separated from a marriage had been older than those who had separated from a cohabitation (31 years compared with 27 years). There was therefore a striking similarity between those who had separated from a cohabitation and those single lone mothers who had cohabited in the past (27 and 25). This confirms the point made earlier that these two groups have many similarities, because the distinction between cohabitation and a non-cohabiting steady boyfriend/girlfriend relationship can be a very fine one.

Table 1.5   Average age on becoming a lone parent among 44 depth interview respondents

	Mean age
Single lone mothers (22)	22
Never cohabited (16)	19
Cohabited in past (6)	25
Separated lone mothers (22)	29
Separated from a cohabitation (6)	27
Separated from a marriage (16)	31

It should be noted that the average ages of our in-depth interviewees was much younger than for lone parents in a cross-section sample. Ford and others (1995) show that the average age of a single, never-married lone parent is 29 and for a divorced lone parent is 37. The reason for the discrepancy between this and our figures is that we were looking at age on becoming a lone parent rather than their current age and, in any case, we were not interviewing a cross-section of lone parents but a particular sample of recent, long-term and former lone parents. Furthermore, our definition of 'single' is different as we only include those who were not cohabiting at the time they had their first baby.

Although there were some women who did not fit easily into the simple divide between 'single' and 'separated', others did fit the 'core' models. For example, some single women had been in very casual relationships when they conceived their first child, including Anita[4] who described her relationship with the father of her child:

I'd known him for a while but not very well, just sort of literally to talk to in the pub.

Jane's relationship with the father of her child had been short-lived and also fairly casual before she got pregnant:

[John] was in prison. I was writing to him while he was in prison, just as a friend... and at the end of March beginning of April he came out of prison and that was it, we were together and like for two or three weeks after that we split up and got back together after about a week and then a couple of weeks after that I found out I was pregnant and I was absolutely gob-smacked.

Charlotte said that she had not had a boyfriend but conceived her baby with a man who was:

a friend, that's all he was, a friend. He lives down the road, 200 yards down the road.

Equally, among the women who had separated from husbands, there were what might be thought of as typical stories of women who married, then had children and then, in some cases many years later, divorced.

We might therefore split our lone parents into four groups as in Table 1.6. At either end we have our 'core' lone parents – those who were clearly single lone mothers and those who were clearly separated or divorced from a husband. Then there are the quasi-singles who were not cohabiting but had a regular boyfriend. Finally, there were those who were quasi-separated, having cohabited before the birth of their first baby or separated from a cohabiting partner after the birth.

Table 1.6   Alternative typology of lone parents

'Core' single lone parents (no regular boyfriend)	8
Quasi-singles (not cohabiting but had regular boyfriend)	8
Quasi-separated (cohabited prior to first birth or separated from a cohabitation)	12
'Core' separated/divorced (separated/divorced from a marriage)	16

But the diversity of lone parenthood means that some women did not fit neatly into this categorisation either, so the report continues to make the more typical distinction between 'single' lone parent and 'separated' lone parent. Overall, women with children who had separated from a cohabiting partner had more in common with women who had separated from a husband than they did with single mothers. Other research, using different methods and definitions, may find that those who separate from a cohabitation had more in common with those who were single and had never cohabited (McKay and Marsh, 1994).

KEY POINTS

- There has been a dramatic increase in the incidence of lone parenthood over the last 20 or so years but little is known about why this has happened.
- In 1971, there were 570,000 lone parents. By 1994, there were 1.5 million. This growth could be due to an increase in the number of people who become lone parents or to an increase in the length of time lone parents remain in this situation.
- In 1972, 6 per cent of children were living in a lone parent family. By 1994–5, this had risen to 20 per cent.
- The growth of lone parenthood has important implications for policies relating to social security, employment, housing and childcare.
- In the 1970s and early 1980s, an increasing proportion of lone mothers were women who had separated or divorced from their husbands. By contrast, in the late 1980s, an increasing proportion were single, never-married women with children. Widows and lone fathers account for a relatively small proportion of lone parents.
- The boundaries around lone parenthood are difficult to define clearly. They depend on a definition of what it means to be 'living with a partner' and what it means to have a 'dependent' child.
- It is important to distinguish between different types of lone parent depending on how they became lone parents. But the difference between single and separated lone parents is not always great and it is unclear as to whether those who separate from a cohabitation should be placed in the former category, the latter category, or a category of their own.

- This book contains the results from quantitative and qualitative research which sought to investigate the growth of lone parenthood through an analysis of entries into, and exits from, different types of lone parenthood.

Chapter 2

Becoming a single lone mother

When lone parenthood is discussed, most concern is usually focused on young single women who have a baby outside a steady relationship. This chapter looks at how and why some women become single lone mothers. The first section documents the growth in single lone motherhood, using evidence from official statistics and previous research. The second section reports on our secondary analysis of the SCELI data. We then turn to our qualitative analysis to explore, in more depth, the process of becoming a single lone mother.

CHARTING THE GROWTH OF SINGLE LONE MOTHERHOOD

In 1971 there were 90,000 single, never-married lone mothers. By 1992 there were 490,000 (Haskey, 1994). These official figures, however, include some women who have separated from cohabiting partners but this chapter is concerned mainly with single women who have a first baby while living without a partner. We deal with those who separate from cohabitations in the next chapter, alongside those who separate from marriages.

Single women face a number of choices which may result in them becoming or not becoming lone parents (as shown in Figure 2.1). For example they will not become lone parents if they abstain from sex or have sex but successfully use contraceptives. If single women become pregnant, they will not become lone parents if they terminate the pregnancy, give the baby up for adoption or cohabit with a man. At each of these stages, women's decisions (and – but perhaps to a lesser extent – men's decisions) affect the likelihood of becoming a lone parent.

The first stage on the road to lone parenthood involves having sex. Research into sexual behaviour by SCPR in 1990/91 found that, in recent years, there has been a progressive reduction in the age at which first intercourse occurs (Wellings and others, 1994). For example, among women aged 55–59 at the time of interview, the median age at first intercourse was 21 years whereas for those aged 16–24, the median age was 17.[5] About a fifth of women first had sex with someone they knew only casually. A further half first had sex with someone with whom they were 'going steady' but not cohabiting. One in ten were engaged to be married, one in seven waited until they were married and only 1 per cent were cohabiting.

The SCPR survey also shows that just under half of all single people reported one or more acts of heterosexual sex in the last four weeks suggesting that there is a significant rate of sexual activity among single people.

It seems likely, therefore, that there has been an increase in sexual activity outside wedlock and this has occurred at the same time as attitudes to such activity have changed. The growing acceptance of premarital sex is illustrated by the fact that, in 1983, 28 per cent of the British general public said that premarital sex was always or almost always wrong. By 1991, this percentage had dropped to 19 per cent (Kiernan, 1992). Attitudes vary considerably with age: in 1991, 87 per cent of 18–24 year olds said that premarital sex was not at all wrong compared with only 29 per cent of those over 60 (Kiernan, 1992). It seems likely that most of this variation is due to generational change in attitudes although it is likely that there is also some age effect, with attitudes becoming less permissive as people get older.

These figures relate to general attitudes to premarital sex, but people may have different views about premarital sex if it occurs outside a steady relationship. They may also have different attitudes to sex between two people where one or both is under 16. So although attitudes appear to be becoming more permissive, we do not know whether certain types of sexual activity are still generally frowned upon and so discouraged.

Having sex when you are single (and female) is the first step on the road to becoming a single lone mother. But if contraception is used successfully then that outcome will not be reached. A recent NOP survey found that about a quarter (850,000) of women between the ages of 16 and 44 were having sex without using any form of contraception despite the fact that they were not trying to conceive.

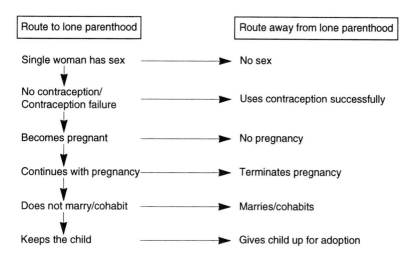

Figure 2.1 Routes into single motherhood

Among this group were approximately 150,000 16–19 year olds. These women may have been married or living with a partner and so may not have been risking lone parenthood, but it is still perhaps surprising that so many women are risking unplanned pregnancies. The survey did not provide any explanations about why this was the case although it was suggested that women were either complacent about the risks of pregnancy or just taking a chance especially at the beginning or end of a relationship (*The Guardian,* 20 September 1996).

OPCS birth statistics show that the total number of conceptions outside marriage more than doubled between 1975 and 1993 from 161,000 to 364,000. Figure 2.2 shows that there was a sharp increase between 1976 and 1979 which then tailed off over the next couple of years before another sharp increase occurred between 1983 and 1989. Since 1990, the number of extramarital conceptions has fallen for the first time since 1976.

The proportion of teenagers conceiving fell in the 1970s but started rising again in the 1980s before falling back in the early 1990s. The rise in the 1980s has been linked to the controversy which occurred in the 1980s, when Victoria Gillick questioned the morality and legal right of doctors to prescribe contraception to girls under 16 without parental consent.

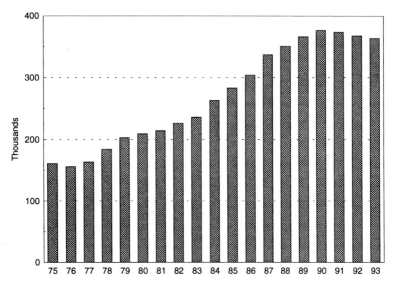

OPCS birth statistics

Figure 2.2   Number of conceptions outside marriage

Conceptions outside marriage, however, do not necessarily lead to births outside marriage. For example, the availability of abortion provides single pregnant women with a choice about whether or not to give birth and abortion is now a fairly common outcome of pregnancy. Abortion became legal in Great Britain after the 1967 Abortion Act. In the early 1970s, about two in five pregnancies among single women resulted in abortion and the overall proportion of single pregnant women who had illegitimate births actually fell from the late 1960s to the early 1970s, precisely because of the availability of abortion (Macintyre, 1977). In 1993 a third of conceptions outside marriage resulted in abortion. In the same year 87,000 teenagers in England and Wales became pregnant and in 1994 there were only 42,000 live births to teenagers. This suggests that about half of all pregnancies to teenagers (most of whom would be single) resulted in either abortion or miscarriage. From 1971 to 1991 the total number of abortions (including those performed on married as well as unmarried women) increased by 43 per cent from 133,000 to 191,000, but there has recently been a decline to 178,000 in 1993.

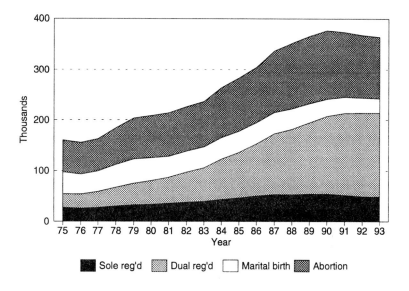

Figure 2.3   Outcomes of extramarital conceptions (numbers)

Figure 2.3 shows the increase in conceptions outside marriage and how the outcomes of these conceptions have changed from 1975 to 1993. Four different possible outcomes are shown: abortion; births within marriage; births registered by both parents; and births registered by one parent only. The number of extramarital conceptions which ended in abortions rose from 63,000 in 1975 to 122,000 in 1993. The number of births within marriage declined from 43,000 in 1975 to 28,000 in 1993. There was a huge increase in the number of births outside marriage which were registered by both parents – from 27,000 in 1975 to 165,000 in 1993. Most (probably about two-thirds) of these births would therefore have occurred within a cohabiting relationship but the rest would not. Those births registered by only one parent would almost certainly constitute the creation (or extension) of a lone parent family and there was an increase in the number of these but to a much lesser extent than the increase in dual registered births. The number of sole-registered births rose from 27,000 in 1975 to 49,000 in 1993.

Figure 2.4 uses the same data as for Figure 2.3 but this time shows the percentage of extramarital conceptions between 1975 and 1993

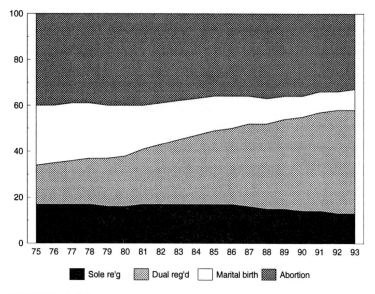

OPCS birth statistics

**Figure 2.4   Outcomes of extramarital conceptions
(as a proportion of the total)**

which ended in different ways rather than the raw numbers. Although the number of abortions rose, the rate of abortion actually fell from 40 per cent of all extramarital conceptions in 1975 to 33 per cent. Given the increase in extramarital conceptions, this means that there was both a larger number and a higher rate of extramarital conceptions which led to births. Figure 2.4 also shows that the proportion of extramarital conceptions which led to births within marriage declined substantially from 27 per cent to 8 per cent. But one of the most significant changes over the period was the proportion of births which occurred outside marriage but which were registered by both parents – from 17 per cent in 1975 to 45 per cent in 1993. The proportion of extramarital conceptions leading to births registered by the mother alone declined from 17 per cent to 13 per cent in 1993. These figures cannot be equated with the creation of lone parent families because some of these births may not be first births. But the figures do show that only just over half of all conceptions outside marriage led to births outside marriage and three-quarters of these were registered by both parents.

So the growth of single motherhood is mainly due to a very significant increase in the number of single women getting pregnant. It is not particularly due to a larger proportion of single pregnant women choosing to have their babies while still single. Single motherhood is therefore being mainly driven by greater sexual activity which occurs either without contraception or with contraception failure.

There is another option for single pregnant women which we have not considered so far. Giving up a baby for adoption is another alternative to becoming a single mother. In 1926 the Adoption of Children Act came into effect, marking a radical break with the legal tradition of inalienable parental rights. Adoption became promoted as a solution to the 'problem' of unmarried motherhood. In 1951, 4,642 babies (under one year old) who had been born outside marriage were adopted by people other than a biological parent. Over the 1950s and 1960s this figure almost tripled to 12,043 in 1968 but by 1977 it had fallen dramatically to 2,786. This reduction was probably due to improved contraception technology such as the pill and the availability of abortion as ways of avoiding illegitimate births. It is difficult to find figures on adoption but *Social Trends* (1995) states that in 1992 fewer than 1,000 babies under one year old were adopted. So adoption is very rare nowadays even though there have been recent calls to promote adoption as an alternative to single motherhood.

Previous researchers have argued (Furstenberg, 1976; Macintyre, 1977) that although single women who become pregnant form a very diverse group in terms of factors such as class, education and ethnicity, the outcomes of pregnancy differ quite remarkably between different groups – see Table 2.1. For example, according to research carried out by Macintyre (1977), cohabitation (and especially marriage) was more common in a particular Scottish city in the 1970s among those in the intermediate social classes and also increased with age up to the mid-twenties before decreasing. Abortion was more common among the higher social classes and those under 16 or over 25. Adoption was also more common among the higher social classes and lower age groups. Women who became single lone mothers were therefore more likely to be from lower social classes and less educated. They were also older, on average, than other women who got pregnant while single.

Table 2.1 **Outcomes of first pregnancies to women single at conception in a Scottish City in 1972, by occupation**

percentages

	Nurses, students, professionals	Clerical	Distributive and skilled manual	Semi- and unskilled manual
Abortion	62	28	22	19
Marriage	31	54	61	48
Illegitimate birth	7	18	17	33

Source: Macintyre, 1977

There may be a number of reasons for these differences in outcome. For example, illegitimacy in the 1970s may have been more acceptable within working-class culture than within lower-middle class culture where the requirement of respectability led to 'shotgun' marriages. As far as abortion was concerned, middle-class women may have been more knowledgeable about abortion and may have perceived higher social and economic costs to having a child, especially an illegitimate one. The womanþs parents may have also been able to afford to pay for an abortion privately. It is important, however, not to forget that the woman is only one of the people involved in this process. For example, there is evidence (Macintyre, 1977) that doctors were more likely to give an abortion to a middle-class single woman than to a working-class single woman even though working-class women who ask for abortions may be more distraught at the prospect of having a baby than their middle-class counterparts. Turning now to adoption, various studies have found that adoption is positively correlated with social class and education of the mother but inversely correlated with age (Yelloly, 1965; Weir, 1970)

The discussion about why there might be differential outcomes from single pregnancy often contain a strong moral dimension. It is sometimes argued that working-class women are more likely to keep their babies and become single parents because there is less stigma attached to them and they have less to lose personally from so doing. It may therefore be argued that these women are part of a subculture which deviates from the main value system which places great importance on marriage. But it could also be argued that working-class women are more prepared to sacrifice their personal reputation and opportunity for personal advancement for the sake of a baby.

According to this argument, working-class women are placing great importance on motherhood, which is firmly rooted in the dominant value system.

Macintyre's findings about differential outcomes are important but are now 20 years old and so it is uncertain whether they are still applicable today. She is also vague about the sample size and it is difficult to know how much confidence we can have in the findings. But Vincent (1954) came up with similar conclusions in the US, as did Illsley and Gill (1968) in Britain. Only Thompson (1956) found that conception while single was primarily a working-class social phenomenon in Aberdeen in the 1950s.

FACTORS ASSOCIATED WITH BECOMING A SINGLE LONE MOTHER

The previous section considered two key stages on the road to single motherhood: getting pregnant while single and then having a baby while still living alone. We will return to these stages when we discuss the findings from the qualitative interviews, but this section deals with the quantitative analysis. This involves reviewing the life histories of the women who took part in the SCELI survey, to see which of them gave birth to a child before they had married, and whilst they were not cohabiting.

The number of never-married mothers has been growing faster than the number of separated and divorced mothers during the past ten years or so. However the growth subsequent to the mid-1980s is not picked up with the dataset we are using in this study (collected in 1986), nor in Ermisch's earlier work using the 1980 Women and Employment Survey (Ermisch, 1991). Some more recent work has used the life-history data collected in 1992 as part of the British Household Panel Survey (Ermisch, 1995).

First births to single women

Women are at 'risk' of becoming a single mother as soon as childbearing is possible, but the data often impose a more or less arbitrary age from which information is collected. In the SCELI study, information on marital and family status is available for each month from the age of 14 years and onwards. The main alternative life path to having a premarital birth is marriage. Of course, some women will never marry nor have children, and many more had not (yet) done so at the time of the interview: these important features are taken into account in the analysis (see Appendix 1 for details about event history analysis).

Table 2.2 shows a basic analysis of women in the SCELI data, in relation to the 'event' of becoming a single lone parent. Of course, all women started as single and childless; 3,379 of them are included in the data, of which 225, about 7 per cent, became single parents, that is, had a baby before they had a partner, and before the date of the interview. The duration of the period at risk varied enormously, but on average, women had 82 months (nearly seven years) between their 14th birthday and one of the events which ended their period at risk: a baby, cohabitation, marriage or the survey itself.

Table 2.2   Women's first destinations

	Number of women	
Total number of women in sample	3,379	
Number of months 'at risk'	276,537	mean=82
Birth (while unmarried and not cohabiting)	225	6.7%
Cohabit (before marriage)	465	13.8%
Marry	2,270	67.2%
No cohabitation, marriage or children at interview date ('censored')	420	12.4%

The analysis has been limited to women who were at risk of becoming single parents after 1945, as there were very few cases among the older cohort. Those over 60 at the time of the survey were not interviewed, and this has a slight effect on the composition of the group at risk in the early years of the period (because a woman aged 61 in 1986 was 20 in 1945, and a potential lone parent). The survey was also limited to women who were at least 20 at the time of the interview. This has a rather more serious effect on the coverage of women who were teenagers in the early 1980s. A 19 year old in 1986 would not have been asked about her life history, even though she entered the age group of interest in 1981.

An important point to note about the analysis discussed in the following pages is that 'single' parenthood has been defined in its narrowest sense. The model does not include women who had a baby while living with a partner in cohabitation,[7] because they did not become lone parents. The period at risk is taken to include only the time that the women remained genuinely single. Births to cohabiting partners have become increasingly common in recent years, however, and some of them may become lone parent families if the couple split up later on. A separate section about births in cohabitation is provided later in this chapter.

Two types of information are available about each woman at risk. The first is fixed information, which does not change from month to month. These are mostly about the woman's background: the area she lived in and her parents' situation. The other type is 'time-varying': as the months and years go by, the woman's age increases; she leaves school and (perhaps) gets a job; the unemployment rate rises or falls and so on. These time-varying items require considerable complex programming and it is rare to see so many (if any) time-varying characteristics in a model, but they can clearly provide a more sensitive measure of the circumstances surrounding the birth of a baby.

Modelling the transition to single motherhood

Ideally we want to look at the impact of different characteristics considered all at the same time, to see which factors have had most impact on entries into single motherhood. This requires a multivariate setting, and the use of survival modelling techniques. In lay terms, this means using a number of items of information about each woman who had not (yet) had a baby or got married, to predict the probability of her becoming a single mother in any particular month. Each woman is considered for the month after her 14th birthday, and then the next month, and so on until she either had a baby, cohabited, got married (or was interviewed). Thus the 3,379 women in the sample were at risk for a total of 276,537 months (an average of nearly eight years per woman). The event in question (a premarital birth) occurred on 225 occasions – a hazard rate of 8.1 births per 10,000 months (or about 1 per cent per year).

Age of the woman

An important first step is to understand how the risk of single parenthood varied as women grew older. The analysis assumes that no woman had a baby before the age of 14. From 14 onwards, she was

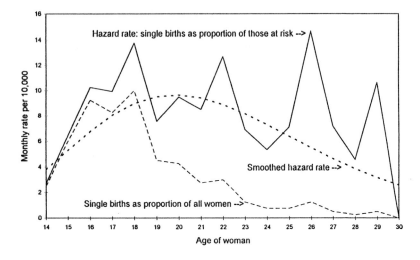

Figure 2.5 Single parenthood hazard rate, by age

'at risk'. The dashed line in Figure 2.5 shows how many members of the survey sample had a baby while single at age 14, age 15, age 16 and so on, in absolute terms. Most of the unwed mothers were teenagers at the time, and the rate of single motherhood looks very low once women were in their twenties. But that is because fewer and fewer women remained at risk by that stage; more and more of them had either married, or had already had a baby, and were therefore no longer capable of having a first premarital child.

The solid line in Figure 2.5 therefore corrects for that, by expressing the rate of single motherhood as a proportion of those who were still at risk at each age. This is the true measure of the hazard rate which will be analysed in detail over the following pages. The risk was low at the age of 14 – the monthly hazard rate was less than 3 per 10,000. It rose steadily up to 14 per 10,000 at the age of 18. The rate fluctuated across the twenties, probably as a result of chance variations in this sample. The overall trend was downwards, but the solid line nevertheless shows that the probability of becoming a single parent remained high well into the twenties – not until the age of 30 had the number of events become so small as to suggest a negligible risk.[8]

The smooth dotted curve in Figure 2.5 plots what appears to be the underlying trend of the hazard rate between the ages of 14 and 30. It is derived from the multivariate logistic regression equation, in which account has also been taken of the date at which the woman reached the age in question, and her social and ethnic background as discussed in the next section. According to this analysis the peak time when women were at greatest risk was at the age of 19.

Table 2.3 shows the full results of the analysis. The first column of the table is based on a straightforward comparison of the hazard rate between categories, using only one analysis variable at a time. The second column provides the results of a multivariate model in which logistic regression techniques were used to estimate probabilities, taking account of all the variables at once. This is designed to show the independent effect of each variable, holding all others constant. The figure R=0.xx against each heading is a measure of the power of each variable in distinguishing between women with high and low risks. None of the Rs is very large (the theoretical maximum is 1.00); this reflects the fact that even high-risk women could go many months and years before they actually became a single mother, and no analysis can expect to explain much of this variance. The sample sizes look very large because the data have been converted from a sample of people to a sample of 'person months'.

The first panel in the table records the effect of the age of the woman, already described. The smooth upwards and downwards curve in Figure 2.5 is derived from the positive sign for log age, and the negative sign for $(\log age)^2$.

Social background

One of the design features of the SCELI data is that it was based in six Travel-To-Work areas, rather than a nationally representative sample. This is an advantage in that it allows the findings to be analysed in the context of local conditions. It is a potential disadvantage in that these towns may not have been typical of the country as a whole. In practice there was not much variation in the hazard rate for single parenthood between the six locations: for the record, the lowest was in Aberdeen, the highest in Rochdale (Table 2.3, second panel). These differences had all but disappeared once the multivariate analysis had taken account of other factors, and no significant independent effect was identified. The lack of local variation among the six selected areas suggests (though it does not prove) that the precise selection of areas

Table 2.3   Hazard rates for the birth of a child before marriage, and outside cohabitation

relative risk ratios

	Simple analysis	Multivariate model	Sample size
Overall average	8.3 per 10,000		
1 Age at time			
Log of age	R=0.059	R=0.060	
(Log of age)^2	R=−0.057	R=−0.058	
2 Area	R=0.014	Not sig	
Aberdeen	0.67		51,246
Coventry	1.16		41,986
Kirkcaldy	1.34		43,091
Northampton	1.16		45,194
Rochdale	1.37		42,158
Swindon	1.00 (=7.6)		41,995
3 Father's occupation	R=0.060	Not sig	
Professional	0.37		49,825
Other non-manual	1.09		13,233
Self-employed	0.65		31,065
Technical/skilled manual	0.78		75,067
Semi/unskilled manual	1.00 (=10.4)		67,511
Not known	1.23		28,969
4 Mother's occupation	R=0.014	Not sig	
Professional	0.48		15,433
Non-manual	0.66		61,092
Self-employed	0.34		3,155
Technical/skilled manual	0.89		37,187
Semi/unskilled manual	1.00 (=9.4)		75,546
Not known	1.09		73,257
5 Tenure at age 14	R=0.094	R=0.091	
Owner-occupier	1.00 (=9.4)	1.00	108,816
Public rented	2.29	2.46	102,772
Private rented	0.90	1.33	33,790
Others	1.14	1.39	20,292
6 Ethnic group	R=0.034	R=0.043	
White	1.00 (=8.3)	1.00	258,322
Asian	0.91	1.14	5,262
West Indian	4.83	5.9	1,995
Not known	0.00	0.04	1,091

continued

	Simple analysis	Multivariate model	Sample size
			relative risk ratios
7 Current housing	R=0.123	R=0.097	
Lives with parents	1.00 (=7.6)	1.00	227,205
Current owner	0.43	2.06	6,168
Current social tenant	6.13	8.5	4,311
Current private tenant	1.07	2.4	11,062
Others/DK	1.56	3.89	16,924
8 Current activity	R=0.155	R=0.136	
Working	1.00 (=9.4)	1.00	148,783
Unemployed	4.45	3.49	4,776
Sick or disabled	1.43	1.24	744
FT education	0.5	0.56	87,780
FT housewife	4.86	7.28	2,403
Not known	0.5	0.51	21,184
9 Local unemployment rate	R=0.081	Not sig	
Up to 2.5%	0.51		183,215
2.5–5.0%	0.81		27,140
5.1–7.5%	0.7		28,267
7.6–10%	1.13		9,373
10.1–12.5%	1.00 (=13.2)		5,289
12.6–15.0%	1.36		4,460
15.1% and higher	1.84		6,986

Notes:
1   In each group, one element has been chosen as the 'reference category' and assigned a relative risk of 1.0; the hazards in other categories are expressed as a ratio to that one. The actual risk (per 10,000) in the reference category is given in brackets. In the second panel of the table, for example, the risk of single motherhood in Swindon was 7.6 per 10,000. In Aberdeen it was two-thirds that.
2   All 14 and 15 years olds remained in full-time education, and the overwhelming majority were living with their own parents. The multivariate model including these variables ('current housing' and 'current activity') was therefore confined to women aged 16 or over.

was not crucial, and that the results may be broadly representative of Britain as a whole.

Other studies have suggested that women from disadvantaged backgrounds were much more likely to have children while unmarried, and/or as teenagers, than others (Ermisch, 1991; Garfinkel and McLanahan, 1986). Analysis of the SCELI data using a measure of social class based on the woman's father's occupation is consistent with this (Table 2.3, third panel): the risk was lowest among women whose father had been in a professional occupation, and high for those from a semi- or unskilled manual background. The high rate of single parenthood among women whose father's occupation was not known might be a further indicator of social disadvantage, as a number of these fathers may have been long-term unemployed; other members of this category may have been lone parent families (that is, there was no father in the household).

Using the young woman's mother's occupation produced a similar, though rather weaker range of variation between professional and semi/unskilled workers' families (fourth panel).

Another indicator of socio-economic position is housing tenure. Indeed it has been argued (Marsh and McKay, 1993) that the cleavage between owner-occupiers and council tenants is now more important than occupational class as a measure of the divisions in British society. That contention is supported by the results of this analysis. Women whose families had been social tenants when they were 14 were more than twice as likely to become a single parent as those from other housing backgrounds (Table 2.3, fifth panel, and Figure 2.6). Not only was this variable more powerful than either mother's occupation or father's occupation; once all three had been included in the same analysis, tenure at age 14 captured all the effect of disadvantaged background, and the occupational variables no longer had any significant influence on the risk of single parenthood.

Another characteristic which women inherited from their family of origin was their ethnic group. There is very strong evidence from cross-sectional surveys that the main minorities in Britain adopt very different family formation – different not only from the white population, but also from each other. The Fourth National Survey of Ethnic Minorities (Modood, Berthoud and others, 1997), for example, showed that Caribbean men and women had low rates of marriage: more than five times as many women of Caribbean origin as white women were bringing up children on their own, having never been (formally) married. In contrast, Asians placed a high priority on marriage, and very few single parents were identified.

Ethnic minorities are quite highly concentrated in certain large cities (Ratcliffe, 1996) and a sample of six free-standing towns, such as SCELI, is a long way from providing a suitable vehicle for studying ethnic variations in any depth. The analysis suggests that the risk of single motherhood was five times as high for West Indian women as for whites (Table 2.3 sixth panel, and Figure 2.7). This is based on

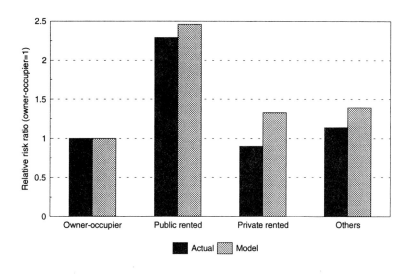

Figure 2.6   Risk of single motherhood, by housing tenure at age 14

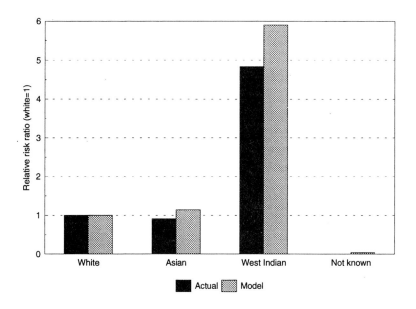

Figure 2.7   Risk of single motherhood, by ethnicity

only five births to West Indian mothers in the sample, but is nevertheless highly significant, statistically; and it stood up to multivariate analysis. Because of the nature of the SCELI design, we would not place much weight on this finding, on its own. But it is so consistent with the results of other research that it can be believed with some confidence.

The woman's situation at the time

The influences discussed in the previous section were all fixed: once the woman in question had reached 14, her parental background remained constant during the following years. The analysis now turns to variable factors, so that it is possible to follow variations in risk as the women completed their education, looked for work, and left the parental home. It is important to think through the implications of any variations likely to be identified here. Some aspects of the woman's situation at any particular time can be considered to have been the outcome of external influences upon her. This is undoubtedly the case for the local rate of unemployment, which is outside the control of individuals. It may also be partly the case for more personal aspects of the woman's situation. The time at which she left home could be a consequence of her family background, and/or of the availability of independent accommodation. Decisions about leaving school and/or getting a job might be affected by the quality of local educational services, and the availability of suitable employment. To that extent, these factors might be considered independent influences on the probability of becoming a single mother. On the other hand, leaving home and/or school might be influenced by factors more directly associated with the woman's risk of single parenthood – her attitudes to parental authority or social convention might influence all three sets of choices. To that extent, associations between her situation and her hazard rate would not necessarily indicate causal influences.

For these measures of the young woman's situation, we certainly do not want to know what she was doing after having a baby; nor even at the same time as that event. The comparison should be made in relation to her situation at the time she was taking actions or decisions which would determine whether she would have a baby – between nine months and six months beforehand (on the assumption that decisions about abortion would mostly be made during that period). The definition of 'current situation' was therefore based on her

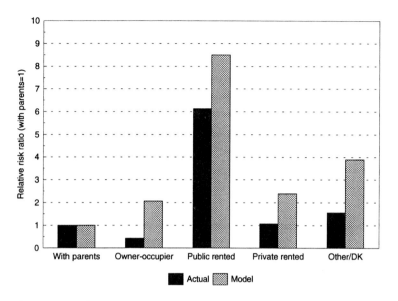

Figure 2.8   Risk of single motherhood, by housing situation
at the time

circumstances nine months prior to the month being analysed as at risk.

There were certainly some strong associations. Only a small proportion of women were living away from their parents and in council housing at any time; but they had a very high risk of single parenthood: six times the rate of women still living with their parents (Table 2.3 seventh panel and Figure 2.8). This rose to eight times when 14 and 15 years olds (almost all at home) were excluded and other factors had been taken into account. The multivariate analysis suggested that the risk of single parenthood was high for all women who no longer lived at home, whatever their destination, though the social tenants still stood out as having a higher risk than those in other forms of independent accommodation.

Relatively few women who remained in full-time education had a premarital baby (Table 2.3 eighth panel and Figure 2.9). The risk was significantly higher for those who had left school and taken a job. But it was exceptionally high for women who were unemployed or considered themselves to be a 'housewife'. All these findings were just as true when other factors such as age and background had been taken into account.

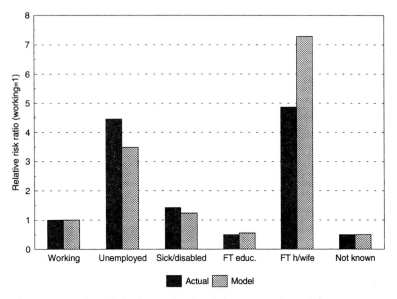

Figure 2.9   Risk of single motherhood, by economic activity (time varying)

Although these situational factors were very strongly associated with women's relative rates of risk, it should be noted that very few women were in the situations associated with high risks, so they did not account for a very large proportion of all episodes of single parenthood. There were 223 pre-marital births in the sample. Of these, 20 were to women who had been living away from their parents in social housing; 31 were to women who were unemployed or 'housewives' at the time. So most babies were not born into these very high-risk situations.

One frequently discussed hypothesis is that young women who perceive themselves to have reasonable job prospects would take many steps to avoid lone parenthood, but that those who foresee a long period out of work or in a routine poorly paid occupation might be more ready to accept the alternative role of motherhood. We therefore looked up the rate of unemployment in each of the SCELI study areas in each year under consideration.[9] It is important to remember that an individual's chances of employment are far more governed by her own educational and training experiences, and perhaps by her motivation and job-search activities, than simply by the availability of jobs in the local economy. Second, the overall unemployment rate might not be a very precise indicator of opportunities available to one particular sub-group of the labour force – in this case, young women. Nevertheless, we were interested to know whether the risk of single motherhood was higher in times and in places of serious unemployment than in times and places when the prospects for work were better.

At first sight, the hypothesis appeared to be confirmed. The final panel of Table 2.3 shows that the risk of having a premarital birth was more than three times as high in times and places when unemployment was over 15 per cent, compared with when it was less than 2.5 per cent. On the face of it, this was one of the most important associations identified in the course of the analysis.

Of course the national rate of unemployment rose over the period under consideration. The number unemployed in the early 1980s was considerably more than the number in the late 1940s and 1950s. Could this be the explanation for the growth of single parenthood – higher risks in later years because of the rising rate of unemployment? On the contrary: when the hazard rate was analysed by unemployment rate within time periods, it was the latter which stood up; the association with unemployment disappeared. Thus the results for unemployment in Table 2.3 are an artefact of the time period over which the data were collected.

Trends over time

Until the last paragraph, all of this analysis has appeared to assume that the hazard rate was fixed over the whole period under consideration, from 1945 to 1984. In fact, of course, it changed substantially over that period, and the title of this book – *The Growth of Lone Parenthood* – emphasises our concern to describe, analyse and, if possible, explain the changes over time.

One technical question was, how to measure 'time'. The analysis was tried two ways. The first compared changes in women's hazard rate between cohorts – defined on the basis of the year they reached the age of 16. The second used the date of the potential event as the basis for comparison. It was not possible to include both of these definitions of time in the same model, as well as age, because if you know any two of these three items of information, the third is determined. Clearly, cohort and current date were strongly correlated with each other, but the date of the month in question gave slightly more robust results. It is also more easily related to outside events such as birth statistics, public debates about morality or the legalisation of abortion.

With 223 births spread over 40 years, the survey data cannot be precise about short-term trends in the way that national statistics can. Figure 2.9 shows the monthly hazard rate recorded for each calendar year. That is, 12 observations of monthly rates have been averaged to provide each point on the chart. Take no notice of the fluctuations from year to year, which have been caused by sampling errors. It is the trends that matter. They seem to have moved over four phases, indicated by the different formats in which the line has been plotted:

- Over the late 1940s and the 1950s, the hazard rate was low and stable. There was no apparent increase in the number of premarital births.
- During the 1960s there was a strong upward trend. The changing attitudes to sexual morality in the 'swinging sixties' really did seem to make a difference. It was at the end of this period that public concern about the number of one parent families (of all kinds) led to the setting up of the Finer Committee which advised on social policy for this growing group (Finer, 1973).
- During the 1970s though, there was a strong downward trend. This seems to contradict a popular view that the number of single births has been rising inexorably for decades. The finding falls into place when two considerations are taken into account. First, the overall birth rate for all women had been falling since about 1960; it was only among teenagers that fertility rates held up, and the downward trend in the 1970s could be seen as teenagers falling in with the pattern of their elders (Ermisch, 1983). Second, legal abortions became available for the first time after the 1967 Abortion Act and, as our earlier analysis of national statistics (Figure 2.4) shows, a large proportion of premarital conceptions in the 1970s were ending in abortion rather than leading to the birth of a child. For example, 40 per cent ended in abortion in 1975.
- The SCELI-based figures for the early 1980s appear to show that the downward trend ceased. The wild fluctuations at the right of the figure are, however, an indication of the unreliability of the data over the end of the observation period: the sample sizes were very small, and excluded young teenagers. Statistics on the number of single-registered births suggest rather a stable pattern at that time.

- Our data do not cover the late 1980s or 1990s and so we cannot
  show the inflow rates during the most recent period. The British
  Household Panel Survey (Ermisch, 1995) indicated that the
  proportion of women who had a first baby before they married or
  started living with a man increased from 5 per cent of those born
  between 1950 and 1962, to 8.5 per cent of those born after 1962
  (whose period of risk would have fallen mainly in the 1980s). This
  suggests that the inflow may have increased again.

If the early 1980s are ignored for the moment, the results of the
SCELI analysis do not suggest a steady increase in the rate of inflow
into single parenthood. A strong rise in the 1960s was followed by a
clear fall in the 1970s. The fact remains, though, that the hazard rate
was higher in the second half of the period under review than in the
first. Before 1967 only three annual observations exceeded 8 per
10,000; after 1967 only three observations were below 8 per 10,000.
The overall average in the first half of the period was 4.8; in the
second half, it had more than doubled to 12.4 per 10,000.

Table 2.4 shows that the increase was especially marked among
'under-age' mothers aged 14 and 15 – the risk for them was four times
as great after 1967 as it had been before, though they remained less
likely to have a premarital child than their elders.

**Table 2.4   Increase in the risk of single motherhood, by age of
woman**

	monthly hazard rate, per 10,000		
	1945–1966	1967–1984	Ratio
Age 14 or 15	2.0	7.9	3.9
Age 16 to 18	6.7	16.2	2.4
Age 19 to 21	4.8	11.9	2.5
Age 22 to 30	5.4	11.4	2.1
Sample size (woman-months at risk)	138,754	126,916	

The crucial question is: how far do the associations identified between
single parenthood and the other factors included in this analysis
explain the trends over time? As explained, one hypothesis was that
the rise in unemployment might have been associated with the growth
in single motherhood, but it turned out that the apparent link with
unemployment was the result of an increase in both phenomena over

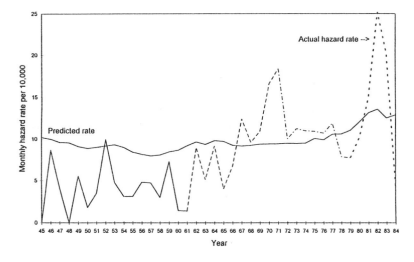

Figure 2.10   Hazard rate of single motherhood, 1945–1984

the same period. The associations with social background, ethnicity and current situation were genuine, though: could the changes in the hazard rate be caused by changes in these underlying social factors?

The full multivariate model, shown in Table 2.3, was used to predict what the hazard rate would have been in each year, if it had been determined solely by the background factors in the model. The results are plotted on the smoother flattish line in Figure 2.10. Clearly the underlying social factors were much less subject to sampling error than the hazard rate itself, so that the predicted rate was more stable from year to year than the actual rate. Nor did the predicted rate change much over long periods. There is a suggestion of a fall between 1945 and about 1958; followed by a very slow rate of increase; at the very end of the period, there seems to have been a slightly faster rise in the underlying conditions which have been found to affect single motherhood. You could just about argue that the expected rate was higher in the second half of the period than it was in the first (the average prediction between 1967 and 1984 was 1.5 per 10,000 higher than it had been between 1945 and 1966). The increase in the actual hazard rate was 7.6 per 10,000. It could be said, therefore, that about a fifth of the actual growth had been explained by the multivariate analysis. But a more rigorous inspection of the relationships between the two trends would suggest that the rises (and falls) in lone parenthood were independent of the social conditions which have been measured by the SCELI data.

Births in cohabitation

The analysis of the SCELI survey so far in this section has been concerned with women who were single in the strictest sense of the word – not only unmarried, but also not living with a man as a partner. These are the ones who, if they had a baby, become single parents.

Another group of potential interest are women who had babies while cohabiting, but outside marriage. These births are 'illegitimate' in the formal sense laid down by the church and the state, but they probably do not constitute one parent families in the eyes of the parents, the child or, increasingly, of the general public. Nevertheless, some of the cohabitations break down at some stage, and these then create one parent families – formally classified as 'single' but perhaps closer to 'separated'. The question of whether cohabiting parents do separate is discussed in the next chapter. At this stage, though, it is useful to compare what the SCELI survey had to say about births to cohabiting mothers, with the single mothers already described.

There were 225 first births to fully 'single' mothers and another 45 first births to cohabiting mothers over the period. Only one of these was below the age of 16 at the time, but the cohabiting mothers were quite strongly concentrated among 16–21 years olds – 87 per cent of them, compared with 69 per cent of the single mothers. Married mothers tend to be spread more widely across the age range, and to this extent the cohabitors were rather similar to the single women. Another similarity was that 71 per cent of the cohabitors, compared with 59 per cent of the single women, had been living in council housing at the age of 14, and therefore may have come from less well-off backgrounds. But whereas three-quarters (77 per cent) of the single mothers were still living with their parents at the time of the event, few (16 per cent) of the cohabitors were doing so – they were living independently with their partners. They were just as likely to be unemployed, more likely to be a 'housewife' but less likely to be in full-time education, compared with the single mothers. But that left a very similar proportion – 60 compared with 63 per cent – in work at the time.

The most noticeable feature of the births in cohabitation was their timing. None were reported before 1956. They accounted for one tenth of the events of interest in the middle of the period; but a quarter of them by the end of the period (Table 2.5). The registration statistics reviewed earlier in this chapter suggest that they may now outnumber the genuinely 'single' births.

Table 2.5   Births to cohabiting mothers

	1945–1955	1956–1974	1975–1985
Births to single mothers	25	115	85
Births to cohabiting mothers	0	14	31
Cohabiting as percentage of total	nil	11%	27%

The quantitative research has shown that a number of factors are correlated with single lone parenthood, such as socio-economic background, ethnicity and the woman's current situation. But the analysis does not explain *how* these factors lead to the creation of lone parenthood. One of the limits of quantitative analysis is that it treats entry into lone parenthood as a single, discrete event, whereas in practice it is a complex process with various stages. The next section of this chapter draws on the qualitative research to explore the nature of the process.

GETTING PREGNANT

The two main stages on the road towards 'single' lone parenthood are getting pregnant and then remaining single during and after pregnancy. Figures cited earlier in this chapter suggest that increases in conceptions outside marriage are primarily fuelling the growth in single motherhood, rather than increases in the proportion of such pregnancies which end in lone parenthood. Our quantitative research suggested that age, socio-economic background, housing tenure and ethnicity were all factors which affected the risk of single motherhood. As argued by Macintyre (1977), the socio-economic and ethnic background of single lone mothers may have much more to do with what happens after single women become pregnant rather than before. So the variables highlighted in the quantitative research (socio-economic background and unemployment) may be linked more to why some single pregnant women have babies but may be less relevant to why they got pregnant in the first place. However, there may be some effect on both processes. Women from poor backgrounds who live in poor areas may feel that they have less to lose by getting pregnant and so may be more likely to have sex outside marriage. Once pregnant, they may be less concerned about any perceived social and economic costs (such as stigma and lost earnings).

One drawback with the qualitative material is that all of the 22 women we are focusing on in this chapter eventually became single lone parents and so we have not specifically interviewed any single women who avoided lone parenthood through: celibacy; successful use of contraception; termination; adoption; or cohabitation. We therefore draw on other studies which have included such women (Furstenberg, 1976; Macintyre, 1977). However, we do have some women among our separated lone mothers who cohabited or married only after they became pregnant, while some of our single lone mothers had previously had terminations and so avoided, at that time, becoming a lone mother. We are, in other words, able to address the issues from many angles.

One final point before we embark on the qualitative analysis is that, although ethnicity is a key issue in relation to lone motherhood, our research was not designed to cover this issue in depth. However, there were two black single mothers in the sample and one white single mother who had a black boyfriend. Where ethnicity is shown to be an important factor, this is commented on in the text.

The sexual relationships and living arrangements of single women

There is a popular view that single lone mothers are young women (usually teenagers) who deliberately get pregnant despite being outside a regular relationship, but there was great variety in the types of sexual relationships our interviewees had been having at the time they got pregnant. Some had been in regular relationships and had even cohabited prior to the pregnancy or birth. In the next section, we distinguish four categories of relationship among our single lone mothers (see also Table 1.3 in Chapter 1). It is important to understand the situation lone parents are in at the time they get pregnant because this affects their decisions about continuing the pregnancy and/or cohabiting with the father.

Never cohabited, no regular boyfriend (eight women)

The women in this group could be thought of as the 'core' of single lone mothers. They had the lowest average age of any of the other groups of lone mothers (19) and included two women who were 15 at the time they became lone mothers. Many of the women in this group had casual boyfriends and the difference between a casual and a regular boyfriend depended on how secure the woman felt about the relationship and the degree of commitment within the relationship. Sexual exclusivity also played a part in the distinction between regular and casual relationships as people in casual relationships accepted that their partner might have sex with other people. Women with regular boyfriends did not sanction sex outside that relationship.

One woman, however, said that there had been 'no relationship' between her and the father of her child. This woman had become a lone parent only six weeks before the interview took place. She was distressed by any mention of the father of her child, saying that she did not want to talk about him and only her parents knew who he was. As we shall see later, she was the only woman in the study who had seriously considered giving up her baby for adoption. This case highlights the fact that women can become pregnant without having any kind of 'boyfriend', for example, if they have sex on a single occasion with a man that they hardly know.

Four of the eight were either of school age or in education. For example, Kelly was 15 and still at school when she became a lone mother. She had met her boyfriend, who was a neighbour, when she was 13. He was her first boyfriend, although they were not seeing each other regularly. He was two years older than her and by the time she got pregnant, he had left school and become a manual worker. The relationship was fairly casual:

> it wasn't like we was matched together, he was either going off with other women or making his own rules. He'd not got any responsibility whatsoever.

Julie was also 15 when she got pregnant but she was not at school at the time as she had been expelled the previous year. The father in this case was 23 and was a friend of her older brother. They were not seeing each other regularly.

The remaining women in this group had been working in fairly routine manual or non-manual jobs – one on a production line in a factory, one as an office clerk, one as a carer in a nursing home. All three were still living at home. Jane had first got to know the father of her child when he was in prison and she became his pen pal. Their relationship had been 'on and off' for the two months before she got pregnant.

Heather was 19 when she got pregnant by a man with whom she had had a casual relationship for a couple of years:

> [He was] just somebody who used to drink in the pubs where we used to drink and it was an ongoing thing for a few years really, just a casual thing... I knew that when I got pregnant it was *my* problem.

Never cohabited, regular boyfriend (eight women)

Eight women had been in regular relationships with a boyfriend but were not cohabiting at the time they got pregnant and had their baby. Jenny was a typical example. She had been 'going out' with her boyfriend for two years before she got pregnant at the age of 19. It had started off as a casual relationship but then became more regular. She still lived at home and he stayed over at her place sometimes. Another woman, Carol, had been in a regular relationship with a married man for about seven years from the time she was 18 until she became a lone mother at the age of 26.

In some cases, the relationship appeared to be a very committed one. Barbara had met her boyfriend when she was 18. One year later they had bought a house together which they planned to renovate before they moved. The renovation took four years but before they moved in Barbara became pregnant. Although it might seem unlikely that this woman would become a lone parent, she ended the relationship while she was pregnant. She therefore bears many similarities to the women who will be discussed later who split up from a partner while pregnant, but this woman had never actually cohabited. This case illustrates the difficulty of placing women into simple categories because of the ambiguities when defining partnerships as argued in Chapter 2.

Cohabited in past, separated before getting pregnant (three women)

Two of the three women in this group had been cohabiting with the father of their child at some time in the past but had split up and then embarked on a more casual relationship with their former partner. For example, Elise had moved to London and had been living in a squat where she met and began to cohabit with her boyfriend. She moved back to her home town one year later and although he also moved there, they did not live together:

> [I was] living in a row of squats [in London]... but then I met [the baby's father] and he was living in a horrible tower block... so I was sort of hanging around with him and living with him... when I got back to [my home town] I suddenly thought, 'I don't know if I want to be with this person'.

Diane had cohabited with the baby's father for a while when she was 18 but then moved in with a female friend and just saw him from time to time:

> We lived together in [a village] first, then we split up and moved to [a city] and we were still going out with each other We were on and off for about a year... while I lived with a girlfriend and then we'd actually split up solidly for a month and then I found out I was pregnant.

The last woman in this group, Anita, had previously been in a serious, long-term relationship with a man but ended it when it became clear that he never wanted to have children. She was the oldest woman to become a single lone mother when she got pregnant after sex with a casual boyfriend at the age of 33. As we shall see later, this woman was very unusual in that she consciously planned to become a single lone mother.

Cohabited in past, separated when pregnant (three women)

This group of women had many similarities to those women who became lone mothers by separating from a partner with whom they already had children. Alison had been living with her partner for over two years when she got pregnant. They had always faced difficulties in their relationship, with arguments over money. The news of an unplanned pregnancy accentuated these difficulties and eventually led to the end of the relationship:

> He'd been drawing out the bank and there wasn't enough money for the mortgage and so on. Plus the fact that he was a drinker, not a heavy drinker but he used to drink and when he'd had a drink he used to hit

me... I got thrown down the stairs when I was pregnant – I had to go to hospital.

Jacqui had been living with someone with whom she had a very good relationship before she got pregnant:

There was nothing he wouldn't do for me and we went everywhere together... and we wanted to do lots of things together.

But she was strongly disliked by his mother because she was much older than her partner and was a divorcee:

I was the older divorced woman taking away her little son and it was making him live in sin.

When she fell pregnant unexpectedly, her partner was not very pleased and his parents even less so, apparently believing that she had got pregnant deliberately to 'trap' him. They split up when she was six months pregnant.

In the final case in this category, Andrea had been married for 12 years before getting pregnant at the age of 34. She had previously had several problems both getting pregnant and completing a pregnancy successfully. Her husband had frequently been involved in extramarital affairs but promised that he would stop these once they had a baby. She was happy with this promise but after she got pregnant she found out that he was seeing someone else and so she asked him to leave before the baby was born and he did, albeit reluctantly:

He'd always had affairs for years and years and years but we always said when [our baby] came along – because it took us seven years to get him – and I just said, 'right, enough's enough, it's got to stop, you know, you've had your free time, you've had your play around'... [but] he was having an affair with one of the girls in [a local village] so I kicked him out six weeks before [the baby] was due.

Both Jacqui and Andrea had been married in the past and so would not count as 'single' lone mothers in official statistics, but both were living on their own when they had their first child and so are defined as single lone mothers for the purposes of this study.

Contraception use

Having sex when you are single is the first step on the road to becoming a single lone parent. But if contraception is used successfully then that outcome will not be reached. This section explores why contraception was not used or not used successfully among the lone parents in our study.

Non-use of contraception

Nine of the 22 single mothers had not used contraception at the time they conceived. Only two of these women said that they had deliberately set out to become pregnant. Andrea had been trying unsuccessfully for seven years to conceive and bear a child with her husband. And Anita had split up from a long-term partner because he did not want children and then started having sex with another man without using contraception:

> I'd had my coil taken out when the other relationship finished and... I thought [my new sexual partner] knew the situation. I thought he was aware of the fact that I wanted a baby... I had said as much, presumably he just hadn't taken it in.

The remaining seven, however, had not wanted to get pregnant and so it may seem irrational for them not to have used contraception. One of the two 15 year olds had not used contraception. She explained that:

> It wasn't lack of knowing anything because I was always taught the rules, the books, the birds and the bees and everything from my mum and dad... I wasn't [using any form of contraception] because I didn't expect any part in a sexual relationship.

Even though this young woman was having sex, she did not identify herself as a sexually active woman who might use contraception and her 17 year-old boyfriend did not mention the subject to her. She had been unwilling to prepare herself for sex because this might have identified her as promiscuous.

Two women said that they had sometimes used condoms but, again, had not done so on the occasion they got pregnant. As one explained:

> We did used to use them but not at this particular time... you say to yourself, 'no it won't happen to you'.

Two points are worth emphasising about this example because they are common to many other women in the study. First, that a method of contraception was used sometimes but not always. And second, that the woman thought that the longer she had sex without contraception and failed to get pregnant, the less likely she would be to get pregnant on the next occasion. As she explained further:

> I didn't think I was capable [of getting pregnant], does that sound silly? But when you're 16 you just... it was very much a trust thing with me.

This woman had been on the pill but had experienced side effects and so stopped taking it 'and then we didn't use anything.' When the interviewer asked her if she had considered using condoms, the woman replied: 'I didn't know what condoms were.' This was in 1993 when she was 16.

One woman got pregnant the first time she had sex with her boyfriend. She considered herself very unlucky to have been 'caught' even though they had not used any form of contraception.

Mors-Rains has argued (1971) that single women are reluctant to use contraception because such use implies promiscuity. Young women try to maintain a view of themselves as conventional, virtuous and non-promiscuous and are willing to risk pregnancy rather than risk the loss of their own self-image and possible loss of reputation. Furstenberg (1976) also argues that young women left contraception to the men they were having sex with who then rarely bothered. Ignorance was not therefore the sole, or even main, reason for non-use of contraception.

These two studies, however, took place over 20 years ago, before the pill became as widespread and accepted as it is today and well before HIV led to the promotion of condom use. But the findings from this study show that, for some women at least, the link between self-image and contraception non-use still exists. The issues of risk-taking and trusting a partner are also important in explaining how single women get pregnant. But our evidence also suggests that there was some ignorance of the risks and mechanics of conception.

Contraception failure or misuse

Thirteen women had been using contraception when they got pregnant but many of these had not been using it correctly. And it is not always easy to know whether to define people as contraception non-users or misusers. For example, one 15 year old was aware of different forms of contraception but disliked most of them and so had settled for a very haphazard form of rhythm method. She seemed unconcerned about the risk of pregnancy:

> I can't take the pill because I get depressed or I feel sick and I didn't want a coil because I'd heard that you get an infection sort of creeping up into your womb... and then the injection I didn't like the sound of either... [I use] sort of rhythm method, but not... I don't really pay that much attention to it, I sort of know when it's alright and that.

She did say that she had also used the cap from time to time but when she got pregnant she must have either not used it or it failed.

Carol had been having an affair with a married man for seven years and he had told her that he was physically incapable of having children. However, he also said that it would be a good idea to use the rhythm method just in case:

> He always used to be careful round about period times, you know, the first few days before and the few days afterwards and I says to him, 'I thought you couldn't have kids?' and he says, 'oh, it's better to be safe than sorry' so we'd used that method for seven years and it worked – but it's ironic that we fell out and I found I was pregnant!

As well as these examples of rather haphazard use of the rhythm method, other couples made similarly risky use of another unreliable technique – withdrawal. One woman, who was 17 when she became a lone mother, explained:

> I didn't know that much about sex... and sometimes he pulled out and other times he didn't because the first two months we'd been alright we'd never thought that we wouldn't be.

This woman trusted her partner, who was five years older than her.

Some women simply could not explain how they got pregnant while on the pill, others admitted to missing the pill on some occasions, others said that they had been sick and others said that they had taken antibiotics which may have reduced the pill's efficiency. One woman explained why she sometimes missed taking the pill:

> I was on the pill but... the pills were at home... and I wasn't going home [every day]. It sounds stupid now, but I just missed them out and then next day took two and it just happened.

Another woman had a similar story, although she thought she had only missed the pill on one occasion:

> What it was, I moved from my mum's to my dad's and all my stuff was in bags and... that night I didn't take a pill and had sex and the next morning took two pills... and that's the only thing I can think of.

Other women had taken the pill regularly but had had its effects counteracted by taking antibiotics:

> I hadn't long moved to the [new] doctors... and the doctor prescribed me some antibiotics and I just didn't bother to question it about is it compatible with my pill... because my [old] doctor knew that I was on the pill and she always gave me what I should and I just assumed that because I'd been to see [the new doctor] for a repeat prescription pill that he'd done exactly the same.

This section suggests that these single women were not deliberately planning to get pregnant and evidence from a quantitative survey in 1993 reinforces this point: 86 per cent of single mothers (by our definition) did not plan to get pregnant when they had their first child (Ford and others, 1995). But although pregnancies were not generally planned, women were aware, to some degree, that they were taking risks and that they might conceive. There was also little sign that the risk of pregnancy concerned them greatly. This suggests that lone parenthood may not have been seen as particularly problematic. The next section reviews their reactions when they discovered that they were pregnant and they were faced with the prospect of becoming a lone parent.

CHOICES DURING PREGNANCY

Getting pregnant while single does not automatically lead to lone parenthood (as Figure 2.1 illustrated). If single women are unhappy being pregnant, there are three main ways in which they might avoid becoming a lone parent: having an abortion; giving up the child for adoption; and cohabiting with a man. This section discusses the choices open to single pregnant women but begins with a review of their reactions to pregnancy.

Reactions to the pregnancy

Only one of the 22 single women had consciously planned to become a lone parent. Anita was 33 and had left a stable relationship because her partner did not want children. She had deliberately avoided using contraception with her new sexual partner. At the time she got pregnant, she was a qualified nurse, living in a boys' boarding school where she was working as the matron. So she was far from the stereotype of a feckless teenage girl, with few economic prospects, who deliberately gets pregnant to get a council flat. In her book about women who chose to 'go solo', Renvoize (1985) argued that women who become lone parents through design were likely to be a middle-class product of the women's movement in the 1970s which encouraged women to make positive decisions in relation to their bodies – whether this meant deciding to have children or not.

None of the other women interviewed had planned to become lone parents. Most knew about contraception and also knew that there was some chance that they might get pregnant, though they thought the odds were low. Others thought that there was no risk even though their contraceptive use was, in some cases, rather haphazard. There was a great deal of variety in the reactions that these women had when they found out they were pregnant. Most were initially surprised (because they had not planned to get pregnant). Some were very shocked.

Following the initial surprise or shock, some women soon reconciled themselves to the idea of being pregnant and were quite happy. This was mainly true of those who were not using contraception at the time they got pregnant and might suggest that although these women were not consciously planning to get pregnant, they were similarly not taking great pains to avoid pregnancy. At one level, they knew that they were taking risks. This may be for a number of reasons, such as finding it difficult to discuss contraception with their partner or not considering lone parenthood a fate to be much avoided, but the end result was an unexpected pregnancy.

Those who had thought that they had been using contraception reliably, found it more difficult to accept the news of their pregnancy and were quite distraught. Most of these women were working in service sector jobs as receptionists, office clerks and bar attendants. Some were working on factory production lines. Some were in school or receiving further education or training. Not only had they not planned to become a lone parent but the prospect had never previously entered their heads. Most had wanted a more conventional route to family life. Heather was 20 and working in a factory when she became pregnant:

> I always thought I'd have a career and then have children when I was late 20s, early 30s.

Gillian was 19 and also working in a factory when she became pregnant. She had thought her future would be a traditional one. She had also not expected to become a lone parent. She said that she:

> always saw myself as getting married, settling down, having a nice house and old man going out to work.

Lisa was 19 and training to be a nurse when she got pregnant. She was very shocked:

> I would have liked for [my baby] to have a mum and a dad in a relationship, something a bit more secure. I certainly didn't think I would end up a single mother, that was the last thing I expected, not me, no! I always thought if I had children it would be with someone that I was married to or someone that I was in a relationship with. I never dreamt that I would have a child on my own.

Jacqui had been in a traditional relationship when she was younger but divorced her husband after suffering violence. She then became pregnant with a younger boyfriend from whom she then separated before the baby was born:

> I had a mortgage, we had two cars, we had lots of money... it is probably snobby values, I just didn't want to be a council tenant on my own with a baby. I never visualised it. I never in my wildest dreams ever thought that this would happen.

Another woman described herself as 'numb' when she found out she was pregnant:

> I thought, 'I can't cope with a baby. How the hell am I supposed to bring a baby up? The relationship had finished... I had my future ahead of me. What could I give the baby? I couldn't give it anything. I had no security.

One woman started having symptoms of the pregnancy but tried to tell herself it must be something else:

> I went into total denial and thought I was really anaemic and that. I had a bit of a drink problem so I was convincing myself that it wasn't sort of pregnancy... then I was round his mum's house one day and she said, 'you're pregnant'... marched me up the doctors and sure enough...

Another woman went through a similar process of denial when she became pregnant because she had only missed the pill once:

> I went straight down to the doctor, [the doctor] said, 'yeah, you are' so I started crying. I was a right state... so I left there and went straight up to the chemist and bought two pregnancy tests, took them home and done them. They both said I was, so I went and got two more... I was in such a state. I thought, 'there's no way I want this child'.

One woman was scared about the pain of childbirth and also about the longer-term financial and social consequences of having a baby:

> We didn't plan it... it was just sort of one of those things... I was thinking about the money situation, well I'm never going to be able to go out because I'd always... done what I wanted to do.

One woman, who refused to talk about the father of her baby, said that she had been 'suicidal' when she discovered that she was pregnant.

Although many women were in work or training and had not envisaged becoming a lone parent, in two cases, the prospect of becoming a mother (even if that meant becoming a single mother), gave them a role in life which was preferable to the one they already had. Elise had left school before her GCSEs and had been living in a squat in London when she found she was pregnant at the age of 19:

> I was waitressing and bar work and it was during that time that I realised I was pregnant so really I hadn't had much time between leaving school and then becoming a mother. I really don't think I fitted in much... and then when I found out I was pregnant I was really happy because I'd always loved children... so I think I felt it was quite exciting.

Kristin, who was 15 at the time she got pregnant, had gone through a difficult childhood with her mother often in hospital and her father frequently having affairs. She was happy about being pregnant because she felt that the baby would be 'something what I could love for myself and that person would love me back.'

Most women had not planned to get pregnant and were shocked at the prospect of becoming a lone parent. Why, then, did they not avoid lone parenthood by taking up one of the following options: having an abortion; giving up their baby for adoption; or living with the father of the child?

Abortion

Abortion is one way in which a single pregnant woman can ensure that she does not become a lone parent and it is now a fairly common outcome of pregnancy. As mentioned earlier in this chapter, the proportion of conceptions outside marriage which end in abortion has decreased over the last 20 years but a third of conceptions outside marriage still resulted in abortion in 1993. The growth in lone parent-hood is not solely due to more single women getting pregnant but, to some extent, to more single pregnant women deciding not to have abortions.

Only one woman among the 22 interviewed had positively wanted an abortion. Alison had split up from her partner during the pregnancy and by that stage it was quite late to have an abortion:

> I actually went for an abortion, to be honest with you, after we split up. I thought, 'there's no way I'm going to be able to cope having two babies [twins] on my own'. So I went to see about having an abortion but they actually showed me a photo of how they were. I was five months then and I couldn't have gone through with it. Because if I wouldn't have seen that picture that the doctor showed me I probably would have gone ahead with an abortion.

Five other women said that, by the time they had split up with their partner or by the time they knew they were pregnant, it was too late for an abortion. But none of these said directly that they wanted one. Three of these women had previously had abortions. Lynn had been in a violent relationship when she got pregnant at the age of 17 and decided to have an abortion. When she got pregnant again at the age of 21 she had doubts about how she would cope with the baby but felt that she was now old enough to try and did not want to have another abortion. Jacqui had also previously got pregnant during a violent relationship. Her (then) husband forced her to have an abortion on that occasion and she now regretted it:

When I was married I fell pregnant and [my ex-husband] beat me black and blue until I agreed to go to the clinic and get rid of it and... I told [my new partner] all about it and I said to him, 'if that happened again I just couldn't do it'.

Two years ago, Gillian had had an abortion forced on her by her parents and would not consider having another:

When I was 17 I got pregnant... and he was black and mum and dad went crazy because... they're very racist... when mum and dad found out I was pregnant, 'You will get rid of it!' So I had an abortion... when I first had it done I locked myself in my room every night for months and months and, I don't know, sometimes I look back and think, 'oh, what would it be like?'

Sixteen of the women who were single when they got pregnant found out early enough to have an abortion. Only four of these gave it any consideration. One said that she was scared about the physical process of having an abortion and decided against. Another thought about it very briefly but decided that she could not go through with it. One woman, who was 15 at the time, faced pressure from her parents to have an abortion and so considered the option but she decided against because she became keen to have a baby. Kristin had gone through a very unsettled childhood and thought that a baby might provide something in her life that had previously been lacking:

The reason why I didn't like get him terminated or get him adopted was because my mum was going in and out of hospital all the time, I was in a foster home, my dad was going off with any Tom, Dick or Harry and I just wanted something what I could love for myself and that person would love me back.

Another woman, Catherine, who refused to talk about the father, was a Catholic and her family was opposed to the idea of abortion but, given her particular circumstances (which we do not know about fully) they had considered abortion very seriously:

When we first confirmed it, I think it was more, 'we don't agree with it but we do think in your circumstances that maybe it's the best thing to do', and I went to the clinic and arranged things... but in the back of my mind I was just thinking, 'I can't do this, I can't do this' and I think then we just sat down together one night and we said, 'it's not the thing to do, it's not the thing to do at all'.

Another single teenager, Charlotte, had also felt some pressure to have an abortion but she said that this had come not from her parents but from the medical profession:

> The medical profession really do look down on you, midwives look down on you, doctors look down on you and it was almost pressurised on me to have an abortion, even up to the last minute it was offered.

In Lisa's case, parental disapproval of abortion reinforced her decision not have an abortion and although she said her mother would have supported her if she had decided to go through with an abortion, it is difficult to say whether she might have had one if her mother's views had not been against the idea:

> My mother was very supportive... I know she doesn't agree with abortions but she did say that if I did want to she would stand by me but I knew that she didn't want, that's not what she wanted me to do.

Parental attitudes were very important to many women in deciding what to do. In most cases, parents were fairly neutral towards abortion and appeared to leave their daughters to decide for themselves, saying that they would support them if they decided to have the baby. This proved crucial to many who had assumed that their parents might disown a lone parent daughter. But after the initial shock, most mothers of the pregnant daughters began to feel more relaxed about the situation. Fathers took longer to accommodate themselves to the news.

Kelly, who was 15 when she got pregnant, recalled the reaction of her parents:

> The first thought in my head was absolute panic about my mum and dad because I was so young... and I didn't actually tell them until I was four months pregnant... and my mum, she took it quite well, being the mother-figure they do, but my father wasn't so optimistic about it. He was quite mad actually... I was his little girl... shattered all his dreams.

But after a while:

> I had their full support, what I wanted. If I wanted to carry on through with the pregnancy it was perfectly fine. If I wanted to terminate the pregnancy they'd go with me either way. I was under no pressure at all really.

Kelly decided against an abortion because:

> I think it was like a bit of a fairy tale really, being so young... I thought having a child so young would make my life easier in the future... I didn't look at the impossible side.

Some women did not approve of abortion and so, once the initial shock of conception had worn off, became more comfortable with the idea of giving birth and did not consider the option seriously.

Adoption

In contrast to abortion, adoption is very rare – with fewer than 1,000 adoptions of babies in 1992. The evidence suggests that single pregnant women rarely consider adoption seriously. Four of the 22 single pregnant women briefly thought about giving up their baby for adoption. Two of these were the 15 year olds who were put under pressure either to abort or adopt. In one case, the pressure came from the pregnant woman's father but in the other, it was medical staff who tried to encourage the pregnant woman, during labour, to consider adoption. However, with the support of her mother, Kelly managed to resist the pressure applied to her:

> I had a lot of pressure actually in the hospital... from a lot of the nurses, there was a few doctors as well... During labour, they brought me a load of forms and I could see 'adoption' and 'options', different options. And I says, 'no, you can take them away'. I was really gob-smacked, I didn't realise any of this. And my mum absolutely hit the roof in the hospital.

A 23 year-old woman had separated from her partner when she was pregnant with twins. Alison had considered but rejected the idea of abortion but did not feel that she would be able to cope on her own and her social worker mentioned the possibility of adoption:

> My social worker was asking me about [adoption] and, I don't know, I was in two minds, didn't know what to do to be honest. I was all confused.

This woman's parents had also mentioned that adoption might be the best course of action because:

> They knew what type of girl I was. They knew that I was independent on my own and going out to work and that – and my own car and all that. So they... probably were thinking, 'well, she's only 23'... so they were probably thinking about my life, that it would ruin my life.

But although adoption had been considered by this woman and her parents, when the twins were born, all parties changed their minds about it.

Alison's primary reason for considering adoption was that she had not thought she would be able to cope with bringing up her twins on her own. There was only one other case where adoption was seriously considered. This was Catherine whose primary motivation for considering adoption was concern about the baby's future well-being. Catherine was 23 when she got pregnant and she moved away from her home town so that she could conceal her pregnancy from her friends. She considered abortion but this went against her Catholic upbringing. When she had the baby, she was living in a church-run hostel for single mothers. Catherine seriously considered adoption because she thought that her child should be brought up in a secure nuclear family, just as she had been:

> I've always thought of the family unit as a mum and dad and then the children. And after seeing my mum and dad together – there's such a closeness there... and I was going to deprive that child of a father and that's why to me adoption just had to be the thing to do... and I thought, I just didn't want people to know at all.

Her parents, particularly her father, were also keen on adoption as a solution to their daughter's 'problem':

> All along, I don't think he was real to my dad – the baby – when he was inside me, you know, he never actually acknowledged there was a baby. To him, it was just – once the baby's born, then it'll be adopted and then we'll go back to just how everything was.

However, once the baby was born, she began to change her mind:

> As soon as he was there... I just used to think, you know, I can give him as much as anybody else can give him. It might not be what I wanted for him originally, but there's no reason why I can't give him everything that I wanted.

But she still felt she needed her parents' approval before converting her change of mind into a change of action:

> Even though everyone said, 'you've got to do what you want'... I did definitely want my family with me – my immediate family, because I didn't

want to hurt them. If they'd said to me, 'have him adopted', even when I said I'll keep him... I think I would have changed my mind.

Adoption had not really crossed many other women's minds. Most had felt that their choice had been between keeping the baby and abortion. Once they had ruled out abortion, they became reconciled, and in some cases excited, about the prospect of having a baby. Abortion was more widely considered than adoption because women felt that they would develop a bond with their baby during pregnancy and be unable to part with it after the birth. Giving up a baby for adoption went against too many moral codes and contradicted the self-image of women as potential mothers and carers. It was almost synonymous with abandoning a child. A typical comment was: 'There was absolutely no way I could do it.' Abortion, by contrast, involved a 'foetus', not a 'baby'. Abortion also had the extra advantage that it could be kept more private. Few people might find out about the abortion whereas adoption would become a much more public issue and the risk of stigma consequently much greater. It is probably no coincidence that the woman mentioned above, who most strongly considered adoption, had moved away from her home town during the pregnancy, to the refuge of a church hostel for single mothers. This would have maintained the secrecy around the adoption and thus reduced any stigma she would otherwise have felt. But the woman had nevertheless internalised the reactions that people might have had if they had known and she felt that she had to justify her consideration of adoption:

I just thought some people could get really angry with me, adopting a baby, 'how could you do that?' but I wasn't doing it for selfish reasons, I was doing it because I thought at the time it was the best thing for him.

In many ways, adoption had a much greater stigma attached to it than did lone parenthood. This is in contrast to the situation in the 1950s and 1960s.

Cohabitation or marriage

If abortion and adoption are rejected, the final way of not becoming a lone parenthood is to live with, or marry, a man. In an early study of lone parenthood, Marsden (1969) pointed out that, in the 1950s and 1960s, 'shotgun weddings' were relatively frequent when single women became pregnant. However, he also pointed out that these ceremonies often merely postponed the creation of a lone parent family as the couple might separate fairly soon after the wedding. As mentioned earlier in this chapter, the 22 single lone mothers could be divided into different groups depending on the relationships they had with men at about the time they got pregnant and this would affect their chances of cohabiting during pregnancy and once the baby was born.

Cohabited in past, split when pregnant (three)

Three women had split up with partners during their pregnancy and so the separation was either more important, or equally important, along with getting pregnant, in becoming a lone mother. However, these women could, in theory, have got back together with their partners before the birth. In Jacqui's case, there was no chance of a reconciliation as the separation had been directly caused by the (unplanned) pregnancy. The partner, and his parents, felt that the woman was trying to trap her (much younger) partner by having a baby.

The situation was more complex in the two other cases. Alison had split from her partner after she found out that she was pregnant with twins. She was not at all keen on the prospect of coping on her own with the babies and had considered abortion and adoption. She also considered getting back together with her partner (who had physically assaulted her in the past) but both her parents and his parents had counselled against such a move:

> My mum told me not to get back after what he's done, you know. And then his mum told him, says, 'don't go back for the kids because it'll never work', so... his parents were saying 'no' and my parents were saying 'no' you know, 'after what he's done, how can you go back?'

This woman's parents were more concerned about the individual happiness and welfare of their daughter than any stigma which might attach either to them or to her, if she were to become a single mother.

Finally, Andrea had left her husband during pregnancy because she discovered that he had been having an affair even though he had promised that he would not do so if she became pregnant. Her partner wanted to get back together with her and it is interesting that both Andrea and her partner used the same argument – the best interest of the child – to justify their own positions:

I didn't have to be a single parent. It was a case of, as my husband put it, 'so I shag around a bit, but at the end of the day, you don't want for anything and [the baby's] got his dad', that is his attitude, you know. My attitude was, no, it had to stop because it's not fair bringing him up, causing rows and arguments. Like he was saying, 'put up and shut up' and I wasn't prepared to do that.

Cohabited/married in past, split before pregnant

Three women had been in cohabiting relationships at some time in the past, but not at the time they got pregnant. In two cases, the father of their baby was the man they had previously lived with but now only saw from time to time. In Diane's case, the father asked her to marry him. This led to a short-lived revival in their relationship:

As soon as I told him I was pregnant he asked me to marry him – I think out of duty, almost out of duty. And I said, 'no' but we got together for a couple of weeks and it wasn't going to work at all. And so we agreed to go through the pregnancy and birth together – but not 'together'.

The other father felt no such 'duty'. He was unhappy about the pregnancy as he had only just been involved with another single woman who had got pregnant with him and then had the baby adopted. As we shall see in Chapter 5, however, this man eventually got together with Elise after the birth and they stayed together for about a year.

Anita had deliberately set out to get pregnant because she was 33 and was desperate to have children. She was having a fairly casual relationship with someone when she found out that she was pregnant. She informed the father and said that he could be involved in the birth and up-bringing of the baby if he wanted to:

I got back in touch with [the father] and said, 'yes, I'm pregnant. I realise I don't know you that well. I don't want to tie you down but how do you feel about this? Do you want to be involved?'… and I just didn't get an answer. For about three or four months I heard nothing.

Although her relationship with the father had been quite casual and she had planned to be a single parent, Anita had wanted the father to be involved. But she was quite prepared for him to want little to do with the child:

I didn't have any illusions about the father of the child. I didn't have any illusions that he was necessarily any more involved than having slept with me without a condom. I was kind of sussed about that one. I didn't think he had any rights... If you're not involved, if you're not supportive, if you're not sharing the decisions and that, I don't think you're a father – you're simply a sperm donor – it's that simple to me.

She found out, when she was pregnant, that he apparently had three other children by different women. He eventually asked to take part, in some way, in the pregnancy, but he failed to turn up to pregnancy classes when he said he would and then he stopped seeing her altogether.

Never cohabited/married, regular boyfriend (eight women)

Women with a regular boyfriend might be in a good position to avoid lone motherhood. However, in six of the eight cases, the relationships broke up at about the time the woman became pregnant. In some cases, the relationship may have ended anyway. In other cases, the news of the pregnancy was the catalyst which hastened its end.

In one case, Lynn had ended the relationship before she found out she was pregnant. Even so, the baby's father reacted in what might be considered a traditional manner:

He said, 'we'd better get married' which I thought was pathetic [laughs]. I mean, we'd been apart and we'd rowed like crazy and there was obviously nothing worth saving and certainly not for the sake of the baby. And I had by that time decided that I was going to do it [have the baby] and if it meant doing it alone, I'd do it alone and I was quite prepared to do that.

Carol had been having an affair with a married man for the previous seven years. She had also ended the relationship before she knew she was pregnant:

I just decided that I'd had enough of the relationship and at the Christmas I told him, 'that's it, all finished' and in the February I found out I was pregnant and no way did I want anything to do with him. So I decided to have [my baby] on my own. But I'd got my parents' support at the time to have [my baby] on my own.

Once again, parental support was often a vital ingredient in enabling women to cope with the process of becoming a lone mother. But some women carried on with pregnancies without such parental support and also without the father.

Della became pregnant when she was 19. Her boyfriend asked her to marry him and her mother was keen for this to happen:

> My mum's got quite strong sort of Christian views... [she] had kind of like suggested it but I sort of explained to her that having a baby was one thing, but getting married... she didn't push it on me though... he had asked me to marry him but only because two of his friends had got married recently.

She decided to decline his offer of marriage, even though her mother had thought this was a good idea, because:

> He was just really young and immature and... not the marrying sort of material... he was completely irresponsible – never around, going off for days on end... oh, he also slept with my best friend... that was before I got pregnant... I wouldn't get married to him, yeah, because he was totally untrustworthy.

Parents were not always keen for their daughters to marry the prospective fathers. In Gillian's case parental opposition to a marriage was very fierce. She had previously had an abortion because the father of her previous baby had been black and her father had forced her to terminate the pregnancy. She was determined not to do the same this time, even though the father of her current baby was mixed race and her father's attitudes were no more enlightened:

> I was arguing with my dad... and he said, 'I'm not pushing the little black bastard down the road in a pram', and I says, 'well, dad, you're not good enough to push my little black bastard down the road in a pram'... and he was saying... I should go and live with [the baby's father's] mother because she was a nigger lover and I'd be alright with her. And I just says, 'well anything's better than living with you white shit'... I knew then that I was going.

In a couple of cases, the relationship carried on in the same way as it had prior to the pregnancy. For example, Jenny had been with a regular boyfriend for two years before she got pregnant. During this time, she had been living with her mother, who was ill. They decided to postpone any decision about cohabitation until after the birth:

> I think we both decided to keep it as it was, see how we went when she was born.

Although her mother had not initially been supportive about the pregnancy, she soon came round:

> At first she was, I suppose, a bit angry. But she soon got used to the idea and she was all excited and, you know, she loved her and spoilt her.

Never cohabited/married, no regular boyfriend (eight)

None of the prospective fathers in this category asked the pregnant women to marry them. Charlotte had wanted to marry the father and discussed it with him but he was not willing to go ahead:

> I didn't particularly want to be single and he said, 'you don't have to be married these days'… and I just went along with that.

They stayed together, on a casual basis, and he went along to some of the pregnancy classes with her. However, most women were not particularly keen on the men who got them pregnant. As Heather said:

> All he thinks about is his mates and his drink so I don't think I'd have wanted a life with him. I wouldn't have had a very good life if I'd had a life with him.

Lisa also said:

> When it was too late, I realised that he was absolutely no good, you know, and there was no question of 'oh, I'm pregnant, is he going to stay with me?' because I didn't want him to stay with me… I knew he was no good, I just found out a little too late… He's got no idea about responsibility.

Her mother supported her in this and both mother and daughter appear to have been influenced by the mother's own experience of an unhappy marriage. She did not want her daughter to go through the same experience as she had and the daughter felt the same:

> My mum and dad had a bad marriage and to me there was no way I was going to stay with someone just for the sake of a child and go through hell.

The two 15 year olds who had not had regular boyfriends had both had sex under the age of consent. One was with a 23 year-old man. The other was with a 17 year old. Although it might be thought that the older man was more culpable, it was the 17 year old who was prosecuted, primarily it seems, because the woman's father in this case was particularly venomous towards the man who had impregnated his daughter. The 23 year-old prospective father had encouraged his girlfriend to have an abortion. She did not go along with this and they continued their 'on and off' relationship.

So there was some evidence that women had quite high, traditional standards for prospective partners. They wanted a man who would be a responsible breadwinner and father but their current boyfriends did not live up to this ideal and most of these women preferred to have their baby on their own rather than compromise their standards. Some women, however, had no choice but to do so as there was no man who was prepared to live with them. These men, apparently, were keen to pursue their own individual happiness rather than conform to more traditional pressures to 'make an honest woman' of their girlfriends.

SINGLE LONE MOTHERHOOD: A PROBLEM OR A SOLUTION?

We saw, in the previous section, that few of the single women in the study planned to get pregnant and yet they all kept their babies and remained single. So although they did not appear consciously to plan to become lone parents, it could also be argued that they did little to avoid such an outcome: they failed to use contraception successfully during sex; they chose not to abort or give up their baby; and they did not cohabit with the father (or any other man). To some extent, therefore, these women can be said to have chosen to become lone parents. Their choice may have been highly constrained but there was usually some element of choice available to them. This might lead us to conclude that lone parenthood is not a problem which these women sought to avoid but, in some way, a solution or a welcome avenue down which they are prepared to venture. Motherhood has traditionally provided women with an identity and a socially-valued role and so has generally been viewed positively as an appropriate path to follow. Unmarried motherhood may not be viewed quite so positively, but in the absence of a 'breadwinner' it may be seen as more desirable than being a single woman without children or a mother who is living with an undesirable man.

Expectations of financial support and housing

It is sometimes argued that single women have babies so that they can receive (more) support from the state in the form of social security and housing. Various research projects in the US (see Hoynes, 1996) and comparative research carried out in Britain (Whiteford and Bradshaw, 1994) have not supported this assertion. Our research also suggests that single women do not deliberately plan to get pregnant, but there is some evidence that they do not see lone parenthood as a situation which they should try hard to avoid. This section looks at their expectations of financial support.

Some form of social security has been available for lone mothers, at least since World War II, and so it would seem surprising if the mere existence of social security provision had had an effect on the growth of lone parenthood in the last 20 years. But Marsden has argued that, in the 1960s, there was a 'conspiracy of silence… which effectively conceals the availability of support… for the unmarried mother who wants to bring up her child alone'.

If there was such a conspiracy in the 1960s there is certainly no longer one – the availability of social security for lone mothers is very well-known – as are government plans to cut such support. For example, short of any last minute reprieves, lone parent premium and one parent addition to child support will be unavailable to new lone parent claimants from April 1998. Although social security for lone mothers is not new, there were reforms in the 1970s and 1980s which may have made some impact on lone parenthood. For example, the Fowler reforms in 1988 removed benefits from 16–17 year olds except in certain circumstances – one of which was lone parenthood.

All the women interviewed had known, prior to becoming lone parents, that they would be entitled to social security, but most expected that they would not be receiving very much money and that life would be very difficult. None of the women had made enquiries into exactly how much they would receive. They knew that there would be enough to survive and the prospect of becoming a mother and having to cope with a newborn baby overshadowed any other consideration. Money was simply not in the forefront of their minds, either as an important advantage or disadvantage to becoming a lone parent. As Jenny recalled:

> At first I was panicking thinking, 'Am I going to be alright?' 'Will I be able to cope'… to be honest I thought it was going to be a lot harder than it has been.

Once pregnant, most of these women felt that they had little choice about becoming a lone parent, regardless of the financial consequences. They were either too late or not prepared to have abortions, and adoption was rarely even considered. Some had separated from partners or boyfriends and so cohabitation was not an option.

But although social security was certainly not considered generous, there were some signs that life as a lone parent on benefit was seen as preferable to the alternatives. Jane had separated from her partner before the birth because she preferred to be a lone parent on income support in her own right than part of a couple on income support:

> He was on income support to start with, it was all just put in his name so like the cheque every week was just given straight to him and I had to ask him for money, that was part of why we finished and that... because I had to go to him for money and he's such a tight bastard.

Della had not planned to get pregnant but once she discovered that she had conceived, she thought that she would be better off as a lone parent on income support than as a 17 year old on a Youth Training Scheme:

> When I was in the YTS you only get paid for the day you went so I was probably on about £13 a week most weeks so, yeah, better off [on Income Support as a lone parent]. It was a secure, stable income of money.

Only four of the 22 women had stayed on at school after 16 to do A levels. The rest had either got pregnant while still at school or had left school with minimal qualifications. These women had gone on to work in factories, hotels and offices, receiving relatively low pay.

Living on benefit was therefore not a tremendous drop in living standards and becoming a mother provided a valuable role in life. Diane was one of the four women with A levels but even she said that she had 'found herself' and gained 'a real feeling of wholeness' through having her daughter.

A couple of women admitted that they had not expected life to be too difficult as a lone parent. The idea of becoming a mother was exciting, particularly for the younger women in the study. As Diane said:

> I was slightly unrealistic at times. I thought of having a baby and travelling here and travelling there and doing all kinds of things... and I always knew that having [the baby] wouldn't stop my life – and it hasn't done, I still

have my own life... but I was a bit unrealistic in how it wouldn't stop my life.

Generally, these women made few concrete plans at the time of their pregnancy. Most assumed that they would be living on social security for some time after the birth and then they would, sooner or later, get a job. Only Anita, who had planned to get pregnant, had also planned to return to her job in a boys' school after the birth.

None of the women expected to be financially better off than before having their baby but they knew that they would be able to survive because of the existence of social security and the help supplied by their families. Social security provided a bare minimum for survival but help from parents often made the difference between mere survival and being able to live.

Although most women expected that they would be able to get council housing once they had their babies, they had fairly low expectations about the standard of the accommodation. Some preferred to stay living with their families where there was usually a ready supply of childcare provision which enabled them to work and/or socialise. Like many women, Heather had applied for council accommodation because she knew that it was available but she was quite happy at home with her parents. Alison had also been in two minds about taking up an offer of accommodation from the council when her twins were four months old:

> I didn't want to go because I knew I'd lose help from my mum and dad and I thought, well, I'm on my own then. But the other part was I wanted to go to give my mum and dad a break because they were getting older.

Most women took up their offers of council accommodation because they realised that they would have to be independent of their parents at some point and so took the opportunity when it arose. But council accommodation was not a big incentive to become a lone parent. Kristin lived with her mother for three years after her baby was born:

> I didn't really want to move out but I felt that my mum was like getting really over-protective... I would say something to [my baby] and she would like say something totally different and undermine my authority... so I said to her 'I need to get out, I need my own space' so she wrote to the council and saying that she was kicking me out.

As we shall see later, there is strong evidence that lone parents, and single mothers on benefit in particular, are stigmatised in society. Such attitudes might deter women from becoming lone parents but, as we shall also see, these women did not identify themselves with lone parents who had deliberately planned to become lone parents. They therefore considered it morally acceptable for them to have a baby and receive state support.

Reactions of family and friends

For many pregnant single women, the reactions of their family was vital in determining their course of action. The attitude of parents was more important than the attitude of wider society. In the main, parents, and especially mothers, were very supportive of their daughters.

Parents were often shocked initially but then soon grew accustomed to the idea that their daughter was pregnant. This may have been partly because in only eight cases out of 22, the lone parent herself had been brought up by a married couple who had stayed together. The experiences of the lone parents' mothers often meant that they were not overly shocked by unconventional family arrangements and there was evidence that this was different from previous generations. Jane's mother had got pregnant when she was an unmarried 16 year old in the late 1960s. There followed a shotgun wedding:

> She'd only been with my dad a little while and she was 16 and… my dad said, 'right let's go down and tell your mum and dad' and they went down and… my mum's parents just said, 'you're getting married', sort of like booked the church and the flowers all in one evening sort of thing. My dad was stunned.

The (fairly unhappy) marriage then lasted 18 years before the couple finally split up. Jane herself had only recently begun what was quite a tempestuous relationship with a boyfriend who had initially been keen on the idea of living with her and the baby. Jane was not so keen and although she decided to keep the baby, she did not want to keep the father. Jane's parents, now living apart, reacted to this situation very differently from the way Jane's grandparents had reacted 30 years before. They were very supportive of whatever she wanted to do:

> I wouldn't know what to do without my mum and dad, not at all. I wouldn't
> have got my house. They kitted it all out for me and they bought me
> everything. Oh God, yeah, if it weren't for them...

Julie's mother had also had an unconventional family life. She had had
two children with one man then married another man with whom she
had Julie. She was now with a different man. She was very supportive
of Julie's situation and happy to endorse whatever she chose to do.

Elise's upbringing had also been unusual for the time. Her mother
had been a lone parent after separating from her partner in the 1970s.
They had moved to a remote part of the country and Elise
remembered feeling stigmatised when she was a child:

> We had quite a hard time from the other children in the village, that was
> quite hurtful... because she was a single parent and different from all the
> other families. I don't think there were any other single mothers.

Elise had felt that things would be easier for her now because there
were more single parents around in general and, in any case, she was
living in a more urban area where there would be even more. Far from
encouraging her to become a lone parent, Elise's mother had initially
encouraged her to think about having an abortion because she knew
that life as a lone parent would still be a struggle today, but when it
was clear that Elise wanted to keep the baby her mother was
completely supportive.

In other cases, parents had stayed in unhappy marriages, at least
until their children had grown up. Heather had been adopted when she
was a baby. Her adoptive parents had not had a good relationship:

> They were just a habit marriage and I used to think there's got to be more
> to life than this.

At the time Heather got pregnant, her mother left her father. Heather
barely considered living with the father of her child whom she had
little respect for. Her parents, especially her mother, said that they
would support whatever she wanted to do.

Bernie had been fostered at certain times during her childhood and
her mother had remained in an unhappy marriage. When Bernie got
pregnant, her mother was keen for her daughter not to make the same
mistake that she had:

> My mum was my inspiration to leave [my ex-boyfriend] because my mum
> stayed in a marriage which is not happy. She's not happy... if you look

closely at [my parents], at their personal relationship without their children, there's nothing. Nothing there at all... she didn't want me to wake up 40-something and my life be over, the best years of my life be over.

And the longer you stay, the harder it gets to go. So I went down one Sunday morning and she was preparing lunch and I said, 'please tell me to leave him'... and she wouldn't – she said it had to be my decision. And I said to her, 'if you were me, what would you do?', and she said she'd find happiness... she wouldn't dedicate her life to her children again because it wasn't worth it because we all grew up and left. And you have to keep parts of yourself special.

This quote shows how important the parents' views are to many women. It also shows that the pursuit of individual happiness has become more important to some women than perceived duty towards fulfilling the traditional role of wife and mother.

Kelly's parents had also had an unhappy marriage. They had separated when she was 12 but they still lived in the same house. Kelly's father was initially shocked when he found out about her pregnancy but eventually her parents were very supportive:

He was quite mad about the situation... I was his little girl and, you know, shattered all his dreams... I had their full support, what I wanted. If I wanted to carry on through the pregnancy it was perfectly fine. If I wanted to terminate the pregnancy, they'd go with me either way. I was under no pressure at all.

In the 1950s Carol's mother had had her first baby before she got married to the father. They then stayed together and supported Carol when she became a single parent in the late 1970s. Her father was not initially pleased but eventually said that she could remain living at home. There was little option for Carol to marry the father because he was already married and, in any case, Carol had recently ended the relationship. Her father's decision to allow her to stay at home was the turning point for Carol. If he had refused this, she was not sure what she would have done.

Having parents who had experienced unstable or broken marriages was no guarantee of support however. Diane's mother had left her husband in the early 1980s because he was violent towards her. Like Elise's mother, this affected her reaction to her daughter's prospects when she became pregnant at the age of 21:

Because she's done it, because she's brought three of us up on her own, she was in a way a bit gutted that perhaps I was following the same path that she was... she was, I think, a bit upset for me, knowing what was coming up and knowing what sort of things I was going to have to get through. But by the time she got back from holiday, she was fine.

Laura was 19 when she became a lone parent. Her parents had always lived together but never married. This did not mean, however, that her father had liberal attitudes:

My dad didn't want me in the house. He was really upset about it even though I'd have been with the dad something like three years... he called me everything from a tart to a prostitute and he told my mum that if I didn't go he was going. So I got a bedsit. I went to live in a bedsit and then I was in a one-parent family unit.

Gillian suffered a similar reaction from her racist stepfather who objected to her bringing 'a black bastard' into the house:

I didn't see my mum and dad for about four months once I actually left and went into homeless families. They didn't know where I was. I just thought, 'stuff you!' which wasn't fair on my mum because, my mum, although she's a racist as well, she's a lot calmer than my dad.

Going back two generations, Della's mother had been illegitimate and had been ashamed of it all her life. She encouraged Della to marry the father of her child:

My mum's got quite strong sort of Christian views. She didn't push it on me though.

When Della resisted this pressure, her mother eventually supported her. Della believed that her mother had come to terms more with her own illegitimacy through her realisation that having unmarried parents was now more acceptable.

So parental opposition on its own was not enough to discourage a woman from becoming a lone mother. But outright opposition was fairly unusual. Even parents who had stayed together and had reasonably happy relationships were supportive of their daughters. Catherine's experience of a happy, stable upbringing with her parents made her uncomfortable at the prospect of becoming a lone parent. However, cohabitation with the father was not an option and the family's traditional and religious values made abortion difficult to consider seriously. Catherine was planning to give the baby up for adoption but changed her mind after giving birth.

Andrea's parents had always been together and held quite conventional views. These views led them to support Andrea when she decided to leave her husband who was continuing to have affairs despite the fact that she had just become pregnant:

> They knew what a wanker he is… if I get stuck my mum and dad are there straight away.

Social stigma

In the past, the stigma of having a baby 'out of wedlock' was very great. Parents (and fathers in particular) demanded 'shotgun weddings' to avoid the shame of their daughter giving birth to an illegitimate child (Marsden, 1969). We have just seen that some parents of single pregnant women were initially shocked by the prospect of having a lone parent in their family but most eventually supported their daughters and if the issue of marriage was raised, this was rarely in the form of a demand, more as a suggestion for a way to make life easier. This raises the question of whether these parents were ignoring the views of wider society and refusing to conform to social norms or whether these norms have changed so that lone parenthood is less stigmatised than in previous years.

There was evidence that, once they became lone mothers, these single women were viewed negatively by other people and, in some cases, were harassed because they were single parents. Lone parents had not expected this before they had their babies, largely because they had received support from their families and, after the birth, they coped with the reactions of wider society by distancing themselves, in their own minds, from the lone parents who were most heavily stigmatised.

Elise had thought that she and her daughter would be less stigmatised than her mother and herself as a child had been. Elise was living on an estate where there were many other lone parents but, in her case, this did not reduce the stigma, it merely gave some people a greater target for venting their frustrations:

> You are made to feel like the scum of the earth, living on an estate, being a single parent. You've got other children that are coming from huge

families that just ring your bell and constantly torment you and you feel harassed by a group of 8 year olds. And you can't do anything about it.

Elise's daughter often bore the brunt of the harassment:

My daughter was picked on constantly, bullied constantly. There was no male, you know, to try and protect us. I would go out there and try and rescue her but they would just laugh at me as well and if you dealt with the other parents they just didn't want to know.

Della also felt that lone parents were typically used as scapegoats for social problems:

People round here… there were some cars smashed out the front and they were going, 'oh, it's these flats up here, they put single parents in them'.

But although the concentration of lone parents in one area made them an easy group to scapegoat, Della felt that this also made it easier to cope with negative attitudes because she was not facing it alone:

[Lone parenthood]'s becoming more and more common. The last place I lived in, you were kind of like strange if you had a partner, you know, nobody did.

There was also a view that different types of people had different views about lone parenthood. Heather felt that she was more likely to feel 'ashamed' about being a lone parent with 'older people… and perhaps a higher class of person, more professional person.' This was because:

People of their own type, it's not rife is it? So they don't experience it… and people just see a situation, they don't see the people behind it… they don't think, 'well, yes, that did happen to her but she was a nice girl and she managed'.

Like many lone parents, Kristin blamed the media for fuelling unfair images. She remembered the media coverage over the murder of James Bulger and the emphasis which was put on the fact that one of his killers had been the son of a lone parent. Della also blamed the media:

You see things on the radio about how much single parents are costing the welfare state, all this and all that, and they [people round here] haven't got the knowledge to come up with conclusions other than those that are slammed in their face by the media.

Dependence on the state

As well as being seen as the cause of social problems, such as antisocial behaviour on the part of the children, lone parents also felt they were being blamed for being a burden on the state. Lynn felt that lone parents were:

> seen as – 'they scrounge from the state. They don't want to do anything. They're quite happy sitting on their bums and they complain when their kids are on holidays. They complain they've got no money.' That is how I think lone parents are perceived by a large majority of people in society.

Carol had become a lone parent in the late 1970s. She felt that: 'we're blamed for everything!' Partly because of this, Carol felt that she could not complain about her circumstances:

> At that time, we managed on social security. I never moaned about the amount of money I got. It wasn't enough but I never moaned because I always considered myself very lucky that someone was giving me money for doing nothing – just looking after two children that I should never have had in the first place. So I always felt grateful. I didn't feel that they owed me a living.

Carol felt that women these days were less likely to feel grateful. She felt that, since the 1970s, there had been in a change in the reasons why women became lone parents:

> There are those girls that get pregnant because they want a house... and they don't go out to work so they decided, 'oh, well I'll have a baby, social security will give me the money'... so yeah, there are the single parents that give others a bad name.

It is interesting that the main cause of negative attitudes to lone parenthood was the fact that lone parents were seen as 'burdens on the state'. Bringing up a child single-handed was not, on its own, viewed very negatively. But dependence on social security rather than on a husband was the real source of disgrace. Charlotte, who eventually got a job working as a nurse, made a distinction when asked to say how people viewed lone parents:

It depends what [the lone parents] do. If they're sat at home doing nothing, then even I... this might sound silly but even I look down on them in a way because I know it's not as hard as they say [to get a job].

Teenage mums: a modern folk devil

It was also felt that some types of lone parent were viewed more negatively than others. The main 'folk devil' was the teenage girl who deliberately got pregnant to secure both council accommodation and a living off the state. The single parents interviewed universally believed that such women existed and gave the rest of them a bad name. None, however, felt that they conformed to this stereotype. Heather 'looked down on' women who deliberately got pregnant:

> I know people myself who I went to school with, their only aim in life is as soon as they leave school or when they're at school is to have baby and not make anything of themselves really... just go out there and have babies and keep having them and having them and having them and not improving the quality of life for their other kids and it just gets on people's nerves, I suppose, and they just see everybody like that.

Gillian made a similar point:

> I've had comments like, 'oh, yeah, young girls get pregnant and get houses, don't they' and I'm not saying that some girls don't because I'm sure in the past decade or whatever, that has happened... if mum and dad had been alright I would have stayed at home, you know. At that time, I never saw myself in my own house, sitting there on my own with a baby and no furniture because I don't think that's fun for anybody and anybody who does want that must be mad in their head.

Although it was generally agreed that there was still a great amount of ignorance and prejudice about lone parenthood, many people believed that there was much less now than there had been in the past. Both Diane and Elise felt that their mothers had faced much greater public shame than they had, even though they felt that general attitudes were still negative.

Some women felt that, far from being stigmatised, they were viewed positively, for managing to bring up their child(ren) on their own. Those women who had become lone parents at very young ages and those who had gone out to work while being a lone parent were most likely to feel that they were viewed positively, mainly by their friends and members of their family.

Alison gave birth to twins after splitting up from her husband. She said that most people were:

> ...pretty good actually because they, like, say, 'well you've done very well. I don't know how you've managed'.

Kelly became a mother when she was 15 in the mid-1980s. She recalled that there were few such single mothers in those days and people were generally supportive. She felt that negative media coverage in the following decade had changed general views and that, consequently, there was now less support for young women in the same situation. But Laura, who also became a single mother in the mid-1980s felt that it had been more difficult then because there were fewer similar people around with whom she could share her experiences and difficulties.

KEY POINTS: BECOMING A 'SINGLE' LONE MOTHER

- In 1971 there were 90,000 single lone parents. By 1992 there were 490,000.
- In the late 1980s the proportion of lone mothers who were single women grew faster than any other type of lone parenthood.
- Becoming a single lone parent is a process involving a number of stages: having sex; not using contraception or not using it successfully; getting pregnant; not having an abortion; not getting together with the baby's father (or any other man); and not giving up the baby for adoption.
- In 1993 there were 364,000 conceptions which occurred outside marriage. About a third of these ended in abortion. About one in ten led to births within a marriage. About half led to births which were registered by both parents and the remaining one in ten led to births which were registered by one parent only. Only about 1,000 babies were given up for adoption.
- The number of single lone mothers has not been growing continuously since World War II. In the 1940s and 1950s, the number of women becoming single lone mothers was fairly low and stable. It increased quite dramatically in the 'swinging sixties' but then declined in the 1970s. This decline was probably due to the

availability of legal abortions in the 1970s and also to generally declining fertility rates. Evidence suggests that the number of women becoming single lone mothers began to rise again in the 1980s.

- Single women who were from a poor socio-economic background were much more likely than others to become single lone parents. The risk of single lone parenthood was lowest for daughters of men in professional occupations but high for daughters of men in semi- or unskilled manual work.

- Women in full-time education were least likely to become single lone mothers. Those in a job were more likely to do so but those at most risk were women who were neither in education nor employment.

- Housing tenure was an important variable linked to single lone motherhood. Women who had been living in council houses or flats at the age of 14 were more than twice as likely as other women to become a single lone parent at some point in their later lives.

- Women from West Indian backgrounds were much more likely than white or Asian women to become single lone mothers.

- There was some association between high rates of unemployment and high rates of lone parenthood, but detailed analysis suggests that this association is due more to coincidence than any causal effect: single lone parenthood has, by coincidence, increased most during periods of high unemployment.

- Despite the identification of some socio-economic variables with the growth of single lone motherhood, it is difficult to explain more than a small part of the growth by these variables. Much of the trend has occurred independently of such variables.

- Some single lone mothers got pregnant after fairly casual sex. Others had regular boyfriends whom they were not cohabiting with and others had been cohabiting in the past but separated from their partners at some point before the baby was either conceived or born.

- Only one woman in the qualitative study deliberately planned to become a single lone parent. She was older and more middle class than the other single lone parents. But there were signs that the risk of getting pregnant did not greatly concern the young women in the study.

- Some single lone parents got pregnant because they did not use contraception even though they did not particularly want to conceive. This was mostly due to: trusting in a partner; taking risks; and an eagerness not to feel, and be seen as, promiscuous.

- Some single lone parents got pregnant because their contraception use was unsuccessful, for example they missed one or more pills or they had been taking antibiotics which reduced the pill's effectiveness.
- Abortion is a much more common way in which some women avoid lone parenthood. Those who did not have terminations usually disagreed with it and, in some cases, had had previous experiences which they did not wish to repeat. Some women, however, simply became accustomed to the idea of having a baby while single and did not see it as a problem which needed a solution such as abortion.
- Most women did not consider their boyfriends suitable for marriage, mostly because they were not seen as very industrious or trustworthy. Some women did want to live with their partners but their partners did not wish to do so.
- Adoption was very rarely considered by single pregnant women. It was incompatible with their identities as women/carers and was more stigmatised than lone parenthood.
- The parents of the lone parent were usually shocked on first hearing the news of their daughter's pregnancy. But most were generally supportive. Some of the lone parents' mothers had, themselves, been lone parents. Most mothers valued their daughter's individual happiness more highly than any idea of social duty.
- Most women expected to receive social security once they became lone parents. They did not expect this to be generous but in some cases it was seen as preferable to the available alternatives, such as living on YTS or living on income support as a couple.
- Support from parents was very important for single pregnant women in deciding to carry on with a birth while remaining single.
- Stigma against lone parents was rife in the community and was directed, in particular, against the 'folk devil' figure of the teenage girl who deliberately gets pregnant to acquire social housing and social security. None of the women interviewed felt that they conformed to this model but some of them believed such women existed and they, themselves, looked down on them.

Chapter 3

Becoming a separated lone parent

Although most concern about lone parenthood is usually directed towards single lone mothers, the most common route to lone parenthood is still separation and/or divorce from a partner. This chapter looks at how some women become separated lone mothers. As with the last chapter, we begin by using official statistics and previous studies to chart this growth before reporting on our secondary analysis of SCELI. The final sections of this chapter discuss our qualitative findings. Although we include separations from cohabitation in our definition of separated lone parents, it should be remembered that most of the official statistics exclude these and much of our quantitative analysis also concentrates on women who separate from a husband.

CHARTING THE GROWTH OF SEPARATED/DIVORCED LONE MOTHERHOOD

In 1971 there were 290,000 lone mothers who had separated or divorced from a husband in Britain (Haskey, 1994). By 1992, this figure had more than doubled to 730,000. Table 1.1 in Chapter 1 showed that between 1971 to 1986, divorce lone parents were becoming a particularly important component of lone parenthood, while between 1987 to 1992, separated lone parenthood became more prominent.

The figures on the increasing number of separated and divorced lone mothers are, not surprisingly, mirrored by the figures on divorce – with just over 58,000 decrees made absolute in 1970 rising to 165,000 in 1993. In 1970, 0.47 per cent of the married population divorced compared with 1.4 per cent in 1993 (see Figure 3.1). This

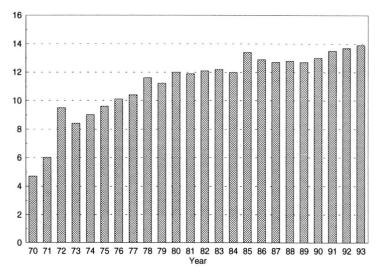

Source: OPCS marriage and divorce statistics

Figure 3.1 Persons divorcing per 1,000 married population

figure shows that there was a steady rise between 1970 and 1979 which, apart from a one-off increase in 1984–85, plateaued in the 1980s before rising again in the early 1990s. The trend in divorce is therefore rather different to the trend in extra-marital conceptions which, as we saw in the previous section, increased in the late 1980s but has been falling in the early 1990s.

There was a particularly dramatic rise in divorces between 1971 and 1972 reflecting the 1969 Divorce Act which came into effect in 1971. In principle, changes in divorce law could have a number of different effects. At a minimum, they would affect the ability of those currently separated to get a divorce. Changes in divorce law do affect the number of divorces granted immediately after their introduction. However, this does not necessarily mean that they affect the likelihood of separation. It is sometimes suggested that easier divorce undermines the character of marriage, reducing people's propensity to stay married during difficult times. An alternative suggestion is that easier divorce encourages people to get married without full consideration of the consequences. In fact, there is little evidence to support these views and although it is true that the number of divorces rose

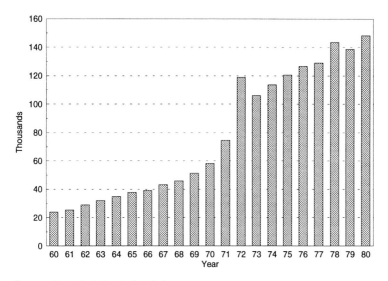

Source: Annual abstract of statistics

Figure 3.2 Decrees absolute

sharply when the 1969 Divorce Act came into effect in 1971, there had been a long-running increase in divorce prior to 1971 and this was precisely the reason why the Act was introduced (see Figure 3.2). Furthermore, if these divorces merely mark in law the separations which have already occurred in practice, divorce law will have little impact on the growth of lone parenthood.

It is worth noting, however, that the 1984 Matrimonial and Family Proceedings Act reduced the minimum period after marriage that a petition for divorce could be filed from three years to one. Once again, this may not have had any effect on actual separations, but there was an increase in the proportion of divorces which were of marriages of short durations. In 1993, 8 per cent of divorces were of marriages which had lasted under three years (Central Statistical Office, 1996). This has also meant that the number of children under five who have been affected by divorce has increased.

Not all divorces involve couples with dependent children but the proportion which do (about three in five) has remained fairly constant over the last 20 years. This means that in 1993 just under 100,000 divorces occurred which involved one or more children under the age of 16.

In 1993 women were about two and a half times more likely than men to petition for divorce. And where a divorce was granted to a woman, over half were for unreasonable behaviour and one in five were for adultery. Where a divorce was granted to a man, the most common ground given was adultery (Central Statistical Office, 1996).

The following factors have been identified as increasing the likelihood of divorce:

* early marriage (Ermisch, 1991)
* premarital cohabitation (Bennett and others, 1988)
* premarital birth (Martin and Bumpass, 1989)
* having children early in marriage (Ermisch, 1991)
* childlessness (Ermisch, 1991)
* couples from poor economic backgrounds (Ermisch, 1991)
* couples with low educational achievement (Ermisch, 1991)
* couples from different social classes (Hart, 1976)
* experience of marital breakdown among close family (Hart, 1976)
* having been married previously (Martin and Bumpass, 1989)
* experience of living apart (Hart, 1976)
* access to alternative partners (Hart, 1976)
* access to an alternative home (for example, parents) (Hart, 1976)
* ethnicity, that is, black women have a much higher risk of becoming lone parents compared with white women (Guttentag and Secord, 1983).

As we can see, many factors have been identified as being associated with divorce and there have also been some attempts to explain the nature of the relationship between these factors and separations among couples. For example, Burgoyne and others (1987) have argued that getting married early may lead to divorce because it is related to other factors, such as coming from a poor background and having a premarital birth or conception. So the inter-relationship between factors is important and makes it difficult to establish cause and effect.

Some factors have been identified as being associated with decreasing the likelihood of divorce. For example, Seccombe and Lee (1987) found that couples were less likely to divorce where the father was more involved with childcare. Linked to this, is the fact that fathers are more involved in childcare when they have sons and the presence of sons has also been identified as reducing the probability of divorce (Morgan and others, 1988).

Most of the studies which have identified factors relating to divorce concern all married couples not just those with children. Nevertheless they are informative. Few studies have looked specifically at separations among cohabiting couples which may or may not be similar to reasons for separations among married couples.

When talking to those who have separated from a partner, people give very personal reasons for the end of their relationship, such as finding a new partner, having financial difficulties, and having problems stemming from alcoholism, lack of communication and infidelity (Bradshaw and Millar, 1991). The challenge for researchers is to link the personal factors which people themselves use to explain the end of their relationship, with the micro and macro socio-economic factors which quantitative analysts have identified as associated with relationship breakdown.

FACTORS ASSOCIATED WITH THE GROWTH OF SEPARATED LONE PARENTHOOD

Although 'single' parents have captured the headlines and their numbers have been growing most rapidly in recent years, the majority of the 'stock' of lone parents have separated from a partner. In this section, the life histories from the SCELI survey will be analysed to estimate the rate at which married couples with children separate; to analyse variations in that rate by the characteristics of the marriage and the partners; and to look for evidence of changes over time in parents' tendency to split up.

Separations/divorces among couples with children

The analysis is based on women who had both married and had children, since these were the women who were 'at risk' of becoming a lone parent by separation; childless couples are ignored. So are parents after the point at which all of their children had reached the age of 17. In common with Ermisch (1991) the analysis focuses on couples whose first child was born after 1960; and the observation period is automatically closed by the date of the SCELI interviews in 1986. The details of the sample are shown in Table 3.1. For most of this section, we concentrate entirely on couples who were married when their first child was born; there is a short discussion of those who were cohabiting at the time of the first birth, at the end of the section.

There were 1,813 couples who had a first child while married: 327 of them separated or divorced while their children were still of dependent age, and these are the 'events' subject to detailed analysis in the following pages. Other women became lone parents as a result of the death of their husband, but these are not counted as 'events' for our purposes, on the assumption that factors leading to the death of a husband would have little in common with the influences on separation or divorce.

Table 3.1   Outcomes of first partnerships with children

	Married couples		*Cohabiting couples*	
Total number of women with children	1,813		49	
Number of months 'at risk'	265,209		3,318	
	mean=146		mean=68	
Separation or divorce (before children grew up, and before interview)	327	18%	19	39%
Widowed	37	2	nil	
Children reached 17	196	11%	7	14%
Still married/cohabiting and with children at interview date (censored)	1,253	69%	23	47%
Monthly exit rate				
All exits	21.1 per 10,000		78.4 per 10,000	
Separation	12.3 per 10,000		57.2 per 10,000	

Note: The technical complexities required were too great to include the small number of second or third partnerships in the analysis.

For 196 couples, the possibility of becoming a lone parent was ended by the fact that their children had grown up. At first sight it is surprising that the number completing their spell as a parent couple was actually lower than the number who separated or divorced. That does not mean that the latter is the more common occurrence overall; but it takes a minimum of 17 years for a period of parenting to end through the ageing of the children, so only those who entered the sample during the early to mid-1960s would have had a chance for this to have happened by 1986. In fact two-thirds of all the married couples interviewed were still together and still had dependent children when the survey took place, and we do not know how the spell was to end.

As before, the analysis deals with that by dividing each spell into monthly segments – the first month after the birth of the child, the second, the third and so on. It is the probability of separating in any month that is the key variable to be studied.

A complication is that the survey did not distinguish as clearly as it might have done between separation and divorce. One third of those who had done either said they had divorced; women who had been through both stages might have recorded only the divorce, which may have occurred months or years after the separation. To the extent that they did so, the estimates of duration of the marriage will be too high, and the estimates of exit rates too low.

Modelling break-ups among married couples with children

The analysis of the monthly hazard rate in the following pages is confined entirely to the couples who were married at the time of the birth of their first baby. It considers, first, what characteristics of the marriage itself were associated with high and low rates of separation and divorce: the age at which the woman married and when the baby was conceived (both fixed), plus the duration of the spell so far (time-varying). Separation rates are then compared in terms of the woman's social background (fixed) and the couple's current situation (time-varying). Finally, the evidence from the SCELI survey is used to examine the growth of entry into lone parenthood by this route. The results are summarised in Table 3.2. As in the previous chapter, the first column shows the results of an analysis of the hazard rate by each variable, taken one at a time; the second the results of a model in which the effect of each variable is measured after taking account of all the others. The figure R=0.xxx is an indication of the power of the variable in helping to explain the hazard rate, with a theoretical maximum of 1.00. Once again, sample sizes look very large because they represent 'person-months' rather than individual people.

Characteristics of the marriage

Other studies have found that marriages that take place at younger ages tend to be shorter (Price and McKenry, 1988). The analysis here takes the birth of a child as the starting point of the spell, but it is still clear that the mothers who had married younger had a high hazard rate. (We do not know how old the fathers were when they married.)

Table 3.2   Hazard rate for separation or divorce among married couples with children

relative risk ratios

	Simple analysis	Multivariate model	Sample size
Overall average	12.3 per 10,000		
1 Log of age at marriage	R=−0.125	R=−0.090	
2 Conception of first child	R=0.106	R=0.034	
Before marriage	2.83	1.61	47,382
Within 1 year	1.47	1.24	88,686
More than 1, up to 5 years	1.00 (=8.3)	1.00	105,699
More than 5 years	0.89	0.84	20198
3 Duration (months since start of period)			
Duration	R=0.025	R=0.025	
(Duration)^2	R=−0.032	R=0.042	
4 Area	not sig	R=0.030	
Aberdeen		0.65	43,961
Coventry		1.36	41,390
Kirkcaldy		0.96	46,225
Northampton		0.95	41,532
Rochdale		1.47	43,216
Swindon		1.00	45,641
5 Ethnic group	not sig	R=0.041	
White		1.00	253,477
Asian		0.12	6,387
West Indian		0.25	1,499
Other/not known		0.01	602
6 Partner's activity	R=0.091	R=0.023	
Working	1.00 (=11.3)	1.00	250,413
Unemployed or scheme	3.31	1.81	7,927
Sick/disabled	0.61	0.52	1,432
FT education	2.35	3.21	752
Other/not known	3.61	1.95	1,441
7 Local unemployment rate	R=0.051	not sig	
Up to 2.5%	0.63		75,303
2.51 to 5%	1.16		45,503
5.1 to 7.5%	0.99		57,482
7.51 to 10%	1.36		20,568
10.1 to 12.5%	1.00 (=12.3)		21,423
12.51 to 15%	1.3		13,318
Over 15%	1.49		28,368

continued

relative risk ratios

	Simple analysis	Multivariate model	Sample size
8 Current housing	R=0.154	R=0.153	
With parents	6.93	7.82	8,266
Owner-occupier	1.00 (=7.1)	1.00	155,103
Public rental	2.37	1.79	72,386
Private rental	3.15	3.91	13,683
Others	2.13	2.07	12,527

Note: In each group, one element has been chosen as the 'reference category' and assigned a relative risk of 1.0; the hazards in other categories are expressed as a ratio to that one. The actual risk (per 10,000) in the reference category is given in brackets. In the second panel of the table, for example, the risk of separation was 8.3 per 10,000 for a couple whose first child was conceived between 1 and 5 years after they married. For those whose child had been conceived before marriage, it was nearly three times that.

Figure 3.3 shows the shape of the relationship implied by the term 'log of age at marriage' – there was a big difference between the women who married very young and those who were rather older; but not much difference between those who married in their early or later twenties.

The raw effect of age at marriage was one of the strongest influences on separation rates; but it was reduced substantially once other factors had been taken into account.

Previous research (Ermisch, 1991) has also found a marked difference in rates of separation by whether the first child was conceived prior to the wedding. We reach the same conclusion, illustrated by Figure 3.4. Rates of separation were twice as high where a premarital conception took place, compared with couples who delayed starting a family for at least a year. This may link back to single lone motherhood – shotgun weddings may have been seen as a way of avoiding lone parenthood, but the marriages were not necessarily stable, and would sometimes merely have delayed the process. On the other hand, we also found high rates of separation when the first baby appeared to have been conceived within a year after the marriage.

The timing of the baby was less important a factor in the multivariate model than when examined on its own. Many of those who married young also had early pregnancies, and it was the combination

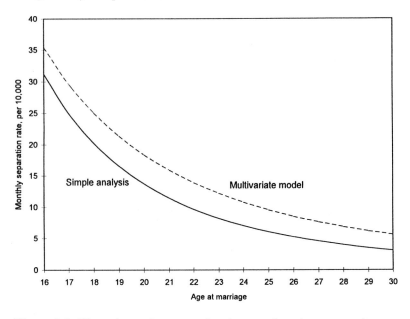

Figure 3.3   Hazard rate for separation, by age of mother at marriage

of the two which had the strongest effect on the probability of separation.

Most analysis of the duration of marriage starts counting at the date of the wedding, whereas the spells under consideration here started at the birth of the first child. In effect, therefore, duration is simply the (eldest) child's age. Figure 3.5 shows the pattern implied by the relationships calculated between the hazard rate and the combination of duration and duration-squared: the chances of separation were below average immediately after the birth of a child; rose gradually to a peak when the child was about 7 or 8; and then steadily declined.

Family background

The simple analysis in Table 3.2 suggested that the six towns in which the SCELI survey was undertaken had broadly similar rates of marital breakdown. But the multivariate model showed that there were differences once other factors had been taken into account, and the conclusion is that the rate of breakdown was lower in Aberdeen and higher in Coventry and Rochdale than might have been expected,

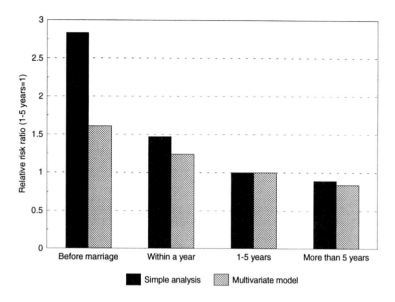

Figure 3.4   Hazard rate for separation, by timing of conception

given the other characteristics of the women who were interviewed there. In the absence of much fuller information about the special features of those towns, in comparison with all other locations, we can only speculate about what it was about Aberdeen, Coventry and Rochdale which made them stand out; the only interpretation that can be placed on the finding is that geographical variation may be an important influence on separation rates.

The findings in the previous chapter were consistent with other research which suggests that marriage is very important to people of South Asian origin, while those of Caribbean origin place a lower weight on marriage as an institution than white people (Modood, Berthoud and others, 1997). Here, it appears that both Asians and West Indians were substantially less likely to separate than white women with otherwise similar characteristics. For Asians, this is consistent with other findings; for West Indians it is inconsistent. It was pointed out earlier that the six-town sample was unlikely to provide a representative sample of members of minority groups, and little weight should be placed on the result for West Indians.

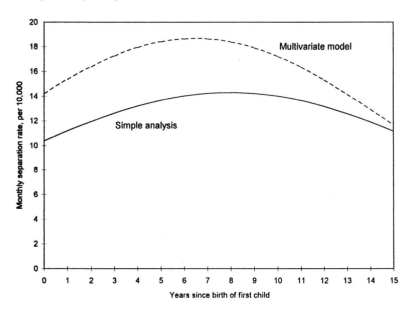

Figure 3.5 Hazard rate for separation, by duration of spell since birth of the child

Surprisingly, neither social class of origin (as measured by the respondent's father's occupation when she was 14) nor the woman's own educational achievement was associated with variations in the risk of separating from a marriage with children. It is known that both these indicators of disadvantage help predict marriage at an early age, and premarital conceptions (Garfinkel and McLanahan, 1986; Ermisch, 1991). There was some sign of that relationship in our data,[11] but it was not strong enough for social and educational background to make any contribution to the explanation of separation rates.

Current situation

The SCELI life histories also provided information about the economic and housing position of the couples in each month of the period under study, and this can be used to show whether the risk of separations was influenced by their recent experiences.

One hypothesis was that women with jobs might be less financially dependent on their husbands, and could therefore feel more confident about supporting themselves if the marriage was in trouble. A counter

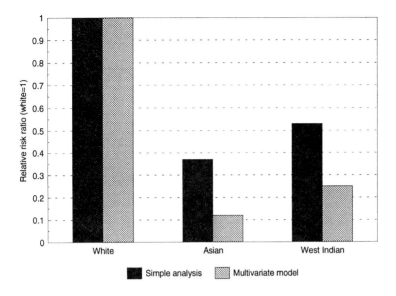

Figure 3.6   Hazard rate for separation, by ethnic group

hypothesis was that where the woman was employed, the family's finances would be in good shape, and this might reduce the risk of personal tensions. It turned out that the mother's economic activity was not associated with separation hazard rates, either way.

There was, though, an important association with the child's father's economic activity. The samples of women whose partner had been sick, in education or in 'other' activities were too small for much notice to be taken of the figures for those categories. If the husband was unemployed, though, the couple were three times more likely to split up than if he was in work (Figure 3.7). This is strongly indicative of financial stress being associated with the creation of one parent families. An alternative interpretation, though, might be that when couples are already on benefit, the prospect of the mother and children turning to income support may not be such a disincentive to separate from a partner.

It should also be noted that the unemployment effect was substantially smaller when the multivariate model took account of all other factors. The indications are that couples who had married young and had children early may have had high rates of unemployment.

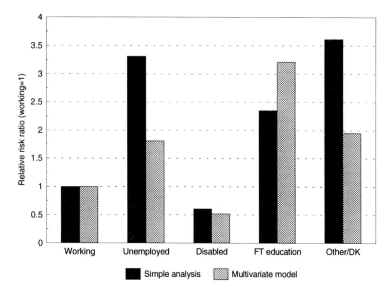

Figure 3.7 Hazard rate for separation, by economic activity of the husband

Unemployment nevertheless retained an independent association with the risk of separation, after controlling for the other variables.

The basic tables suggested the possibility that separations were more likely at times and in places of high unemployment, but this association disappeared once other information about the couples was taken into account.

There were substantial differences, though, between couples in different sorts of accommodation. Not many lived with the young woman's parents, but those who did had a very high risk of separation. An initial interpretation was that couples who had married young and in a hurry might have been most likely to turn to their parents for shelter, and they might well have been unemployed too. But the effect held up strongly after these things had been taken into account, and it seems likely that it is specifically associated with the crowding and potential personal tensions likely in a domestic situation which is not customary in Britain.

Less striking, but more important numerically, couples in council housing and, especially, in privately rented housing, were substantially

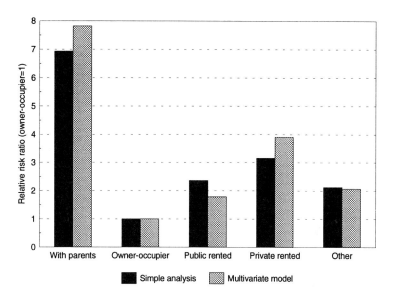

Figure 3.8 **Hazard rate for separation, by housing situation at the time**

more likely to separate than those who were buying their own home. This is another indication that couples who were able to secure a conventionally prosperous lifestyle had better prospects of staying together. The rate of separation for families in council housing reduced somewhat when other aspects of disadvantage were taken into account. But, overall, the Rs in Table 3.2 showed that this was easily the most important correlate of separation, whether it is the simple analysis or the multivariate model that is being considered.

Changes over time

The analysis so far has covered all the months 'at risk' of separation by married couples who had their first child in 1960 or later, up until the time of the survey in 1986. It is important to see whether there was a consistent trend towards a higher or lower incidence of separation and divorce, and so towards the creation of lone parent families.

A technical difficulty is that the sample of couples at risk was not the same at all times through the period. The problem is illustrated in

Table 3.3 Diagram showing changing composition of sample at risk of separation

				Period of observation					
Date of birth	1950	1955	1960	1965	1970	1975	1980	1985	1990
1950	x	x	x	x	x				
1955		x	x	x	x	x			
1960			o	o	o	o	o		
1965				o	o	o	o	o	
1970					o	o	o	o	c
1975						o	o	o	c
1980							o	o	c
1985								o	c

Key: x = excluded   o = observed   c = censored

Table 3.3, where each row represents a married couple who had a baby in a particular year. For the purpose of the diagram, each period of potential risk is assumed to last 20 years. The columns of the diagram represent the years in which we might wish to observe the separation rate. In 1960 there were many couples who had started their period as a two parent family before then, but they were excluded from the data being analysed. The 1960 sample consists entirely of people whose child was born that year. By 1985, on the other hand, the sample includes not only those whose child was born in 1985, but also those whose children had been born at any time since 1965. In general, therefore, the earlier years of the survey cover only those who had recently entered their spell; while the later years contain a range of short and long durations. Exactly that effect is observed in the data itself, where the cases at risk during the first five years of the period average only 27 months duration, with a standard deviation of 14. Those at risk during the last five years averaged 137 months duration, with a standard deviation of 79.

What this means is that a straightforward analysis of the rate of separation observed in any year would not make sense. It is essential to control for the varying durations of the spells experienced prior to each year. This can be done simply by including the known association between duration and the hazard rate as well as the date in a 'mini' multivariate equation.

The continuous jagged line in Figure 3.9 shows the estimated separation rate in each year of the period under analysis, after

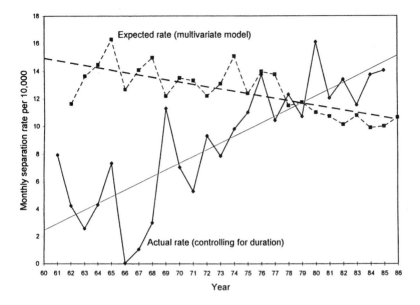

Figure 3.9 Hazard rate for separation, by date

controlling for the duration effect, as just described. There is an indication of a fall in separation rates at first, but this is the least reliable section of the data, and the overall impression is of a fairly steady rise in separation rates. In the case of single parenthood (Chapter 2), there was not a single trend in the rate of entry; it rose and then fell. For entry to separated lone parenthood, the year-to-year figures could be summarised as a steady trend. The straight continuous line plots the best fit between the yearly points, to suggest that the hazard rate rose steadily from about 2.5 per 10,000 in 1960 to 15 per 10,000 in 1986. This is a sixfold rise.

Can this growth be 'explained' in terms of changes over the period in some of the other characteristics of couples at risk – such as their age at marriage, timing of conception, rate of unemployment or housing situation? The full multivariate model (right hand column of Table 3.2) can be used to predict what the hazard rate would have been each year, taking account of changes in the number of couples who had married young, had children early, were unemployed or were not living in owner-occupied accommodation, but if the rate of separation had remained unchanged. In fact the only two 'predictor' variables which changed significantly over the period acted in opposite directions: the rise in the number of unemployed partners would have increased the separation rate; but the rise in owner-occupation would have reduced it. It turned out that the latter was the stronger influence. The dashed line in Figure 3.9 shows that the 'expected' rate of separation fell by about 4 points per 10,000 over 16 years. The fact that the actual rate rose by 12 points is all the more surprising: the underlying trend must have been even stronger to counteract the changing expectation.

Even that clear conclusion requires some interpretation, however. The proportion of married couples with children who were separating rose over the period. On the other hand, the total number of married couples with children may have been going down, as a result partly of the reduction in fertility rates, and partly of the increase in the proportion of children born outside marriage. A rising proportion of a shrinking total means that this source may not have made as important a contribution to the overall growth of lone parenthood as at first appears.

Cohabitations

The text of this section so far has described couples who were married when their first child was born. Table 3.2 recorded some parallel information about women who said they were living with their partner at the time of the birth. Although unmarried, they did not immediately become single parents, because the child was living with both parents. They could, however, separate later: their official status then would depend on whether they had got married in the meantime, but for our purposes they should really be considered separated, rather than 'single'.

Cohabitation, and births to cohabiting couples, have become increasingly important elements in the pattern of family formation in Britain in recent years, as well as in other countries (Kiernan and Estaugh, 1993; Dormor, 1992). It should be recognised that cohabitation is not the same as marriage and can span a variety of relationship types. Although a number of studies have focused on this group (McRae, 1993), it remains far from clear how cohabitation fits into the pattern which previously divided single people unambiguously from married couples. Some couples turn out to be using cohabitation as a preliminary to formal marriage; others split up without marrying;

only a small proportion remain together so long that the condition should be seen as a long-term alternative to marriage (Ermisch, 1995).

From the point of view of lone parenthood, the important question is: what happens in the years following the birth of a child to a cohabiting couple? If they marry, or as long as they stay together, they remain a two parent family. If and when they split, a one parent family will be formed; if the couple still have not married by then, the family will be categorised as 'single' parent, although its origins may be more similar to those of a formerly married mother and children. Ermisch (1995) has used the BHPS life histories to analyse the outcomes of first births to cohabiting couples. He estimated that by the time the child is ten years old, half of the mothers will still be with the father – most of them will be married to him by then. But the other half of cohabiting couples will have split up before the age of ten – before s/he left primary school. Similar analysis of BHPS couples who were married at the birth of their first child suggests that only one in eight would separate within ten years (Table 3.4). On the other hand Murphy (1995) has made a strong case that there is insufficient evidence that cohabitations break up more quickly than marriages, once account has been taken of other factors.

Table 3.4   **Life-table estimates of the proportion of couples who separate in the years following the birth of their first child, by marital status at the time of the birth**

	Cohabiting		Married	
	SCELI	BHPS	SCELI	BHPS
Within 2 years	20	na	4	na
Within 5 years	33	42	11	7
Within 10 years	na	50	19	12
Number of separations contributing to analysis	19	39	159	123

column percentages

Notes
1   BHPS cohabitation figures from Ermisch (1995); BHPS married figures calculated by Ermisch and Francesconi at our request.
2   SCELI married figures confined to births occurring after 1974. BHPS married figures confined to women born in 1950 or later.

The problem for this study was that there were only 49 cases in which a child was born to a cohabiting couple. Also, the SCELI survey only asked whether the woman was cohabiting during each year of her life history, and this does not fit well with other information which was accurate to the month. Of the 49, 19 had separated following the birth of the child, and this does not provide a sound base for the sorts of detailed analysis required. The raw separation rate was 57 per 10,000 months for the cohabiting couples, compared with 12 per 10,000 for the married ones (see Table 3.1 earlier). Some analysis suggested that the separation rate was increasing over time. Table 3.4 shows that one in five cohabiting women with children separated from their partner within two years of having their first child, while one in three separated within five years. The comparable figures for married couples were one in 25 and one in 10. These figures appear to provide strong support for Ermisch's findings, but cannot be read as conclusive proof until larger sample sizes allow both types of couple to be included in a single multivariate model.

If confirmed, the higher rate of separation among couples whose first child is born outside marriage would have important implications for our study of the growth of lone parenthood. The chapter on single mothers showed that, although the number of babies born to mothers who were neither married nor cohabiting was higher at the end than at the beginning of the period of observation, there was no consistent upward trend. A short section on births to non-married mothers who were cohabiting showed, however, that most of them had occurred at the end of the period. There is other evidence – such as the number of registrations of 'illegitimate' births by both parents – that births to cohabiting couples have been increasing through the 1980s and 1990s. This chapter has shown that the rate of separation and divorce by officially married couples with children increased steadily over the 1960s, 1970s and early 1980s, and that trend may have continued. But if couples who have a child while cohabiting really do have much higher separation rates than married couples, that could provide one of the strongest explanations for the growth of lone parenthood in recent years. The trend may be concealed by the fact that this important group is consistently misclassified in official statistics, because the mother's marital status is typically recorded as 'single' rather than 'separated'.

PERSONAL EXPLANATIONS OF RELATIONSHIP BREAKDOWN

The quantitative research looked at variables associated with separations among couple with children, but the only way of understanding the process by which relationships end is to talk to people who have gone through the process to find out what happened and why. The task then is to unravel these personal explanations and see how more 'objective' factors such as social class, age and economic activity have had an effect on people's personal lives. The other task for the analysis is to explain how and why personal difficulties within a relationship eventually lead to separation rather than being resolved or accepted by both members of the couple.

Among our interviewees, the most common relationship problems mentioned were: disputes over the control and spending of money; domestic violence; and extramarital affairs. But it is important to explain why these problems led to separation rather than being resolved or accepted. We also need to explain why relationship breakdown has become more common among couples with children. Is it because the incidence of problems has increased – and if so why? Or is it because partners are less likely to resolve or accept problems and are more likely to separate – and if so why? It is important to remember that we have only the woman's version of the reasons for the relationship breakdown. Talking to the men would probably have provided a different version (see Bradshaw and others, 1997).

It is also worth remembering that among our 22 'separated' lone mothers, six had separated from a cohabiting relationship and the remaining 16 had been married. The group were also diverse in terms of the length of time they had spent in their relationships and the year in which they had separated from their partners. Ten women had lived with their partner for five years or less before splitting up. Seven had been together between six and 10 years and five had been together for more than 10 years. The majority (13) had split up since 1991 but seven had separated in the late 1980s and two had become lone parents in the early 1980s. There were three ex-couples where the mother was white and the father was black.

Although quantitative research has suggested that the presence of young children can prevent or postpone separation, in 14 out of 22 cases the youngest child was less than 2 when the couple split up. Seventeen of the women had been in their teens or early twenties when their relationship had begun so these women had begun to cohabit at an early age. In 16 cases, the woman said that it had been she who finally ended the relationship, according to her.

Conflict over money and gender roles

Arguments over money and conflict over gender roles were often at the centre of the difficulties in the relationship and were usually related to each other. As suggested by the quantitative research, problems sometimes began, or were intensified, if the man in the relationship became unemployed. Valerie believed that their problems had been triggered when:

> My partner had a series of bad backs and he had to have surgery and it worried me constantly because the money wasn't coming in because he wasn't working so it was like financial pressure.

Vicky's partner was out of work for over a year, during which time, unbeknown to her, their debts were increasing. But even when he got a job they were no better off because he was constantly out, socialising.

Lack of money by itself could cause tension within a relationship but it was more often the case that, with little money to go round, some women resented the fact that their partners appeared to be spending too much on themselves. There was also a feeling that little effort was being made to get back to work. Some of these women were working themselves and so further resented having to be both breadwinner and homemaker while their partner was doing very little. Their men were thought to be irresponsible and were seen as a drain on the family rather than making a positive contribution towards it.

Susan's problems also began when her husband was made redundant. But in her case, lack of money was not the cause of difficulties:

> While he was in regular work... he was absolutely fantastic. I mean he was brilliant with money. Bills were always paid. We didn't go without or anything like that... but then once he had all this [redundancy] money [about £18,000] he just seemed to, I don't know, lose a lot of responsibility on his part. He'd go and buy a car, quite a bit of money, keep it three months, be bored with that, see something else he wanted, sell that car at a loss to buy the next car.

Ros's partner had been in work but there were still tensions over money:

> [My ex-partner]'s not a responsible person so money became one of our huge problems because although we could afford the house and we could afford everything and me not work as long as we were really careful... he wasn't really careful... this is like 50 quid in the pub on a Friday night... and then I'd go and look in the bank to make sure we'd got enough money to pay one of the bills or something and we wouldn't have and he would hide it from me.

As well as being irresponsible about money, women also thought that their men were irresponsible, or had little interest in their children. Maria's partner had been made redundant. She managed to get a job to help the family out financially and he was supposed to be looking after the children until he found work but he did little in the way of child-care and they were still unable to meet their mortgage payments, eventually losing their home:

> He was supposed to look after the children but it came out in the light, he was letting me go to work and then dumping the children on the in-laws and going off with his mates.

Terri's partner was a heroin user and dealer who had never had a regular job. She said that she never knew when he would be home and when he would be away and he was, apparently, not interested in looking after his child:

> It was about a month or so after [our baby] was born and I was just fed up with him. It was twice as much work for me looking after [the baby] and him... he started going out and staying out days on end. I was just exhausted, pleading with him to stay back and help me take care of [the baby] and he wouldn't do it basically. To him it was baby-sitting and I couldn't make him understand that spending time with your son was not baby-sitting. It all went down-hill from there.

So lack of money on its own was not always as much of a problem as control of money and disagreements over how it should be spent. Such problems were more apparent when money was short but they could also cause difficulties when people were in jobs. The arrival and presence of children could produce or increase tensions over money and gender roles. This was because there would be less money to go round and the man would generally be the one in control of the money. Furthermore, the men appeared to expect that the relationship would now convert towards a more traditional breadwinner/homemaker model and this was not quite what the women expected. Pat explained what happened to her:

> We was fine until we had children. When we was both working, when we was both earning we was fine because we was on an even par but once I packed up and my income wasn't coming in any more he started getting a bit funny with money. As far as he was concerned, he went out and earned the money and it was entirely up to him what he spent the money on. And I didn't mind that to a certain extent, but when it came to the fact that he was going out and buying himself really good clothes to wear, as soon as the kids wanted something, he'd never got any money for them... And then we went through a patch where he threatened that he wasn't even going to give me housekeeping money...

Sarah's relationship with her partner also changed for the worse (as far as she was concerned) on the arrival of their first child:

> We used to do a lot more together... he'd go out and do the garden while I made the tea or he'd go out and wash the car while I made the tea... but all of a sudden when I had [the baby] things changed... he used to cook, but all of a sudden when I had [the baby] that all stopped – it was my job then for some reason... I don't know whether [my partner] thought I was just sitting at home all day and doing nothing.

When Sally left work during her pregnancy, conflict over money and gender roles became very apparent:

> I had to give up work when I was pregnant obviously towards the end. It was 'oh, how much of my money have you spent?' you know, very much like that, and, 'my tea should be on the table, you shouldn't be round at your friends talking'... and he'd even say things in front of his friends, things like, 'oh, you'll never guess what she went and spent my money on today!'

Arguments over money and gender roles were often increased when there were changes in the employment situation of one or more of the partners in the couple: for example, if a man lost his job or if a woman left work to care for children. There were also examples where conflict originated from a woman starting a job, as in Tessa's case:

> I did for a long time... let him be the boss and I had to do as I was told but when I got the job working in the bar I seemed to get a little bit more con-

fidence and... being behind a bar you have to be a bit assertive anyway. And I suppose I just got a bit more confident in the way that I didn't need him to tell me what to do all the time or what to wear and all the rest of it.

Escaping responsibility and having affairs

As we have just seen, arguments over money were often linked to the woman's view that the man in the relationship was irresponsible with money, spending too much on himself and not enough on the children. Linked to this, some women said that their relationship had broken down because their partner had left to find more fun and independence. The quantitative research suggested that people who married young were more likely to split up. The qualitative research suggests that this is because people, mostly men, regret the loss of their youthful freedom. The arrival of children was often the catalyst which caused difficulties because there was both less time and money to spend on oneself. Furthermore, women expected their partners to 'settle down' and behave more responsibly once children arrived but this was not always what the men wanted to do. Among the 22 cases of 'separated' lone parents, only six of the relationships had been ended by the man. Five of these had been ended because the man was seeking an escape route from what he saw as his oppressive family ties.

Paula recalled that when her ex-husband was in his late 20s and already had one child, he started mixing with:

18, 19 year olds, driving round in their XR3is, clubbing it every night. And looking back on it, I'd done all that, and for some reason I think he thought he hadn't.

He left her when she was pregnant with their second child and moved in with a 19 year-old woman whom he had met at work:

A lot of it was the responsibility which he didn't want to handle, which again didn't really make sense because if that was the case, why didn't he go [when we had the first baby]?... But looking at the way he has behaved since, that seems to have been the problem.

Vicky had a similar story to tell about her ex-partner, whom she moved in with when they were both 18:

> He started a job and he was working in a bar and it was like the worst thing he could have done because he was hanging round with people and I think he thought about what he was missing out on.

Valerie also had a similar tale about her ex-husband whom she married when she was 18:

> My partner... thought he was missing out on things. The grass was greener on the other side and it was all work and no play. And it was mortgages and families and things like that. And, you know, he just decided that maybe married life wasn't what he wanted and what he wanted was to be able to go out and enjoy himself and have other female company.

In most cases, it was the man who had wanted to escape family responsibilities. But there was also one case where it was the woman in the couple who had been seeking more excitement. As Penny explained:

> I'd been with [my ex-husband] from when I was 15 and by that time I was 25... I'd come straight from family to him, no in between time... he'd got boring. He just wanted 2.2 children, nice house... and I was 26 – I don't want this! I don't want to be like my mother and father at 26 years old.

The turning point came when Penny started having an affair with the manager at the shop where she worked:

> With him, it was – pop down to the warehouse, quick bonk, bottle of wine and 'who was he seeing tonight? Have a good time – see you when I see you'. And it was great because it was like, really good friends but it completely changed my outlook on everything... there was more to life, like... the sex was unbelievable. I didn't know these things existed and it was like, 'I don't want you [husband] no more. You're boring, get out!'

In a rather different case, one woman had sought to escape from the responsibility of caring for her partner. He had developed a severely debilitating illness and was unable to leave his bed. Samantha found herself caring full-time for two children and a partner and said she found it too 'strenuous'. She was not seeking 'fun' but an escape from spending all her time and energy as a carer.

The search for excitement often led men (and one woman in the study) to having one or more affairs. A study by Lawson (1988) found that about two in five British men and women had engaged in extramarital affairs at some point in their lives. This figure was considerably higher than for some other developed countries but was not based on a randomly selected sample so it has to be treated with some caution. The figure in the US was about one in three. It is interesting that, although attitudes to premarital sex have become increasingly liberal, attitudes towards extramarital sex have barely altered over the years. According to the 1990/91 SCPR sexual attitudes and behaviour survey (Wellings and others, 1994), four out of five people believe that extramarital affairs are always or mostly wrong (79 per cent of men and 84 per cent of women). Disapproval of sex outside a live-in relationship is also very high – about two-thirds of men disapprove and three-quarters of women. Attitudes towards extramarital sex do not vary greatly by age. Those aged 16–24 have similar attitudes to those in their late forties and fifties. These strong attitudes appear to be at odds with actual practice and the SCPR survey shows that about half of those who have ever engaged in extramarital sex say that it is always or mostly wrong. So disapproval of certain behaviour does not necessarily mean that someone will not behave in that way.

Seven women said that their partners had been involved in other sexual relationships while they were living together. The consequence of having an affair was sometimes that the man would leave his partner because he thought he might be happier in a different relationship or he might leave so that he felt more at liberty to have casual relationships. Another consequence was that his partner might find out about the affair and end the relationship. However, it was rare that the discovery of an affair would be enough, on its own, for a woman to end a relationship with a man. Usually there were other problems such as domestic violence or disputes over money. The accumulation of problems would eventually reach some kind of boiling point and lead to the end of the relationship.

Pat first found out that her partner was having affairs when they had their first baby but she did not feel that she had the strength to leave him and cope on her own, even though she had strong views on the subject:

> It might sound old fashioned but I believe that when you marry somebody, you marry for keeps... to me, how can you love one woman and sleep with another and then come home and expect your wife to sleep with you at the same time?

She did not think that her husband would have left her over any of the affairs:

> The funny thing about him was, he'd have these affairs but he didn't want the women. It was just something he wanted to do. He always wanted me. And even now, I know it might sound conceited, but he still does want me.

His affairs continued and their arguments over money became more frequent. When their three children were aged five, three and one, Pat felt that she would now be able to manage on her own and decided that she had had enough and left him.

Domestic violence

There is a great deal of controversy over the measurement of domestic violence, but a survey in the US in 1975 found that at least one violent incident had occurred in the past year in 16 per cent of the couples interviewed. And if the sample is restricted to married couples, the figure rose to 28 per cent (Straus, 1981). Although about two-thirds of these incidents involved 'minor' assaults such as slapping and throwing things, over a third were serious assaults such as kicking, hitting with an object or assaults with a knife or gun. This suggests that domestic violence was fairly common. A repeat of the study in 1985, however, showed that the incidence of domestic violence had declined by about a quarter. No similar survey has been carried out in Britain but it seems unlikely that the increase in separations is due to an increase in domestic violence. If anything, women may be less likely to remain in violent relationships than in the past.

In half of our cases (11 in total), domestic violence was cited as a contributory factor in the relationship breakdown. And four out of the six cohabiting relationships had broken down mainly because of violence. Once again, violence was often only part of the problem – along with conflict over money and gender roles. Mandy summarised what happened to her relationship:

> He was an alcoholic, he did actually get fired from the hotel where we both worked and we decided to come back to [Midlands town]. Things just got worse... you were waiting for him to come home with his wages. He'd never come. He'd spent all his money on drink... and eventually I felt the kids were suffering so I just called it a day, you know. I mean the police used to be out four or five times a week because I used to get beat up and,

you know... the good hidings got worse, and I think I eventually one day I just snapped and I give him back what he give me and he didn't like it, you know. In fact he did try to do me for husband battering... I mean that's not the kind of environment I think you should bring kids up in.

Ros's partner had been aggressive before the birth of his son but his aggression then turned to violence:

He got really drunk... and he beat the living daylights out of me. He tried to kill me, he strangled me... and it went on for ages, 20 minutes of him doing that and eventually I managed to get away and go next door and they'd phoned the police who came round and arrested him and I went to hospital... and that's what happened, that's why we split up.

Sarah's partner also became more violent after the birth of his son. Sarah felt that this was because he was jealous of the attention she gave to their new baby. On one occasion he went to hit Sarah and accidentally caught his son. Although he had not meant to harm him, Sarah decided that she could not stay any longer and so left him.

Rachel had been beaten up 11 times in the 10 years that she had been with her partner. After the birth of their child, the violence became more serious and 'the last straw' for Rachel came when her three year old son became a witness to the violence.

Experience of domestic violence did not always lead to the woman ending the relationship. Martina sometimes suffered brutal beatings:

I could be in bed asleep, yeah, and someone would upset him when he was out in the pub. And then he'd come home, drag me out of bed by my hair and start hitting me while I was sound asleep.

Her partner was also having affairs and was in and out of work, rarely providing any financial security. Despite all this, Martina stayed with him for 15 years. She said that she did this for the sake of the children and also to avoid the stigma of divorce:

Try and make good so people won't talk about you.

Although she did not leave him, Martina made it clear to her partner that she was very unhappy and refused to cook for him or even talk to him. Eventually he left her for another woman.

Maxine also experienced severe abuse. At one time, when she was seven months pregnant, her partner threw boiling water over her which resulted in a miscarriage. He also used to 'slap' their daughter, leading her to hide from him in cupboards. Nevertheless, Maxine had also stayed with him for 15 years and he eventually left her when their daughter was four years old. In the cases of both Martina and Maxine, there was parental disapproval of divorce which only wavered when their parents were told about the extent of the abuse they had suffered. But neither Martina nor Maxine had wanted to reveal their abuse to their parents (or anyone else) and their parents' disapproval of separation may have discouraged them from splitting up.

Maxine said that her mother:

> ...thought it was terrible, me going in for a divorce... I don't think she tried to stop me but she didn't like it very much... [she said] 'have another go at it and see if you can sit down and talk and have another go'.

Rona eventually left her abusive partner but she had initially hoped that the relationship could be saved:

> He was in and out of prison a lot when he was with me... He'd come in and I'd be asleep and he'd just start punching me and kicking me in the stomach... But I wanted to stay with him because we had a child together, you know, and I still thought I could change him.

As argued above, the growth of 'separated' lone parenthood could be partly due either to greater incidence of violence or to a reduction in tolerance of violence among those who experience it. Evidence from this, and other studies, suggests that it is a reduction in tolerance of domestic violence which has been most important. For example, Tessa's mother had been a victim of domestic violence but she had never left her partner. Tessa said that this was partly because the norms of the time discouraged separation and society treated the issue very differently from today:

> It was just the normal thing to do then [stay with your partner] even if there was violence. It was normal. There was nowhere to go. Nobody helped you. I mean, plenty of times my mum, the police turned up and they just didn't want to know... it was a case of, 'sorry, it's a domestic, we don't get involved', whereas nowadays they do.

Women, society in general and authorities such as the police, appear to be less willing to accept domestic violence than they have been in the past.

WHY PEOPLE SEPARATE RATHER THAN RESOLVE OR ACCEPT THEIR PROBLEMS

People may be unhappy in a relationship but this does not necessarily mean that the relationship will end. They may be able to resolve any conflict so that their unhappiness ends or they may decide to live with the unhappiness rather than end the relationship. The growth of lone parenthood which is due to mothers separating from partners could therefore be due either to a growth of discord within relationships or an increase in the proportion of unhappy relationships leading to separation. In the past, the stigma against divorce and the pressure to do one's duty to social norms rather than seek individual happiness may have reduced the number of separations which would otherwise have occurred. Such social pressures may now have declined. For example, the British Social Attitude Survey in 1992 found that very few people (only 2–3 per cent) agreed that 'it is better to have a bad marriage than no marriage at all'. And a majority (over 70 per cent for women and 59 per cent for men) agreed that it is better for a couple to end an unhappy marriage. But these percentages fall when children are involved (Scott and others, 1993).

All 22 couples in this study decided to end the relationship and so we do not have any comparison group to see why some people continued the relationship. However, we can look at the extent to which people tried to resolve their difficulties or were prepared to accept their problems.

Attempts to resolve or accept problems

There was a general view among the women interviewed that women today were less likely to stay in an unhappy marriage than they would have been in the past. Nevertheless, some women had been prepared to put up with a great deal and had not ended the relationship at the first sign of conflict.

Maxine (now 43) had stayed in a very violent relationship for 15 years during the 1970s and early 1980s. Despite the violence, she did not leave her husband – he eventually left her. Even then, Maxine initially hoped and expected that he would return and only started divorce proceedings after he had been away for a year and was living with another woman. Sian (now 47) had stayed with her husband for 20 years during the 1970s and 1980s despite a continual deterioration in their relationship. She was unhappy but he finally ended it in 1990 when he returned to Ireland. After taking advice from lawyers, Sian reluctantly divorced her husband. But she still considered herself married and, although she had not been happy with him, was prepared to have him back if he would come.

In other cases, women had also been reluctant to end relationships even though they were unhappy. In some cases, it was the man who initially left the family home. He then returned fairly soon afterwards, but in the meantime, his partner had gained the confidence to realise that she could manage on her own and she refused to take him back. Valerie had been with her husband for more than a decade when he left her for a next door neighbour. She took her husband back once but refused to do so a second time:

> He stayed living next door for a good six months I would think. And then that relationship came to an end and, having talked, we decided to try and make another go of it, which we did, which seemed the right thing to do – having a young child. But unfortunately within a couple of years a situation arose where he did exactly the same thing with another next door neighbour... and that relationship lasted 12 months or so. At that time, I actually found out that he had actually had affairs with others of my friends... so at that time I thought, 'this is it now' and so that's when I decided to call it quits and actually go for a divorce.

Natalie's relationship with her partner had been rather precarious. He had left her a number of times, including on two occasions while she was pregnant. She had always taken him back. But Natalie eventually decided that she did not want to live with his volatility and so when he left her again, soon after the baby was born, she finally ended it.

Sally had been unhappy in her relationship but was scared to leave her husband because she was not sure how she would cope alone. He had been in the Army and was posted abroad for six months during which time Sally realised that she could be happy again and could manage alone. When officials in the Army knew about the problems in the relationship they offered counselling but, by then, Sally had made up her mind to leave, and there was no turning back.

Some women had put up with an unhappy relationship for some time but then eventually decided that they would no longer do so. Sarah had been in a violent relationship for four years and she ended it when her partner hit her and accidentally hit their son at the same time.

For many women, however, there was no single trigger which led to them breaking up from their partner. Somehow, the steady accumulation of unhappiness continued until it reached a level which they could no longer bear. Mandy had been in an abusive relationship for eight years before she ended it:

> I'd just had enough. I mean I was coming up to my 40s then, well in fact I was past 40, and I used to look at other people and think to myself, 'they're in their 50s now, look what kind of life they've got', you know – the kids are off their hands, they're both together, still walking down the street arm in arm, what a wonderful life! What am I doing, sitting here and taking a life like this? There's no need for it, you know. I mean, alright, I'll have to bring three kids up on my own but anything is better than the life I've got now.

Pat reluctantly accepted her husband's affairs because she did not initially feel that she could cope as a lone parent but she grew in confidence until the day she decided to end it. In one last attempt to save her marriage, Pat and her husband went to Relate for guidance but, if anything, it helped Pat to end the relationship rather than helping her to remain in it:

> It did help me, I had never been able to speak my mind so freely... and it really made me feel better... and he [Pat's husband] never opened his mouth... and we went for the last session and the lady said to me, 'well I hope that we've helped you to save your marriage' and I says, 'no, I still want a divorce', so she says, 'well, why?' I says, 'because he has never opened his mouth once when we come here and I know for a fact he's still seeing this other woman'. And he couldn't deny it.

Susan's father had had many affairs and her mother had stayed with him. Susan thought that her mother had been 'weak' and should not have stayed but when she found herself in the same situation, Susan realised that it was not so easy to end a relationship as she had once thought. She eventually ended it after eight years.

Terri's relationship had been deteriorating but when she discovered she was pregnant she wanted to ignore the problems and hoped that things would improve:

> As it gets closer to the time of giving birth, you just want it all to be right and even though he'd been such a bastard to me, I just wanted it to be perfect... [after leaving hospital with the baby] he was almost nice to me for two weeks and then it just all went downhill again.

In other cases, there was a particular incident which led to the end of the relationship. Martina stayed in an unhappy relationship for over 15 years. Her husband had been violent and had several affairs. She had stayed with him because she thought it was the best thing to do for the children. She was also frightened of being stigmatised as a lone parent and divorcee. She felt that couples generally were too quick to separate and she was proud of the fact that: 'I did try, no-one could have tried harder'. The last straw came when he gave her a severe beating in front of their daughter. Martina decided at that point that 'enough's enough'.

Some couples did make particular efforts to avoid separation. Samantha had become unhappy with her bedridden husband. She decided to try for a baby son as a way of improving her life and their relationship, but even while she was pregnant it was clear that the birth of a new child would not bring them together and she left her partner.

Other couples tried reconciliations. Penny had left her husband because she felt she had missed out on the fun and excitement which she might have had in her teens and early twenties. After six months, Penny was unhappy again:

> Then I thought the grass isn't so green on the other side... I'd be going out with friends and they'd be stood in night-clubs and bars and everybody stood there, looking for a bloke... and I thought, 'I had a perfectly good bloke, what am I doing this for?'... and so we got back together to give it another go ... I said to him, 'I feel totally stifled. I need a life of my own. I need to do things. I just feel like I'm somebody's wife or somebody's mother. I'm not actually me.' And things were fine for about nine months.

But then Penny became unhappy again and felt that they had fallen back into the same routines and patterns that had led to her leaving him the first time. So she asked him to leave and this time it was for good.

Pat had also given her marriage another go, after her mother-in-law put pressure on her to do so. But Pat did not really believe the relationship would improve and her husband continued with an affair. Pat found it even more difficult to leave a second time, believing that her mother-in-law would now blame her for not trying hard enough rather than blaming her son for having affairs. She now felt desperate:

> I could have walked under a bus. I just kept walking and I thought, 'well, if I go under that bus I won't have no more problems' but it was the thought of the children that pulled me back. When I got home, I told him, I says, 'you're going to have to go', I says, 'I can't live like this'.

Although most relationships continued for some time after the initial problems appeared, some ended dramatically, giving one partner at least little time to try and repair any damage done to the relationship. Paula's husband had started going out a great deal and she had some idea that he was not particularly happy but when he left her one day, without any warning, it was like a bolt from the blue. He had moved in with another woman and never attempted to talk to Paula about his dissatisfaction with the relationship.

Rona left her partner soon after she had their baby because he started hitting her and she was not prepared to tolerate any violence.

Rita (now 47) had separated from her partner in 1981 after 11 years of marriage. On reflection, she felt that she not done enough to save the relationship:

> I wasn't desperately unhappy. I was totally unaware that he was unhappy, which proves to me that I was a very immature sort of person to not even notice... and I don't think I tried and I don't think he tried either.

So most women were reluctant to end their relationships even if they were unhappy. Attempts were made to resolve or accept problems but there was a limit to what would ultimately be accepted. Many women felt that, in the past, there had been virtually no limit to the unhappiness that women would accept within a relationship. As we shall see in the next section, the difference in more recent times was that there was now a limit, even though that limit was still fairly high.

The main reason why there was now a limit to the unhappiness which women would put up with was that they now felt less economically dependent on men. All 22 women had worked before they had children and most intended to go back to work at some point, although the exact timing of the return to work varied greatly from woman to woman. They knew that social security would enable them to survive if they felt unable to work immediately after splitting up with a partner but, more important, they believed that, at some point in the future, they would be able to provide for themselves and their families, through work.

Divorce law was not a factor which affected decisions about separation. Divorce was usually only considered once separation seemed final. In some cases, divorce occurred soon after the final separation. For many women it just seemed like the logical thing to do – the end of the process. As Penny remembered:

> It was the next step... I didn't want him having any hold over me.

Rita had always hoped that her husband might come back to her but eventually she gave up hope and accepted that the separation was final:

> It was five years before I said, 'right, that's it! I'm fed up of asking you to come back, I want a divorce'... because I couldn't really get on with my life until I knew what was happening.

There is a view that people are encouraged to divorce because the law made it easy for them to do so. But our interviewees said that they had known very little about divorce law before going through the process and none had expected the process to be easy. Some of them said that their divorce had been much easier than anticipated, suggesting that they had embarked on divorce despite the fact that they expected it to be problematic.

Reactions of parents

As with the 'single' lone parents, the attitudes and experiences of the women's parents were important for a number of reasons. In nine cases, the lone parents had 'lost' a parent through death or, more commonly, parental separation and this experience affected their attitudes towards their own relationship breakdown. It also meant that their parents were generally sympathetic to their daughter's situation. Other parents had stayed in unhappy marriages and now advised their daughters not to make the same mistake they had.

'Separated' lone parents were older than the 'single' lone parents and were not living at home with their parents while they were married or cohabiting, so in some ways, the attitudes of their parents were less important than they had been for the 'single' lone mothers. But they still had an effect and, because they were older, some of these parents had more traditional views than the parents of the 'single' lone mothers. Such traditional views sometimes meant that women felt they should stay in unhappy situations for reasons of social duty.

Given her mother's experience of an unhappy marriage, Susan decided to leave her unfaithful partner, and her mother supported her in doing this.

> My mum, she's quite a weakish person, she's very much a hypochondriac and her excuse for letting my dad have his affairs and what have you, was she wasn't going to chuck him out because she didn't want to be old and on her own. And here she is, she's on her own anyway because he died.

Whereas their mothers had stayed in unhappy relationships, the daughters did not. This was mainly because the daughters had greater confidence in general and also had greater financial and emotional independence from men. Experience of employment was often the key to such feelings of independence. Valerie's mother had also stayed with her unfaithful husband. She had done so because she was financially and generally dependent on him:

> My father had an affair and my mum found out about it and she had a lot of support from the family but mum was different [from me] because she didn't have any work... the house was not in her name for a start because the husband had the house then... and mum couldn't drive so she couldn't get herself from place to place... but she did say [to me] 'don't put up with it, you'll be better off without him'.

Tessa's mother had been through '22 years of hell' with her father, who was violent towards her. Tessa said that her mother had stayed with her husband:

> for the children... but the years of hell my mum went through was never worth it.

Although Tessa found herself in a similarly violent relationship, she was not prepared to stay in it and felt that it was actually better for her child not to stay.

Mandy's father had also been very violent to her mother and she had witnessed many distressing incidents. Mandy stayed with her violent partner for eight years before leaving him.

The women's mothers-in-law were generally much less keen for the relationship to end than their own parents. This was partly because they worried about their sons having to fend for themselves and partly because they did not wish to lose touch with their grandchildren. Martina's mother had thought her daughter should end her violent relationship sooner than she did. But her mother-in-law encouraged a reconciliation, despite knowing about the violence:

> His stupid mother used to keep ringing me up, saying, 'have him back, have him back!' and all that, but that was because she didn't want him.

Although most parents were supportive of their daughters, some were less so. Penny left her husband because she wanted more fun and excitement in her life. They had been childhood sweethearts and both family and friends were shocked that they were splitting up:

> Family were absolutely gutted, and friends. They were shocked because it was always imagined as, 'they'll be together forever, can't possibly split up'.

Penny's parents had had a reasonably happy marriage and had very traditional views. They found it difficult to understand the reasons behind the split and could not blame her husband who had not been violent, unfaithful or unreasonable. His only 'crime', as far as his wife was concerned, was to be rather boring. Her parents tried, unsuccessfully, to help:

> Mother was like, 'I'm sure there must be something you can do' and I said, 'No, mother, it's over'. 'Well what is it?' And I explained and I said, 'I don't even want to sleep with the man. It's disgusting, it feels like incest'. 'Well, if you go to a sex therapist I'm sure they'll sort you out.' 'I don't want to because it will only get back to exactly the same in a couple of years.'

Pat's parents had been happy together and, as far as she knew, faithful to each other. She had expected the same from her marriage which was why she found it difficult to accept her husband having affairs. Her mother was dead by the time Pat decided to end the relationship. But her mother-in-law pressurised Pat to attempt an unsuccessful reunion.

Rona's mother had encouraged her daughter to stay in her marriage, mainly because she had suffered the shame of being born illegitimately in the 1920s. Her own unhappy childhood led her to stay in a rather unhappy marriage because she placed greater value on social respectability and social duty than she did on her individual happiness. As Rona explained:

My mum was raised in a single parent family herself and it was a much worse thing in those days... and she got picked on and teased a lot because there was only her mum – her dad had gone off with someone else... My mum and dad don't actually get on that well, even though they're still together... but it's very important for her that they do stay together because of the sort of stigma attached to splitting up.

The existence of violence in a daughter's relationship usually meant that her parents were supportive about the end of it but this was not always the case. Maxine's mother had fairly traditional views and was in her sixties when Maxine wanted to end her violent relationship. Her mother found this difficult to accept even though Maxine had suffered a great deal of violence at the hands of her husband.

Expectations of financial support

Views about future financial support for lone parents might affect whether or not a couple decides to separate. For example, a woman may decide that she is not sufficiently unhappy in a relationship to trade in a reasonably comfortable financial existence for the uncertainty of life on benefit and, possibly, maintenance. Alternatively, a woman who is currently living on benefit with her partner may feel that she will not be much worse off, if at all, receiving benefit in her own right and so she may be less prepared to stay in an unhappy relationship. Men, too, may also be affected by financial considerations. For example, they may feel more able to leave their partners if they know that the state will provide for them. Or they may feel less able to leave their partners if they are concerned about the costs of maintenance.

In the previous section, we quoted research which suggested that social security did not encourage women to become lone parents (Whiteford and Bradshaw, 1994; Hoynes, 1996). Marsden (1969) however, argued that women stayed in unhappy relationships for a long time because they did not know about the availability of social security. He argued that they were also concerned about the possibility of losing custody of their children. Such concerns would be very few now as custody is rarely given to fathers.

In cases where a partner left without much warning, women had little chance to consider what life would be like, financially, as a lone mother. But, as argued above, their partners may have felt more able to leave because of the availability of social security.

Most of the women who had taken the decision to end the relationship had thought that they would be mainly reliant on benefit and that this would be difficult, but they thought that there would be enough money to survive on and they preferred independent survival on benefit to their current situation of unhappiness. In 12 of the 22 cases, the women's partners had been in and out of work – mostly out. When they were in work, these men had fairly low-paid insecure jobs, for example, one was a nightclub bouncer, one had been a labourer and two had worked in the hotel industry. Some of these men had criminal records and had been in prison before. One was a heroin addict and drug dealer. Another was an alcoholic. These men provided little financial support to their families and so the prospect of life on benefit posed few financial concerns. As argued above, lack of money and lack of control of money were often at the root of the couple's problems.

Seven of the 22 women had been living with partners who had relatively secure and well-paid jobs. Interestingly, in three of these cases, it was the man who ended the relationship. Only four women ended financially secure relationships. These women knew that it would be difficult. Ros had expected life to be very hard on benefit but preferred to try this rather than stay with her violent husband. And although her husband had a reasonably secure job, she had considered him to be a poor money manager and there had been arguments over money in the past.

Although there were no signs of, what Marsden called, 'a conspiracy of silence' about the availability of social security for lone parents, some women knew very little about how much money they might receive and did not give it too much thought. Penny's husband had been a metalworker in a reasonably secure job. When she separated from him, she did not have much knowledge about the benefit system. Similarly, Rita had little idea or concern about the financial consequences of separating:

> I didn,t really think about [how things would be financially]. That was the furthest thing from my mind. The fact that I could cope on my own was what was in my mind.

Sally also said that feeling that she would be able to cope emotionally was more important than financial considerations. When her husband went away for six months with the Army, she knew that she would be able to cope emotionally on her own even though her financial situation would change if she was separated.

Some women, however, did have a good idea about how much benefit they might receive because they had relatives or friends who were already lone parents. This knowledge did not particularly encourage women to separate because they knew that benefits were enough to survive on but little else. Samantha's partner had been on Invalidity Benefit and she had thought that they had been quite 'comfortable' on this benefit. She knew that life on her own, on Income Support, would not be particularly easy but that she would be able to survive:

> My sister, she's a single parent... and she sort of managed. I thought, 'I'll manage and that' but it's quite hard.

Turning to housing, the separated lone mothers generally stayed in their own homes and so did not transfer into council accommodation. Some, however, left their home and stayed with their parents or, in two cases, in refuges, so that they could escape their violent husbands. A couple of separated lone parents had difficulty gaining access to council accommodation because they were labelled 'intentionally homeless'. So the prospect of council accommodation was certainly not an incentive to separate from a partner.

Social stigma

In the past, social stigma against separation and lone parenthood would probably have prevented many couples from going their own ways. Does such stigma still exist and does it affect behaviour? The views and experiences of the women interviewed suggests that stigma does still exist in relation to separation and lone parenthood but that there is less today than in the past. Some women had stayed in unhappy relationships partly because they wished to avoid the stigma of having a failed marriage. But there were also strategies which these women used to avoid feeling stigmatised. Like the 'single' lone mothers, 'separated' lone mothers knew that if they went out to work they would be viewed more positively. They also emphasised the fact that they had not been to blame for their relationship ending and this enabled them to feel less guilt and stigma. Finally, they disassociated themselves from other types of lone parents whom they saw as deserving of stigmatisation – the stereotype of the teenage mum. Ros explained:

> There was much more of a stigma [in the past] wasn't there?... I think that people still look at you as if, you know, if you don't wear a wedding ring and you've got a baby, you still see, especially old people, they look as if you've been irresponsible. They don't ever think twice... one old man... said to me 'you shouldn't have had children if you couldn't look after it', or something like that.

Valerie wanted to move house to make a new start, away from the neighbours who knew her history:

> Because of living where I do, I've got this, my divorce, still hanging on because the neighbours are still the same and certain people who live in the area, who my husband had affairs with, are still here, which I have found awkward.

Samantha's neighbours had complained about her children being unruly and she felt that they had implied that, as a lone parent, she was unable to control her children.

Rona's son was being bullied at school and Rona felt this may have been because he had a lone parent mother. She complained to the head teacher, who was very unsympathetic and had some very stereotypical views about lone parenthood:

> The headmistress said to me... 'probably because you're a single parent I don't expect you feed him a very good diet and you probably let him stay up at night and he doesn't have the energy to run away from [the bullies].

Dependence on social security

As with the 'single' lone parents, the main 'shame' about being a separated lone mother was related to dependence on social security. As Paula explained:

> The divorce side of things is not seen as so scandalous these days. I suppose your position as a woman on benefits bringing up children, is looked down upon... basically you are public property now. And I heard this person who lived across the road tell my next-door neighbour, these are his exact words... 'and now we're having to pay her bloody mortgage!' And that's how he saw it because I was on government money, that was his money... and that's how people see it. And I found myself thinking, are they looking at me thinking, 'how can she afford to clothe her children?'... they'd see it as their money that I'm using... and I find that hard.

One way of reducing the stigma is, therefore, to get a job. Penny had not come across negative views of her position since she had been in work (even though she was still receiving social security in the form of Family Credit):

> For the last two and a half years now I've been on Family Credit so as far as I'm concerned, I've been working for my money, the same as anybody else.

Sarah was also keen to distance herself from other lone parents who received benefit:

> I'm not your typical lone parent because that's how they stereotype single mothers is people that live off the social and they get all their furniture off social. I've never had nothing off the social.

Although working can reduce some stigma, lone parents often felt that they owed it to their children at be at home and give them their full attention. So they found themselves in a Catch-22 position – if they stayed at home, they felt guilty about being seen as dependent on the state but if they went out to work, they felt guilty about leaving their children in someone else's care. Paula explained why she was not working:

> It's bad enough that they've lost one parent, then having the prospect of never seeing me as well during the holidays... I'm not about to sacrifice [my children's happiness] for the sake of to be seen as pulling my weight.

So although there was stigma about being on benefit, these women were willing to bear it for the sake of their children, as they saw it.

Teenage mums: a modern folk devil

In the previous chapter, we saw how single lone parents criticised those women who deliberately planned to have babies while single. Separated lone mothers took a similar view and they resented being pigeon-holed alongside 'single' lone parents. They did not feel that they had much in common with these other women. There was a marked lack of solidarity and 'sisterhood' among lone parents. As Susan said:

> It does annoy you when you read it in the paper how they look upon single parents. And they're really degrading on single parents when half the

time, it is not the woman's fault anyway. I mean, OK, it's a different thing when there's a teenager that's just going to get pregnant because they want a council flat or whatever, but they should not categorise everybody in the same bracket.

Paula had similar views:

I'm a mature, divorced woman with two children but I'm lumped with the 16 year old who's gone off and got pregnant and is living in a council house on Income Support. I'm as far removed from her as a married woman down the road... but because I'm on benefits I'm lumped with those people and I resent that. It's not my fault. It's not my choice that I'm in this position.

It is worth stressing that, like other studies, this study found no evidence of teenagers who deliberately got pregnant in order to get into council accommodation. So it is interesting that even lone parents themselves needed a scapegoat and appear to have accepted media images of lone parenthood. Pat described the type of lone parents who have become folk devils in modern society:

You're getting a lot of women now who have no intentions of getting married yet they have children by different men and then they live off the state... and then you get the others that don't care what the children are doing, these are the children that go round stealing cars, mugging old people, causing a general nuisance, smashing shop windows... these are more from the single parents of this generation, not from when I was made a single parent. And I think a lot of these surveys do tend to class us all as being one and we aren't all as being one.

On reading the first few sentences of this quote, it would be easy to think that Pat herself was not a lone parent. It is also interesting that she makes a point of saying she was 'made' a lone parent, as if she had little choice in the matter. Once again, this is an attempt to distance herself from the other lone parents she is describing.

Valerie had little sympathy for 'single' lone parents and felt that there was no need 'these days' to be one – 'they could quite easily have an abortion'. She disliked teenage lone parents, of whom she said:

I'm working full-time and I'm paying for them and it grieves me.

One way of reducing any stigma was for 'separated' lone mothers to argue that they had not been to blame for their situation. They blamed their partners who had left them or whom they had to leave because they had been violent, unfaithful or unreasonable. It is interesting that lone parents feel the need to talk about 'blame' at a time when divorce law has tried to move away from such a concept towards 'no fault' divorce.

Paula's husband had given her no warning before he walked out on her. She felt that she should not have to feel ashamed for her situation:

> I could understand if I'd put myself in this situation but I didn't. I didn't anticipate this, nobody anticipated this and there was nothing I could do to prevent it.

Michelle expressed similar sentiments:

> I never chose to be on my own. I didn't want to be on my own. I don't think anybody wants to bring up a child on their own… I think it's wrong that [the general public] moan about it 'oh, we give them money'.

Although lone parents generally felt stigmatised, they sometimes felt admired and respected for coping on their own, especially if they had jobs. Some also felt admired for finally leaving an abusive partner.

There was a general view that attitudes towards lone parenthood had softened in recent years and that this was partly because there were more lone parents around. Many were relieved about this for their children's sake as they would be less likely to stand out at school than they might have done in the past.

Penny compared her childhood with her children's:

> Years ago at school, I can't think of anybody that had separated parents in my class – one was adopted… The children in my children's class, the majority of them, their parents have separated at some time or they only live with one parent or the parents with whom they live – one of them's a step-parent… there doesn't seem to be that many that haven't been through it.

Many of Penny's friends had now separated from their partners:

> It seems to be one after the other – one does it and they all do it.

In Terri's case, the domino effect was closer to home:

> I've got two older sisters. The eldest one was married when she had her son but split up with the father two years after so she brought up her son

alone... My second sister, her son was only maybe three months when she split up with the father and brought up the child alone... I think it's the norm these days rather than the exception. It's normal to be a single mother.

KEY POINTS: BECOMING A 'SEPARATED' LONE MOTHER

- In 1971 there were 290,000 lone parents who had separated or divorced from a husband. By 1992 this figure had risen to 730,000.
- Separating from a partner is still the most common route into lone parenthood.
- Analysis of SCELI has shown that various factors are associated with increasing the likelihood of separation and divorce. These include: early marriage; having children early in marriage or having a premarital conception; being a social tenant or private tenant.
- Most economic variables made little difference. For example, the woman's socio-economic background (in terms of her parents' occupations) and her own varying economic activity had no impact on separation rates. But her husband's economic activity was important as couples were three times as likely to split up if the husband was unemployed rather than in paid work.
- Those (albeit few) couples who lived with the woman's parents had a very high risk of splitting up and although this was partly associated with early marriage and unemployment, there was also an independent effect due perhaps to crowded circumstances causing or accentuating personal tensions.
- As was the case with the growth of single lone motherhood, there appeared to be clear trends over time which were independent of micro-economic and social variables. In the case of separated lone motherhood, the trend was always in an upwards direction throughout the period under study.
- The quantitative analysis focused on separations from marriage but there is some evidence that cohabitations are more likely to break up than marriages. Hence the rise in cohabitation in the last 20 years might be indirectly leading to a rise in lone parenthood.
- Women themselves cited personal reasons for relationship break-down including conflict over gender roles and the control of money. The arrival of children often produced or accentuated these

difficulties because there was less money to go round. Men were sometimes considered to be irresponsible with money and neglecting their childcare responsibilities.

- Some women, especially those who had married early, said that their partners had felt that they had 'missed out' on having a carefree youth. They wished to escape the responsibility by ending the relationship. Some men also had affairs which contributed to the relationship breakdown.

- Domestic violence was a key factor in a number of cases. Some women stayed in violent relationships for a long time, in some cases until their partner left. Others ended the relationship after some trigger incident, such as their child being caught in the crossfire. Others simply reached the point where they were not prepared to put up with the violence any longer.

- Couples often stayed together for a long time after their problems began. In some cases, there were several temporary separations followed by reconciliations before the relationship ended for good.

- Although women often stayed in unhappy relationships, they felt that they were less likely to put up with unhappiness than their mothers would have been. This was because they generally felt more confident and had greater financial independence – in the form of access to employment.

- Stigma against separation, divorce and lone parenthood did encourage women to remain longer in unhappy relationships than they would otherwise have done. But they felt that there was less stigma than in the past and they developed strategies to deal with that which remained. For example, they got jobs, they blamed their partner for the relationship breakdown and they distanced themselves and looked down on the stereotypical lone parent scapegoat – the teenage mum.

Chapter 4

The duration of lone motherhood

HOW LONG DO WOMEN REMAIN LONE MOTHERS?

It is important to investigate how long women remain lone parents because if women are remaining lone parents for longer periods, this could explain the rise in lone parenthood.

People may stop being lone parents for a number of reasons. Usually this is the result of forming a (new) partnership (Ford and others, 1995). The other 'event' that can mean the end of this status is when the youngest child ages beyond dependency (that is, 16/18 years) or leaves the household through another route (such as going to live with the other parent or going into care). Our analysis focuses on new partnerships as the route out of lone parenthood.

DURATION OF LONE MOTHERHOOD

The objectives of the quantitative analysis have been to estimate how many lone mothers find a new partner; to analyse variations between lone parents in their chances of leaving that status; and to examine changes over time in exit rates. Table 4.1 provides the basic number of cases available from the SCELI survey. Following Ermisch (1991) we have taken into consideration all women who became a lone parent in 1960 or later, 696 spells of lone parenthood (as understood in this book).

Separated, divorced and widowed lone mothers outnumbered single lone mothers by about two to one. About one in seven of the formerly married women said that their husband had died. In principle, we might have wanted to distinguish between separated and divorced mothers, but there is an element of circularity here: a separated woman would have to have obtained a divorce before she could remarry, so that separation and divorce are often two stages in a single process, rather than two distinct states.[13] The two are always combined in the analysis here.

Nearly half of all spells of lone parenthood ended in a (re)marriage. This was more likely if the starting point was a premarital birth, but that was partly because the single women had a minimum of 17 years before their children grew up, where many of the formerly married women would have a much shorter period at 'risk' of finding a partner. A further 80 spells of lone parenthood ended through children growing older; this time, it was formerly married women who were most likely to complete their spell as a lone mother by this route. That left 298 women still lone parents at the time of interview, for whom the eventual outcome is not known.

Table 4.1   Exits from lone parenthood

	All spells		Never married		Previously married	
Total number of women in sample	696		245		451	
Number of months 'at risk'	40,237	av=57	11,824	av=48	28,413	av=63
(Re)partnered (before child reached 17)	318	46%	143	58%	175	39%
Child reached 17 (before survey)	80	11%	3	1%	77	17%
No partner, still with children, at interview date (censored)	298	43%	99	40%	199	44%
Monthly exit rate						
all exits	9.9 per 1,000		12.3 per 1,000		8.9 per 1,000	
(re)partnering	7.9 per 1,000		12.1 per 1,000		6.2 per 1,000	

As with the analysis of births and separations in the previous two chapters, the lack of evidence about the completion of all spells of lone parenthood is dealt with by dividing each spell into a series of months, so that the chances of leaving in the first, the second, the third month and so on can be analysed and compared. The average woman had 57 months at risk – just short of five years. That is not an estimate of the average duration of the period of lone parenthood (because many women will have continued their spell after the interview). But it can be used to calculate an average monthly exit rate of 9.9 per 1,000 from which it can be deduced that half of all periods of lone parenthood would be completed after 70 months – getting on for six years.[14]

The median duration was longer for separated lone parents than divorced lone parents (eight years compared with five), but this is mostly an artefact of the data collection as separated lone parents would have had to divorce first before finding one route out of lone parenthood. The most interesting difference between groups is that the median duration for divorced mothers is nearly two years longer than for single mothers (five years compared with three), and one of the aims of the analysis will be to find out why this should be.

These estimates of duration for particular types of lone parent are rather longer than those suggested by Ermisch (1991) from data collected six years earlier than ours. The gap may have been caused by two factors: differences in the dating of the start and end of partnerships in the two source surveys; or the extension of the observation period into the 1980s when (as will be seen) repartnering rates were lower.

It is variations in the rates of exit that are important. For that purpose, the analysis focuses on occasions when the woman took up with another partner. The end of lone parenthood caused by children reaching non-dependent age is assumed to be determined by the march of time (in the absence of marriage), and is not included in the analysis from now on. Single mothers who were aged 14 or 15 at the time of the birth of their child are considered at 'risk' of finding a partner only from the age of 16 onwards.

Modelling the duration of lone motherhood

As in previous chapters, the analysis goes through a series of stages, each examining the relationship between the probability of a woman re-entering a partnership and one broad category of variables. First, intrinsic characteristics of the lone parenthood – how it started (fixed), how long it had lasted and the age of the mother (both time-varying). Second, information about the mother's home background (fixed), and third, information about her current circumstances (time-varying). Finally, some fairly complex analysis is required to show whether the rate at which lone parents (re)marry had been increasing or decreasing over the period covered by the SCELI survey.

Table 4.2   Hazard rates for (re)partnering

relative risk ratios

	Simple analysis	Multivariate model		Sample size
Overall monthly rate	8.0 per 1,000			
1 Origin of spell	R=0.103	R=0.050		
Pre-marital birth	1.79	1.56		11,694
Separation/divorce	1.00 (=6.8)	1.00		24,107
Widowhood	0.38	0.50		4,313
2 Age at time	R=−0.149	R=−0.140	R=−0.085	
3 Duration (months since start of period)				
Duration	not sig	not sig	R=+0.077	
(Duration)²	R=−0.037	not sig	R=−0.070	
4 Current housing	R=0.026	R=0.110		
Lives with parents	0.77	0.28		6,634
Current owner	1.00(=9.8)	1.00		9,926
Current social tenant	0.71	0.46		19,098
Current private tenant	1.07	0.71		2,964
Others/DK	0.55	0.29		1,492
5 Year at risk (1960=60)				
Year	not sig	R=+0.031	not sig	
(Year)²	not sig	R=−0.039	not sig	

Characteristics of the lone mothers

It has already been seen that single never-married mothers had a higher probability of partnering than women who had previously been married. This, in spite of the fact that the single women tended to start at an earlier age, and fewer of their periods were closed by the ageing of their children. This meant that single mothers were substantially more likely to find a partner than formerly married women were to find another partner. As shown in the first panel of Table 4.2, the 'hazard rate' for single women was four-fifths higher for single women than for separated and divorced women. Widows were less likely to repartner than separated and divorced women – a finding which was replicated throughout the analysis, although there were not enough of them in the sample for this to have a very important influence on the overall pattern of remarriages.

The difference between single and formerly married women's exit rates turned out to be complicated, because it was related to two other factors – age and housing tenure, which operated in opposite directions. The story to emerge over the following pages is that:

- there was not much difference between the two groups' chances of remarrying, age for age;
- but when housing tenure had been taken into account as well, it appeared that single women did, after all, have higher chances of marrying than formerly married women in equivalent situations;
- single women had higher rates of partnering in the 1960s and early 1970s, but by the mid 1980s the two were very similar.

Because the influences on exit rates were rather different, the multivariate analysis is presented in two columns: one for single mothers, the other for formerly married mothers. Results in the centre of the pair of columns are derived from a joint model, covering both groups of lone parent.

For both groups, women had a much higher chance of repartnering when they were relatively young, and the probability reduced as they grew older. The raw comparisons are shown in Table 4.3. Single women aged 16 to 20 had an 'escape' or exit rate of 19 per 1,000. That means that two-thirds of those who were single parents on their 16th birthday would have married by their 21st birthday, 60 months later. The rate fell rapidly and steadily: of the 23 women who were still single at the age of 31, four married in their early thirties, and none at all after that.

Table 4.3   Hazard rates for repartnering, by age

monthly rates per 1,000

	Never married	Formerly married
16 to 20	19.0	nil
21 to 25	12.3	8.7
26 to 30	8.8	12.4
31 to 35	4.3	6.0
36 to 40	nil	5.6
41 plus	nil	0.5

For separated, widowed and divorced women, the pattern was more complicated; the rate of repartnering seemed to rise to a peak in the

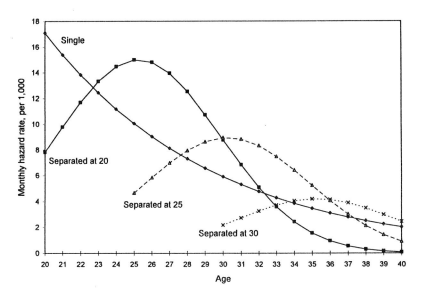

Figure 4.1 Model estimates of hazard rates, by age and duration
of spell

second half of their twenties, before falling to a very low level in their
forties. But the multivariate model suggested that there were two
effects going on at the same time. Women were unlikely to form a new
partnership immediately after their separation. The chances increased
as time went on, up to a peak about five years later, and then
decreased. This is represented in the multivariate model by the
positive sign on duration, and the negative sign on duration-squared.
There was also a straightforward age effect similar to (though not as
strong as) the one influencing the partnering rates of single women.
For a separated woman, her expectations were influenced by the age
at which her first marriage ended. But from that point on, two clocks
were ticking: a lapse-of-time clock which initially raised the probability of her leaving lone parenthood after a few years; and an ageing
clock which reduced it. The outcome is shown in Figure 4.1, which is
derived from models in which age and duration were the only
explanatory variables. The conclusion seems to be that the pattern of
exits from the two types of lone parenthood was rather different, but,
once that has been taken into account, the rates of exit were fairly
similar.

Family background

Unlike rates of entry into lone parenthood, the analysis identified no aspects of the women's family background which were associated with higher or lower probabilities of (re)partnering. Neither the area where they lived, their ethnic group nor their father's occupation were significantly linked to exit rates.

Current situation

We rather expected that lone mothers who were in employment would have either a higher or a lower probability of forming a new partnership than those who spent all their time looking after the home and family. The hypotheses were that a woman in employment would have more chance to meet someone and form a relationship; or that a woman without employment might have more of an economic incentive to join forces with a working man. In practice there was no significant difference in exit rates – perhaps these forces exactly cancelled each other out.

As before, repartnering rates were also compared, according to the rate of unemployment recorded at the time and place of the period at 'risk'. On this occasion, variations were identified which appeared to be 'significant' in the technical meaning of that word; that is, the differences were wide enough for us to conclude that they were unlikely to have arisen by chance from a sample of this size. On the other hand, it was hard to make sense of the variation in terms of contributing to an explanation of the pattern of women's experiences. Over most of the range, when unemployment rates were between 2.5 and 15 per cent, the number of women forming a new partnership each month increased as unemployment increased. But the highest repartnering rate of all was found when unemployment was below 2.5 per cent; and the lowest hazard rate was at the top end of the unemployment scale – above 15 per cent. In the absence of any hypothesis explaining this pattern, we conclude that the unemployment variable was not helping, and it was omitted from further analysis.

There was, though, a substantial variation in outcomes, depending on the lone parent family's accommodation. Women who owned their own homes were much more likely to form a new partnership than those who lived with their parents, on the one hand, or who rented a house or flat, on the other. This was clear from the basic tables of exit rates by accommodation; it was even clearer after multivariate

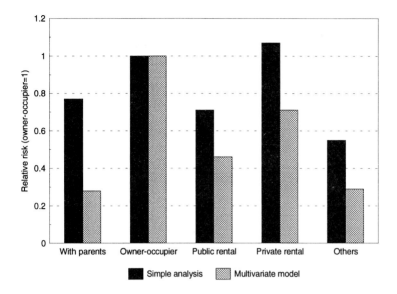

Figure 4.2 Hazard rate for (re)partnering, by housing situation at the time

analysis had taken account of variations by age and duration (Figure 4.2). Much more detailed work would be required to explain this important finding in full. We do not know what were the terms of ownership (whether the lone parent had full possession, or whether her former partner retained an interest), but it is possible that owning a home makes a woman a more attractive economic proposition for potential partners (assuming that other elements of 'attraction' were not affected, either way). One of the findings of the qualitative interviews concerned lone mothers' control of their territories in subsequent relationships, and the greater feeling of independence that this enabled them to assert, compared with first relationships in which they had more often adopted a position of financial dependence.

Remember that the analysis of marital splits in Chapter 3 showed that marriages were less likely to break up if the couple was in owner-occupied housing than in any other form of accommodation. The finding now that women living in owner-occupied housing had high rates of repartnering suggests that lone parenthood is especially rare in this sector: people here are slow to separate and fast to find a new partner.

But this factor also played a role in differentiating between never- and formerly-married women. Table 4.4 shows that about half of both groups of lone parent lived in public housing – at the time of the survey, this mainly meant council tenancies. But whereas a large proportion of never-married mothers lived with their own parents, few of the ex-married mothers did so; a third of them were owner-occupiers.

Table 4.4   Current housing, by origin of spell

percentages

	Single	Separated or divorced	Widowed
With parents	39	9	1
Owner-occupier	6	31	42
Public tenant	46	48	50
Private tenant	5	9	8
Others	4	4	*
Sample size (woman months at risk)	11,694	24,107	4,313

Given that separated and divorced women, and widows, were in the housing situation most likely to lead to the formation of a new partnership, it is all the more striking that their partnering rates were lower, not higher, than those of single women. The apparent difference between them had converged once age had been taken into account (because formerly married women were usually older than single women). But it widens again, now that housing can be taken into account. In council housing (the tenure where both types of one parent family were found in large numbers) the monthly hazard rate for single women was 10.1 per 1,000. For ex-married women, the rate was little more than half that – 5.6 per 1,000.

Changes over time

As in previous chapters, one of the key objectives of this analysis is to describe and explain the changes that occurred over the period covered by the SCELI survey. Increases in the number of people in the 'stock' of any category are often assumed to have been brought about by a rise in the number of people joining the category – the inflow. In practice, it is often the opposite: a fairly steady inflow but a falling outflow leads to an increase in the stock as people remain

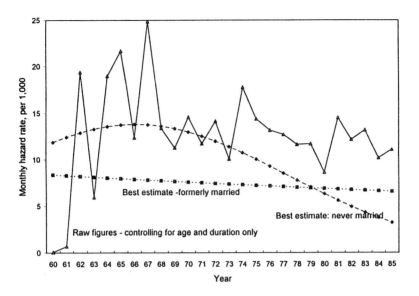

Figure 4.3   Hazard rate for (re)partnering, 1960–1985

longer and longer in the same position. This is true of the number of pensioners, of the unemployed and of disabled people claiming benefits: all of these have increased in numbers because fewer people have been leaving than joining over the past decades. In the case of one parent families, there have been clear increases in the inflow, by both routes; but it remains to be established whether durations have changed over the same period.

As with separations, the data available do not provide a straightforward estimate of the rates of repartnering at each stage of the period under observation. Selecting all spells of lone parenthood starting in 1960 or later means that all the spells observed to be in progress during the early 1960s were of fairly recent origin, and most of the women concerned were fairly young. By the end of the period, the data for the early 1980s contains a mixture both of recent spells and of others which may have started 10 or even 20 years earlier. This means that the only meaningful estimate of hazard rates in each year has to be made after controlling for the age of the woman and the duration of the spell.

Figure 4.3 shows, as a jagged line, the hazard rate calculated on that basis for three-year periods between the early 1960s and the early 1980s. There is some sign of a rise during the 1960s, followed by a fall in the 1970s although it is difficult to perceive any clear overall trend.

The multivariate analysis provides a much clearer picture, principally by distinguishing between never-married and formerly-married women. The smooth lines plot estimated hazard rates for each group separately, after controlling for age, duration and housing situation. For separated, divorced and widowed women, there was no clear trend over this period – the exit rate remained stable at about 8 per 1,000 (for the case illustrated, a council tenant aged 25 who had separated five years earlier). For single women, though, there appeared to be a regular rise in the rate of partnering, followed by a fall, with a peak about 1967–69. At the peak, a hazard rate of 18 per 1,000 is equivalent to a median duration of only about three years. By the 1980s the rate had fallen to 9 per 1,000 – equivalent to a median duration of eight years, and very similar to the formerly married women's experience.

Remember that the analysis in Chapter 2 showed an increase in the rate at which young women became single parents during the 1960s, followed by a fall in the 1970s. The finding, now, that the partnering rate followed a roughly parallel trend suggests that the two may have balanced each other out. The rise and fall in entries was countered by a similar rise and fall in exits, so that the effect on the number of lone parents in the stock was less than it would have been if either trend had occurred on its own.

Overall, though, the analysis suggests that one parent families did not remain longer in that condition in the 1980s than they had in the 1960s. If anything, durations were reduced – the opposite of what happened over the same period to other groups with high levels of dependence on social security.

LIFE AS A LONE MOTHER

There has been very little qualitative research which has investigated the duration of lone parenthood. Our quantitative analysis suggested that few factors, apart from age, length of time as a lone parent and housing tenure were linked to variations in lone parents' chances of taking a (new) partner. In seeking to understand the duration of lone parenthood, our qualitative analysis begins by considering what life is like as a lone parent.

The initial phase

The initial phase of lone parenthood was the period during which women were coming to terms with being on their own with their child(ren). This phase was particularly difficult for 'single' lone mothers. These women were becoming mothers for the first time and yet had no partner with whom to share the joys and woes. Some of these 'single' women had just split up from their partners before the birth and so had been faced with coming to terms with the end of a relationship as well as the arrival of a baby. This initial phase, of becoming accustomed to being a lone parent, could last anything from six months to two years.

Alison was having to come to terms not only with the birth of twins but also with the recent end of her marriage. She recalled that:

> It was hell, for the first two years it was hell. It was horrible and, to be honest with you, I used to look at them and I used to hate them babies. I used to think, 'God, I hate you'. I was so tired all the time and I maybe used to feel sorry for myself, sit there crying, thinking, 'why me?'

Life was difficult for Alison even though she had a great deal of support from her parents. By contrast, Gillian's parents had disowned her and she had to move into a hostel:

> It was awful. I had to share with this lady and her two children because they'd got rooms like for six people... it was horrible... I got really depressed when I had [the baby] because I loved him but it weren't how I thought it was going to be... I just thought, 'Oh, God, I can't stand him crying', you know, 'Oh, God, shut up!' you know. And I went to the doctor and they gave me anti-depressants.

Natalie had split up from her partner soon after their first baby was born. At the time, she had a well-paid full-time job in an accounts department and she was anxious about losing her job so she decided to return to work immediately after having the baby: 'The first year was hell'.

The transition was, perhaps, slightly easier in general for separated lone parents. Many were soon happier than they had been in their previous relationships. These women had always borne most responsibility for their children and their home, often with little or no help from their partners. The absence of the partner therefore made little difference except that there was an end to arguments and, in some cases, physical abuse. Martina said that, when she became a lone parent, life was:

> ...better, much better. It's nice to have peace of mind to think that I can sit in my own house and he's not hitting me. I feel safe now. I never felt safe. I used to lie in bed thinking, 'what's it going to be like tonight? Is he going to start? Is it going to be alright?' You can't imagine what it's like.

For some, however, there was still an initial phase during which their lifestyle changed and they started to grow accustomed to their new life. Bernie initially became a lone parent when she had a baby while single, but then she got together with the baby's father and had another child, only to become a lone parent again when the, sometimes violent, relationship ended:

> The first six months were – denial – I just ignored everything... After six months, it was easier being a lone parent than it was being married and being a wife... it's a control thing – I was in control of my life... my biggest hangup was the boys. I wanted them to be happy so much... I didn't get lost in the pitying – it was me, my sons and I was going to make them happy.

The support of a family certainly made the early days of lone parenthood bearable for many women. Heather found lone parenthood to be easier than expected because of the support of her mother:

> I couldn't imagine how it would be but it weren't as bad – you always imagine 'haven't got enough money to buy food, living on beans on toast, and can't never go out...' but it wasn't like that for me because I was at home, I was lucky... And when I wanted to go out, I just had to say, 'Mum, would you mind having [the baby]?' And... I could go out quite easily. And, like, everything was sorted out for me. I never had to worry about bills or nothing because I was at home. My money was literally my own. I used to give mum a bit every week but apart from that...

The economic life of lone mothers

We saw in Chapters 3 and 4 that most women expected that life as a lone parent would not be easy, financially. Most expected to be on

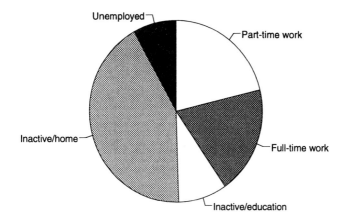

Figure 4.4   Economic status of lone mothers in 1990

benefit. Figure 4.4 is based on data from the Labour Force Survey 1990 and shows that just over half of all lone parents were either unemployed or economically inactive (59 per cent). The rest were working full-time or part-time. But the rate of economic inactivity is higher for single lone mothers, about three-quarters of whom were not doing any work at all. Table 4.5 is based on a survey of lone parents by Ford and others (1995) and shows that in 1993, about four single mothers in five were receiving Income Support compared with about half of those who had separated from a husband.

All the 22 single mothers interviewed were on benefit immediately after having their first baby. But two women had started doing odd jobs to supplement their income and a further eight had found part-time or full-time work within a year of having their babies. Five women were on Family Credit. Eight of the absent fathers paid regular maintenance for their offspring and in five of these cases the women were also in work and so had reasonable incomes. Four of the absent fathers had denied paternity. In two cases, paternity had been proven by DNA tests and the father was now paying maintenance. In the other two cases, which occurred before the availability of DNA tests, blood tests had been carried out and were inconclusive in one case.

Table 4.5   Receipt of social security benefits

percentages

	Income Support	Family Credit
Mothers not previously married		
Always single	79	11
Previously cohabited	73	14
Mothers previously married		
Divorced	56	20
Separated	49	20
Lone fathers	35	7

Source: Ford and others, 1995

Fifteen of the 22 separated mothers were on or went onto Income Support when they became lone parents. In two cases, these women gave up jobs when they became lone parents because they wished to give more time to their children. But in the other cases, these women had not been in work when they became lone parents and carried on without work. Seven women soon began to take on odd jobs and three fairly soon went on to Family Credit. Seven women had stayed in part-time or full-time jobs when they became lone parents. These women generally had older children or relied on parents to babysit.

Money was very short for many lone parents, especially those reliant solely on income support. Maxine's experience was typical:

> Sometimes it's been hard... having to sit and count your money out at the end of the week and then [my daughter] needs something like a pair of shoes and things like that and you think to yourself, 'God! Where am I going to get the money from for a pair of shoes?' But you get there in the end.

Paula's experience was even worse:

> It's impossible. Every month there are three or four bills that you are not going to be able to pay. I spend my whole time on the phone saying, 'I'll pay you that next month' or 'I'll pay half of that'... and leaving things until it gets to the point where – not quite to the point of bailiffs – but you're just buying time all the time... You have never got enough money, ever. There's never a week goes by where I am sitting at the end of a week and there's £5 left in my purse. It's more a case of, 'God, I've got to pay back Monday what I borrowed from someone on Saturday'.

Women felt strongly that the government was not providing them with enough money to give their children a decent upbringing and a decent chance in life. However, despite their financial difficulties, many women felt that they ought to be grateful for what they got. Anita said:

> Every so often, I think, 'shit! I'm on Income Support, having my rent paid. I'm entirely dependent on the state and what my family can offer me. And I'm nearly 40. What kind of a state is that to be in?... How did I get here?'

Some women were very reliant on their families to bail them out every now and then. As Andrea explained:

> If I get stuck, my mum and dad are there straight away and, although they haven't got a lot because they're retired, at the end of the day, they are still there for me, whatever, and if I get a bill through the door that's unexpected, then they pay it.

Kristin was 24 and on Income Support. But she received quite regular and substantial financial help from her parents:

> If it wasn't for my mum and dad, then, well, I'd be in trouble... my dad gives me a payment every week and my mum gives me a payment like every month... if it's just for plain groceries, like, just like a bit of shopping, [my dad]'ll give me 20 quid but if I need to do like a big shop, like cupboard and freezer, then he'll give me 50 quid... but my mum will give me 30 quid a month.

Other women survived financially through various means. After becoming lone parents, they found out as much as they could about the benefit system, such as how much they could earn within the Income Support disregard, how little they could work and still claim Family Credit and how much they would be allowed to keep if they had a lodger. On top of this, there were a couple of cases where women were prepared to break the social security rules and fiddle the system in order to increase their meagre incomes.

Penny knew little about benefits when she first became a lone parent but then:

> It must have been five to six months after the second time we split up that I realised I was entitled to One Parent Benefit – it was just by looking in the back of my book... then I went down the social and got the book on Income Support and other benefits and basically read through on everything... and I got everything.

Penny moved from Income Support to Family Credit and back again as it best suited her. She also had a lodger and knew about all the passport benefits that she could claim. As well as getting everything she was legally entitled to, Penny also worked without telling the DSS about it and she was also living with a partner while still claiming social security as a lone parent. She justified all these activities on the grounds that her children would suffer financially if she did not break the rules.

Andrea was also prepared to work without informing the DSS. But this was not the only kind of illegal activity in which she was prepared to engage:

> I've got shoplifters come in, I buy tins of food off them... and then I bang it out again the other door, with a bit of extra couple of quid on it... I've got outlets that I let it out and I make, say, 20 quid on whatever, but that's just to survive.

As mentioned above, the difficulties of living on benefit encouraged some women to find full-time or part-time jobs. Many of these felt ambivalent about leaving their children to the care of others but felt they needed the money for their children and so had little real choice.

Separated lone mothers often felt better off as lone parents than they had been before, because they were now in control of their finances and able to spend money on what they really needed. About half of all separated lone parents mentioned this as an advantage of lone parenthood. Some women said that their previous partners had been irresponsible with money and so they were relieved to be in control of their money now. As Vicky said:

> Even though when you're in a couple I think you get more money, well we did get more money when we were in a couple, but it's him, he'd spend money like it was water. So I knew I would be better off without him.

Ros had a similar experience:

> I'm not as badly off as I thought I was because I can manage my finances and it's only me that looks after the finances. And I know that it's a bit of a relief because if I spend too much money, I spend too much money but at least it's only me that's spending too much... whereas before, although we should have been much better off, because my husband was so bad with money, we weren't.

Michelle and her previous partner had both been on benefit and so received a regular income. But the cheque went to her partner and Michelle was pleased that, now, it came to her:

> He used to get the giro and, that was it, I wouldn't see any money.

Martina preferred the certainty of the weekly benefit money to the uncertainty of her husband's wages. And even when her husband did receive good wages, she and her children did not always receive much money:

> It's regular money every week whereas [my husband] would work for a few weeks and then he'd be out of work and then he'd work and you never knew where you were. And the money he did bring, I mean he was hitting me and taking it back because he used to want it for drink. And then I used to have to hide the money behind pictures, in ornaments. I had money everywhere.

Mandy had also been in an abusive relationship. She said that when her husband was in work, he would spend his wages before coming home. When he was out of work, she would get up early and wait for the benefit cheque to arrive in the post so that she could be the one to cash it. But even when she had access to the money, she, like Martina, had to hide it in her home to stop her husband from taking it and spending it on himself. Not surprisingly, therefore, she was relieved when she became a lone parent:

> I could cope with things myself. I hadn't got the watching or hiding money or anything else. Because I knew what I'd got there. Everything would get paid. Everything would. And I knew I'd be better off.

Rita felt better off as a lone parent, partly because her husband had been very generous in leaving her the house, the car and a good allowance. This, however, was far from the norm for lone parents.

The personal lives of lone mothers

Some of the main advantages to being a lone parent were non-financial and related to the independence and autonomy which many women, whether single or separated lone parents, said that they valued. Some of the separated women felt a new sense of freedom – freedom in general and freedom from having to answer to a man. As Valerie said:

> I can eat when I want to eat and I'm not answerable to anybody. I can come and go as I please and there's nobody there actually to criticise... plus the fact that it's made me financially independent. There is a great sense of satisfaction knowing that you're in your own house and you can change your house if you want and buy somewhere new and do it all yourself.

Pat had been a lone parent for 15 years after splitting up from her partner. She said:

> I like the freedom. I like to be able to do what I want to do, when I want to do it. And I haven't got, for instance, a time that I've got to be home to have a meal on the table for my husband coming in from work. I haven't got to have a certain shirt ironed and a certain pair of trousers laid out and shoes and what have you... and I haven't got the finicky ways to put up with. I am perfectly happy.

A number of women used almost exactly the same language to describe how they felt about lone parenthood. Penny summed up their views:

> I could do what I wanted, when I wanted. I didn't have to ask anybody. Basically I felt my life was my own again.

Many of the single lone parents had never lived with a partner and so were not comparing their new-found independence with a previous state of dependence on, or obligation to, a man. It may seem surprising, therefore, that many had similar views and expressed themselves in similar language to the separated lone parents. Part of the reason may be that some of these women now felt independent from their parents – having a baby marked an important transition to adulthood for them. But many of these women had previously been involved with boyfriends and were comparing their current situations with what life might be like with a man. Kelly echoed many of the separated lone parents when she said that one of the things she liked about being a lone parent was:

> Not having to worry about a man, as such. Not having to answer to a man. Not having to explain yourself to somebody else.

As we shall see later, Kelly's views may explain why she had never cohabited, despite the fact that she had another baby with the same boyfriend with whom she had her first. Andrea had similar views:

> I go out when I want to go out. If I go in the pub and play up horrendously,
> I don't think, 'Christ, I'm in trouble when I get home'. I wear what I want
> to. I cook when I want to.

Women have traditionally been brought up to care for others and put
others before themselves. These women were still prepared to put
their children first, but no one else. Many equated this with
selfishness. As Andrea said: 'I've become quite selfish minded really'.

Lone parents also mentioned other advantages to being a lone
parent. Separated lone parents now said that they had fewer people to
look after, implying that their partner had been more of a drain on
their caring services than a contribution to them. Ros said, with a
laugh:

> I don't have two babies to look after, I've just got one!

Jacqui made a similar point:

> It's easier in a sense [to be a lone parent], not having two men to run
> around after because a lot of them are so God damn lazy. And even when I
> was with [my previous partner], he never done anything for himself. I
> don't think he knew where any of his clothes were.

Related to this was the sense that these women now had complete
control of their child or children's upbringing. As Vicky said:

> It's nice that I'm solely responsible for bringing the boys up and what I say
> goes.

Some of the single women found that their babies gave them a sense
of identity and purpose which they felt had been lacking before. As
Diane said:

> One thing that I did get that I didn't expect, was to have a real feeling of
> wholeness... I really found myself through having [the baby].

Having control over money, children and life in general, gave many
lone parents a sense of real achievement in having managed on their
own. As a 25 year old, Kelly looked back on her ten years as a lone
mother, and said:

> It has its ups and it has its downs but at the end of the day, you just... you
> have that peace of mind because you've done it on your own.

In many ways, the advantages of being a lone parent were mirrored by the disadvantages. For example, the downside of control and independence was often loneliness and lack of adult company. And although many women liked having sole responsibility for their children, others would have liked someone to share in the decisions concerning their offspring.

Alison said that, although she liked the independence which she had gained from being a lone parent, there were drawbacks to such a life:

> It's not much fun being a lone parent, really. It's just that you haven't got anybody to tell you what to do, 'you're not going there' or 'you shouldn't do this!'... then you've got the other side where you're fed up and you're on your own all the time when your kids are in bed and you're just sitting there and thinking, 'well, what shall I do for tea tomorrow?'... It's monotony, day in, day out.

Kristin had similarly mixed feelings:

> I don't mind being on my own but it would be nice just to like have someone what is like close to you, with you, sort of thing, just to like talk to.

Anita said that she was 'not sure there's much I do dislike' about being a lone parent. But she did mention:

> There's the loneliness sometimes and... there's nobody to get into bed with and say, 'what a horrible day today has been' or 'what a lovely day today has been'. There's nobody to share with, after midnight.

The amount of loneliness felt seemed to depend on the age of the child. With babies, the lone parent was so preoccupied with caring for the baby that there was little time to feel lonely. But when the child or children were at school loneliness could be a problem if the lone parent was not working. With teenage children, loneliness was relatively low because the child could provide some companionship although never in the same way as a partner. With the impending departure of adult children, lone parents became concerned about being both lonely and on their own.

Lack of an adult partner was particularly felt at times when someone was needed to look after the children or where decisions regarding the children had to be made or discipline of the children was required. Diane, who was a single lone parent, said that one of the things she found most difficult was:

> Not having somebody to share the decisions about [my daughter's] life. Because it's quite scary, taking on somebody else's life and having to decide what's best for her character.

Andrea was quite happy most of the time but had times when she found it difficult to cope:

> When you're ill and you're at your low anyway, it really does hit home that there's nobody there to care for you or look after your littl'un. You are on your own.

Mandy split up from her violent partner but still said about lone parenthood:

> I don't think it's a very great life... you've got all the worry of... well, everything. you've got your bill worries – all that's your own. You've got your children – all that's your own. Every worry that you ever get, which everybody gets, you have to deal with it yourself.

Some women received help from family, friends and social workers. This reduced the loneliness and difficulty of making decisions on one's own. But, even those women who were fortunate enough to receive such help, sometimes said that it could not compensate for the lack of a partner. As Vicky said:

> I do miss someone being there. And I miss someone who's as responsible for them as I am. People come and they help out, like grandparents and cousins and even the health visitor, they all come and play with [the baby] but there's no-one who's as responsible for the kids as I am and I miss that.

The sexual side of a relationship was also difficult to replace. But Bernie was unusual when she said that sex was:

> probably about the only thing I missed!

Some women eventually found life as a lone parent too difficult. Julie was 15 when she first got pregnant. She then had another baby when she was 17 and another at the age of 23. All three babies were fathered by the same man although they did not live together (apart from a brief spell before the third baby was born). Julie found that she could not cope when the third baby arrived and so asked the father to take the eldest two. He agreed that they could come and live with him, along with his new partner and their child.

REMAINING A LONE MOTHER

Among the 44 women who were interviewed, 28 were still lone parents at the time of interview. Twelve of these had become lone parents at some time in the last two years and the other 16 had become lone parents more than two years ago. The longest serving lone parent was Carol who had become a single lone parent 16 years ago when she was 25. Pat was close behind her, having become a separated lone parent 15 years ago when she was 28. Elise and Gillian had also made it into double figures and the remaining 12 women had been lone parents for between two and 10 years. As we shall see, however, some of these women had had relationships with men while being a lone parent.

Some women remained lone parents for positive reasons and others for negative reasons. Women valued the independence they derived from lone parenthood and so some positively chose to remain in this state. However, others were lonely and found it difficult to manage financially on their own and so preferred to be in a couple. The reasons they were not in a couple therefore reflect lack of opportunity to find a partner rather than lack of motivation.

A few of the 28 women who were still lone parents were adamant that they did not want a partner. A few were very keen to find someone to live with. But the majority had mixed feelings about the prospect of cohabiting. This section assesses the extent to which these lone parents were looking for a partner and then explores the relationships these women had had since becoming a lone parent.

Reasons to stay a lone mother

Both single and separated lone parents gave similar positive reasons for remaining a lone parent. Many were concerned about losing the independence they currently enjoyed if they were to live with a partner. Barbara felt quite strongly that:

> I just don't want any man telling me what to do any more and taking over my life because it's nice to feel free and able to do what you like.

Valerie had a boyfriend but appreciated the fact that they were not living together:

> You've got your own space and your own house. And you see each other a few times a week and it's nice when you see each other. But it's sometimes very nice to come home and have your own space.

Pat felt that, as the years went by, it became harder to contemplate living with a partner:

> The longer you leave it from one relationship to the next, it gives you that breathing space. You get out of the routine of having to look after somebody else, of being with somebody else all the time... You find other things to do with your life. You find that you haven't got to share your life with somebody to find happiness, that you are a person in your own right. You can do what you want to do, when you want to do it... I'm scared to make that commitment. It frightens the hell out of me.

Kristin had never lived with a man, except for a brief spell (about six months) with the father of her three children. She said:

> That house has always been my space, and then to have someone come into that space, like day in and day out – it's scary!

Having lived on their own, in some cases for considerable lengths of time, these women generally felt that they could, at least, survive financially and emotionally, and, at best, be very happy, without a partner. Men were certainly no longer essential as breadwinners. But these views were sometimes in contrast to how these women had felt as teenagers when they had thought it necessary to have a man. As Ros recalled:

> I can cope with things on my own now so I don't feel like I need to have somebody around to do things, which is what I've always felt like before. I think it's something that's programmed into you a bit. You feel like you need to have somebody around to put up certain things on shelves and whatever... before I was married I just went from relationship to relationship because I always thought that I ought to.

In the past, women may have felt that it was more important to have a male partner if there were children around. But this view was not held by some of the women here – quite the opposite. Ros actually felt that single women without children were more likely than lone parents to feel a need for a man in their lives because lone parents did at least have someone else around and so were less lonely. Gillian also felt that her need for a man had lessened after having children:

I haven't had a man for 12 years. I've had men in my bed but I haven't had a man that brings food in, clothes in or anything like that, and I'm still here!... Years ago, I wouldn't finish with one boyfriend till I found the next one because you wanted to be seen as part of a couple. But when I got pregnant, all of that changed. It all went out of the window. And from then on, I've never thought of myself as needing a man. I don't need a man. I'd like one but I don't need one and I think a lot of women think they need one but they don't!

Jacqui felt that she had less need of a man than in the past:

I think as you get a bit older you realise you don't need [men]. I mean, because I can put up a shelf, I can paint a room and I can do the things that they do, change the oil and water in the car and I don't think we need them like we used to. Like when I was younger, because I always had a boyfriend, I just always did... One after the other when I was younger, but no, we don't need them.

Anita felt that women no longer needed men as breadwinners because:

On a practical and financial level, so long as there's a state who's prepared to keep shelling out money to them, then [women] don't [need men].

Other women were keen to provide for their families through work rather than rely on social security. Diane said that, even if she found a partner:

I'll carry on working, whether it's work in the bar or sorting out my own, you know, ceramics and things, no I'll definitely carry on with my thing as well.

There was a general lack of trust in men, especially among those who had previously experienced violence or whose partners had been unfaithful. This had caused a fear of commitment. In Pat's 15 years as a lone parent, she had received marriage proposals, but had refused them all because she was still unable to get over her previous experience of having an unfaithful husband:

I've never married again because I've never been able to trust a person... I just don't want to experience that hurt again. I don't want it to get to me. I don't think I could stand it.

Barbara's husband had drunk heavily and had been violent. She said:

I don't trust men now. You think they're all going to be the same, don't you? I think I'd rather be on my own, really.'

Among many women, there was a view that men would change for the worse if they went from being a boyfriend to a full partner. Gillian met a man at her workplace:

And eventually I let him move in and that was the only man I've ever let move in and it was the last – the first and the last. Oh, it was horrible, because… they want their dinner at a certain time… and I thought, 'oh, excuse me a minute'. He was nothing like he seemed at the beginning… I think once he felt he was in, he changed… In the end I had to leave where I was working because he was so possessive, so obsessed, that he was threatening people at work that if they come near me, he'd kill them… I should really have got rid of him and kept my job but I didn't… I thought, 'OK, give it a go!' so I stayed at home but he was coming home five days a week, wanting to know where I'd been, what I'd done, who I'd seen… He was a nutter and he was really hard to get rid of.

Many of the women justified their continuing status as a lone parent by saying that it was better for their children. Some who had been physically abused by their previous partners did not want their children to witness such scenes again. When Mandy was a child, she had seen her mother being beaten by her father. Eight years ago, she left her violent partner when her three children were very small. She did not want to risk getting into a similar relationship. Some women were scared to trust men with their children, especially if they had experienced physical or sexual abuse in the past from partners or parents/step-parents.

Some women also felt that they should concentrate their time and attention on their children and should not be distracted by a man, especially if their children were very young. Diane was 22 with a one year old baby. She worked 20 hours a week in various part-time jobs such as childminding, bartending and running a market stall. She said:

I don't actually feel I can commit myself [to a man] at the moment – I haven't got the time or the energy to have a full relationship and to give somebody everything that they need.

If the children were slightly older, women were concerned that a new partner might cause further confusion in their children's lives. As Alison said:

> If I was to have somebody move in, I think it would affect [my children] because they'd be wondering why somebody else was living here and not their daddy. It was strange anyway, because, well the kids, they rule this house really at the end of the day and I can't imagine them accepting anybody.

Elise had found it difficult when her own mother had got together with her stepfather and she did not want her child to go through a similar situation:

> I kind of feel that, through my own stepfather, that my mother's – not that he took her away – but she's very much piggy in the middle, trying to keep her husband happy and her children and I think I would have the same problem. I think any mother who meets another man who is not the father of her children will always feel like piggy in the middle, trying to keep both happy.

Reasons to find a partner

This section considers the views of women who were still lone parents at the time of the interview. Although many of these felt that they had neither the time, nor the energy nor the inclination to find a new partner, some nevertheless felt that there were some aspects of cohabitation which appealed to them. Some felt that they would be better off financially if they had a partner. When Gillian had lived briefly with a man, she felt that the main benefit to her and her children was the extra spending power he had brought with him:

> When [my boyfriend] was here, the one that I let live here, there wasn't any money worries and he could take my kids away, he could buy them nice clothes. I mean they've got nice clothes now but it's a struggle to get the nice clothes. They don't want to go to school in £2.99 trainers, they want Reeboks and they've got them, but it's at a price.

Elise was not necessarily looking for a breadwinner but she said that if she were to live with someone, she would either want him to work while she took care of her children or she would go out to work while he looked after the children. But she would not want someone who was unemployed and making no contribution to the running of the household.

Other women, like Samantha, had more conventional aspirations:

Someone sort of out all day working – typical family really, I suppose...
that would be nice because then I wouldn't have to worry so much about
bills.

As well as money, women wanted to find a partner so that they were
no longer lonely and had a companion to share decisions and jokes and
general experiences. Paula felt that:

You need a man more for yourself than for the children... for sex, the adult
side of things... It's nice just to feel loved.

And Barbara said that she wanted a partner for:

the attention, the love and the feeling close to somebody. Somebody you
can talk to, you just want somebody as a good friend really, don't you,
who's compatible.

Vicky liked the idea of having a man for fairly specific, and limited,
reasons:

mostly for company and that because, like I say, it does get lonely sometimes but then I get lonely in the evenings but it's not a reason to go out
and get someone just for a couple of hours in the evening when *Eastenders*
is finished.

Carol felt that she was capable and independent enough to do anything
around the house that a man might otherwise do but there were some
things she felt she lacked:

The only thing I miss is someone to sit down, put their arm around me and
have a kiss and a cuddle now and again.

Loneliness was a particular concern for women whose children were
approaching independence. Sarah was 36 and had a 10 year old son but
she was already thinking ahead when she said:

I don't want to grow old and be on my own.

Valerie was 35 and had a 13 year old son. She felt the same:

I would hate to think that I'm going to get old and have nobody there at
the end of the day... when you're 35 and towards 40 you don't particularly
want to be on your own all the time.

Some women felt that their children needed a man around at least as much as they personally wanted one. This was particularly true where women had sons. Carol had a 17 year old daughter and a 16 year old son. She said:

> This is the time when I think I need a man around for [my son's] sake, not for my own, but for someone to take him places like football matches and things like that. And I think now is the stage that [my son] needs a man in his life. But I don't.

Diane was keen for her daughter to have a male figure in her young life:

> I would like [my daughter] to have a regular male input into her life as well which I think is important to her.

Whereas some women were concerned that the arrival of a new partner might upset their children, Kelly's nine and six year old sons were very keen for her boyfriend to move in with them. But she was resisting their pressure:

> They have asked me quite a few times – the children – 'why isn't [your boyfriend] living here?' and it's quite difficult to explain to them some-times... but I think they'd be over the moon actually, but I just don't want to do it for the children... I want to find a bit of peace of mind for myself as well.

Alison also thought her kids would benefit from having a man around but she still had mixed feelings:

> It'd be great for the kids but it would be weird after six years of being on our own. Strange to have to cook him a dinner and do the ironing and... I don't know.

Women varied in the extent to which they wanted to find a new partner. They agreed that, if they could find the ideal man, they would live with him. But they had grave doubts that such a man existed so it was a question about how far they were prepared to compromise. Sarah summed up many women's views when she described her ideal man. She felt that she had found different aspects of him in different men in her life but had not, so far, found all the attributes in one person:

> I would probably want somebody who's... that was a good father like [my current boyfriend] is, that was as stable and as hard-working as [my current boyfriend] is, somebody that was as gentle and kind as another partner that I had was... and another partner that I had at one time was that his qualities as a lover were the best.

So, generally, women were looking for someone who was a good father for their children, a good lover for themselves and a breadwinner. Many were not willing to accept someone whom they saw as lazy or had little interest in their children, let alone someone who was drunken or violent. Samantha said that the men she had come across were:

> immature and... picking up girls, getting drunk sort of thing.

Women who were still lone parents tended to be quite relaxed about finding a man. They were generally happy about being a lone parent and so would only go into a relationship if it was likely to be a good one. They were not desperate to find a partner. Kristin's view was typical:

> If something comes along, then it comes along. If it doesn't, obviously it wasn't meant to be.

Some women felt that the ideal situation would be to have a partner but maintain separate homes. This would enable the women to retain a large amount of their independence but also give them access to a lover and their children access to a father. As Pat explained:

> The ideal relationship for me would be that he's got his place and I've got mine and he can have his space and I can have mine. I can't be doing with being crowded.

A few women felt that they had achieved their ideal in their current relationships and they did not want to cohabit with anyone. As Martine said:

> I've still got the best of both worlds now, I've got [my boyfriend], I've still got my house, still got my kids, still got my independence. But I would never lose my independence. I even tell [my boyfriend] that, never, I would never ever give my total life to one bloke ever.

Relationships with men while remaining a lone mother

A few lone parents either wanted or expected to get back together with their previous partners. Alison had separated from her partner before she gave birth to twin boys. At first, he wanted little to do with the children but after a few years his interest in them grew and he had, in the past, asked Alison if he could move back in with her. She had mixed feelings about this because she was bitter about the fact that he had been unfaithful to her on several occasions. But she felt that it would be good for the children if she was with him again:

> I've actually considered [living with him] sometimes… it's for their sake really and then I think, 'well, no! Because you're not thinking of yourself.' But I think, to be honest, I think we will get back together… I still feel something for him because he is the father of the kids, you know.

Kelly had been with her boyfriend since the age of 13. She first got pregnant when she was 15 and her on-off relationship with the father continued. She got pregnant again, by the same man, when she was 19 and although he asked to move in with her, she refused. She felt that she could cope on her own and did not see what she would gain from living with him. She was also unhappy with the fact that, while he was her boyfriend, he was having simultaneous relationships with other women and while she was prepared to accept such an arrangement with a boyfriend, she did not want such a relationship with a partner. She felt that all he was interested in was the fact that she had, by now, acquired a decent council house. A few years later, Kelly started seeing another regular boyfriend and, three years after that, they were still going out together but Kelly said that they did not have a sexual relationship. She was happy with the nature of the relationship and did not want it to change.

Sian had lived with her husband for over 20 years before he left her, and the country, in 1990. Despite the difficulties of being a lone parent, she felt that she was happier than she had been with him and she now had very good relationships with her two children, aged 18 and 20. There were signs, however, that her ex-husband wished to return to the marital home. She was not at all keen on the idea of his return and thought that it would upset her children who had never got on very well with him. But Sian was torn between what she considered to be her duty (to let him return) and what she really wanted (to remain on her own). She felt that, even though they were divorced, her ex-husband was still a part of her:

> I am worried about the fact that he's coming home. I mean, I did think long and hard about how I would feel and I have accepted that I might not have any sort of life... I might be restricted in the friends I have or where I go or what I do, but the alternative – to say, 'right, I'm not married any-more'... that's the worst scenario... [my friends] all think I'm mad but I don't ... [My ex-husband] is half of me, always has been... and irrespective of what I do, I can't do anything about it... I don't see I've got a choice... I made a commitment, I wanted to make a commitment however many years ago it is now, 28 or 9.

Very few other women had such a strong sense of duty and such a traditional attitude towards marriage as Sian did. It was much more common for women to put the happiness of themselves and their children before any notion of conformity to traditional patterns of coupledom.

Most women did not want to get back together with their ex-partners. Women had ended the relationship and, once ended, they rarely wished to go back. But many had new boyfriends. Only a few women had not had any boyfriends since being a lone parent. Terri's baby was only 18 months old and she rarely went out socially so had little time, energy or opportunity to meet men. Sian was 47 and was not used to going out and so had little in the way of a social life.

Most women, however, managed to find the time to go out and meet men or they met them at work or through friends. Diane had had a few boyfriends. She said that she had had some relationships which were 'casual, but almost securely casual'.

There were various reasons why these relationships had not led to cohabitation (and therefore the end of lone parenthood). In some cases, the woman was keen for the relationship to develop but the man was not. In some cases, it was the other way round and this was mainly due to the woman's fear of losing her independence and finding herself in another unhappy relationship.

Ros, 32, had started a relationship with a man who said that he was splitting up from his partner, but it soon became clear that he was not in fact doing so and she ended the relationship. The age difference was reversed in Martina's case. She was 38 and having a relationship with a 23 year old. Given her experience of domestic violence, she was nervous about any new relationship:

> I didn't have any intentions of meeting any blokes. It was the last thing on
> my mind after all what I'd been through. And I mean I kept [my new
> boyfriend] at bay for ages. I wouldn't let him near me and I was ever so
> jumpy because I was frightened of getting hit again.

But she soon came to believe that her new boyfriend was different
from her previous partner and so decided to 'let him near her'.

Pat had had a number of boyfriends, some of whom wanted to
marry her. But she was adamant that she would never marry again and
this view had led to the end of those relationships. Despite this, Pat
had no regrets.

Sarah had been involved with a man for over three years. He had
been married before and had a young daughter who sometimes came
to stay. The presence of the daughter caused tension in the
relationship and Sarah had ended it. She was now involved with
someone else.

Barbara was in what she called a 'serious' non-cohabiting relationship. But, in her case, she was less positive about its future. He had
started drinking and was asking her to move in with him. But such a
move would entail up-rooting her daughter from her school and her
friends so she was not very keen on the idea.

Other women, like Valerie, were hoping that their current
relationships might develop further:

> At the moment I'm seeing somebody and hopefully that will turn into
> something long-standing.

Sally wanted to live with her new boyfriend. But he was in the armed
services and Sally said that they would not be given 'married quarters'
until they were legally married. She was nervous about jumping
straight into marriage without having the chance to test out
cohabitation. She nevertheless expected that they would be together
in the future.

Paula was having a relationship with the man in the next house to
her. In many ways, they were almost living together. She said that
there were some weeks when he was staying every night from
Monday to Friday. He would then return next door to his own home
when his children arrived for the weekend. Although her children
were clearly aware of the close relationship that she was having, he
did not feel comfortable about being so open with his children (and his
ex-wife). Paula was keen for them to live together more formally but

he had been divorced twice and was 'paranoid' about making the same mistake again.

Having children while still a lone mother

There is a great deal of stigma surrounding women who have children while they are still lone mothers. Most of the lone parents in this study were very careful not to find themselves in this situation. Kristin had had several boyfriends but now took a great deal of care about contraception:

> Once bitten, never again. I wouldn't have no more kids.

However, seven women had had further children while they were lone parents. For example, four of the 15 'single' lone parents had had further children while still living on their own.

Carol had given birth to her first child 17 years ago after having an affair with a married man. Although shocked, her parents supported her. However, within a year of having her first baby, Carol was having a sexual relationship with the landlord at the pub where she worked. The relationship lasted three months, during which time she got pregnant again. The pub landlord 'disappeared from the face of the earth' and her parents decided that they could not forgive her twice. They told her that she could no longer live with them and so she seriously considered giving up the baby for adoption. But she 'melted' once she saw the newborn baby so decided to keep it and was eventually given council accommodation.

Gillian was a lone parent when she met a man who was living with someone else with whom he had two children. After a four-year friendship, they slept together once and Gillian became pregnant. She had the baby and her relationship with this man ended.

Elise also had a baby while she was a lone parent. She had been feeling lonely and got drunk one night and ended up sleeping with a man she had met a couple of times. She subsequently found out that he was married but tried to put this out of her mind while carrying on an affair with him. She explained how she got pregnant:

> We did use contraception but there was one time when we didn't. And it was for him, he didn't want to and I took that risk for him and basically live to pay for it now… I'm really happy with my son but from taking a risk for someone else, I was the one who paid the consequences.

The relationship ended before she found out that she was pregnant:

> Basically because he wanted to stay with his wife and basically, he realised that I was taking it seriously and I think that frightened him.

When she found out that she was pregnant, she was:

> Devastated... I'd just got to the point where things were going really well and my daughter was a lot older and I had a lot more freedom.

She told her ex-lover that she was pregnant and he assumed that she would have an abortion. She made an appointment for an abortion and her mother had agreed that this might be the best thing to do but, at the last minute, Elise could not go through with it. She had had an abortion five years before when she had found herself in a similar situation and had always felt guilty about it. She did not feel that she could go through with another one even though her material situation was just the same. After the second baby was born, however, Elise found that she had grounds for a move away from the council flat that she was so unhappy in and she finally went to a council house on a different estate. So life with the two children was not quite as difficult as she had imagined.

As well as the four women who had had babies while single, Charlotte was a pregnant lone parent at the time of the interview. Charlotte's case is interesting because, in a sense, she had planned to have another baby while single. But she had planned it because she had thought that it would provide her with a route out of lone parenthood. Charlotte had been 17 when she originally became pregnant after sleeping with a man who was separated from his wife but had another girlfriend as well as Charlotte. Charlotte wanted to live with this man, but he was only prepared to give her some support during the pregnancy and stay friends after the baby was born. But Charlotte still wanted to be more than just friends. A year or so after the baby was born, Charlotte started sleeping with him again and she thought that if she got pregnant a second time he would move in with her. She did get pregnant but she lost the baby and he had not moved in. She soon got pregnant 'accidentally' again and at the time of the interview, she was awaiting the birth of their child and still hoping that the baby would bring them together.

Two other women who had had babies while a lone parent were now living with a partner – their stories are told below (pp188–189).

LEAVING LONE MOTHERHOOD

Sixteen women were no longer lone parents at the time of the interview. Nine of these had formerly been separated lone parents and seven had formerly been single.

Keen leavers and reluctant leavers

Although all 16 women were now with partners, some had been more keen than others to leave lone parenthood. Some women had felt that they needed a man to look after them and their children, both personally and financially. Julie was 15 when she became a single lone parent 12 years ago. She had been in an on-off relationship with the father for six years after that, during which time she had two more children. They finally split up when she was pregnant with their third child. Ever since then, she had been very keen to find a partner:

> I was just looking for a man all the time to look after me... I was really lonely and depressed... I'd really like to be independent but I just can't seem to get it together... if I could drive and had enough money to support myself maybe I wouldn't need a man.

Laura liked having a man with her at night because she was frightened of being burgled. Tessa had been with her first boyfriend since the age of 14. When she broke up from him she felt that, although she could theoretically cope without a man:

> I was so used to being in a relationship that it just becomes something that is normal... when I was bit younger I was really frightened of being on my own.

This feeling of fear had previously led to Laura being in an unhappy relationship. She was now out of that but was pleased to be with someone else rather than on her own.

Lynn had also been prepared to put up with an unhappy relationship because she wanted to be in 'a proper family' rather than be a lone parent. She had left her council flat to move in with a new boyfriend but he became violent and eventually Lynn decided to leave. She was now with another man and wanted to get married:

> I think it would just be quite nice to know we're a proper family.

But her new partner was not so keen on marriage.

Although some women were keen to find a partner, others had not felt that they needed a man. Like some of the women who were still lone parents, these women had been reluctant to lose their independence and had been concerned about the risk of getting into another unhappy relationship.

Laura had been beaten by her ex-husband and was scared of getting into a similar relationship again when she met her new partner:

> He was keen and I was, like, not so keen, because I liked him but I was wary. I just didn't want to go through what I'd been through before.

Penny had been looking for a man (or men) but not in order to settle down with one:

> I was keen to find several men... I didn't just want one! I just wanted to live a bit. I just wanted to have as much sex as possible!... it was great – I'd meet one bloke in one place and meet another bloke in another place... it was something I'd never done since I was 16 and all my friends had done it from about 16 to 20 and I'd missed out on all that bit and at 26 I was doing it and it was great!

Within a year, however, she met her new partner and they lived together. But she still felt very independent:

> Women don't need a bloke – what for? There is no reason. If you can manage on the money you get or you can get yourself a decent enough job... there's so much more independence... and I think it's good for the kids to see that their mum's doing something.

Lisa met her new partner soon after she had a baby by another man:

> When I was pregnant, the last thing I could think of was another man or another boyfriend. Certainly when I had her I was not interested at all. Meeting [my new partner] was by chance really. It's only that he took a shine to me and paid me so much attention and wouldn't leave me alone for months and months but, no, I was not interested at the time.

When Bernie split up from her violent partner, she had mixed feelings about finding a new man. Part of her wanted a man to look after her. But after a few months as a lone parent she felt able to cope on her own and when she started to become friendly with another man, she drew back from making a commitment:

> When [my ex] left, I wanted someone strong who could look after me...
> that is what I was looking for... but I've learnt to be strong... In the last
> year, I've fought being a couple. I haven't wanted anyone because I've had
> such a bad impression.

Although many women said that they did not need a man in their lives,
this was not necessarily based on antagonism towards men. They felt
that men and women did not need each other in the same way as they
had done when there was the breadwinner/homemaker division of
labour. Some women felt that children could be brought up just as well
by one person (whether a man or a woman) as by a couple. Rosa made
this point clearly when she said:

> I've also got a male friend who's a single parent who's just as good a par-
> ent as anyone else I know, if not better... I don't think he needs a woman
> in his life particularly. He does a brilliant job of raising his kids and they're
> really nice kids and they get everything that all the other kids get. He's a
> really good cook, he sews things for them, you know.

Those women who had not been looking for a partner were prepared
to leave lone parenthood only because they had found a special man.
'Special' in this case meant someone who was one (but usually more
than one) of the following: kind; caring; trustworthy; non-violent; a
good father; in a regular job; willing to allow a woman a certain level of
independence; and willing to share the housework.

Laura was sold on her new partner when:

> I'd only known him about a week and it was [my son's] birthday and he
> came round and bought [my son] this great big truck for his birthday and I
> was, like, shocked. And my mum and dad had never liked any of my
> boyfriends and my mum was at the house when he arrived and mum liked
> him.

Rosa's new partner was also very good with her children:

> He's interested in the children. He's aware of things, like not arguing in
> front of them... he's got more idea of what being a parent's all about, I
> suppose, even though he makes it clear he's not their dad. He isn't their
> dad and he never will be but he's their good friend and he is their male
> role model at the moment which I'm very happy with.

Rosa's new partner was also good for her, personally and financially,
especially in comparison with her previous partner:

I'm not scared of him. He's not a bully. We laugh a lot. We have fun together. I never had fun with [my ex]... He's a nice person from a nice middle-class family. He's got a good job, he's got a degree, he's nice looking, he's polite... he's very good at doing washing and putting it in the drier... but then he could do more – I don't think he's ever cleaned the toilet.

Susan's new partner had a full-time job and yet was also, in many ways, a 'new man':

He's absolutely fantastic. He cooks, he cleans, he looks after the children. He does everything... I'll come home from work, my dinner will be ready for me. While I'm eating my dinner, my bath's being run. I get in the bath and then he'll bring up a Bacardi and Coke.

It is, perhaps, ironic that many of the lone parents had objected to providing the services to their ex-partners that Susan was so happy to have provided for her by her new partner.

The transition from lone motherhood to coupledom

The transition from lone parenthood to coupledom was often a gradual one. At first, the two people would be living in different homes but spending more and more time in the same home (usually the woman's). Sometimes they would be spending more time together than apart but this did not mean that they considered themselves a couple. Having gone through the often difficult phase during which they had established an identity as an independent lone parent, many women were reluctant to lose that identity. But then it was often the man who suggested that they formalise their informal cohabitation which they then did, usually by him moving out of the home which he now rarely used anyway. This transition from informal to formal couple rarely involved many changes in living arrangements but it did often involve changes in financial arrangements. Joint management and control of finances usually took place at a very late stage in the transition to coupledom. Indeed, some couples maintained separate finances even when they were cohabiting formally.

Bernie's new partner was eventually staying over most nights but they had not formally agreed to live together until:

I asked him, 'do you want to move in?'... He said, 'I don't know, it's a big step.' And I said, 'well, do you want to get your stuff from your mum's?'

And he laughed because he realised he didn't have anything at his mum's, it was all here. I said, 'nothing different, we'll live as we have been'.

Bernie recalled that the transition to becoming a formal couple and a family was related more to her new partner's relationship with her children than his relationship with her:

One day he was going back to sleep at his mum's and the boys were crying because he was going... and [the boys] told him they loved him... and I realised that... he was an important part of our lives... I realised that he wasn't my 'boyfriend', he was part of my family now and we were a couple – and then he started to decorate the house...

In Rosa's case, the transition from informal to formal cohabitation appeared to be one of convenience:

To start with he'd just come and stay the weekend or stay a couple of nights of the week... It ended up that he was actually living here but keeping his flat on and then it seemed ridiculous because it was about £300 or £320 a month for an empty flat and we were just letting people stay in it, you know, when couples broke up, we were letting one of the couple stay in the flat.

Rosa's new partner got rid of his flat but not all new partners gave up their own homes even though they were now cohabiting. This sometimes made it difficult to classify the relationship – were they living together or not? Maria said of her relationship:

He virtually lives here apart from the odd night he'll go home.

Paula's partner maintained his home next door to her. The main reason for this was that he found it difficult to admit to his children and ex-wife that he had such a serious relationship with another woman. Natalie was nervous of making the transition from informal to formal cohabitation:

He stays here quite a bit but there is talk about him – he's got a flat and there is talk about him giving up his flat because he's more here than he is at his flat but at the moment it's quite scary for me to do that... he's here nine times out of ten. But it's just that extra step... [I'm scared about] it going wrong again.

Although some women drifted into cohabitations, others were far too wary to allow a cohabitation to creep up on them without a great deal of consideration. Maria was concerned about any possible effect on her children due to the arrival of a new man:

> I just wanted to be sure myself before the children got to meet him. I didn't want the children meeting every boyfriend I had and thinking, 'oh, here's another one mum's got!'

Michelle found out all she could about her new partner before agreeing to move in together:

> I wanted to know what he'd be like – and you don't just ask him – you ask his friends, his family… I even spoke to his ex-wife about him. Of course, she never heard a good word said about him so I thought – well she's like that anyway. And I spoke to his family and his mum and dad and everybody and they all said, 'he's great. He don't mind housework, he don't mind cleaning, hoovering, cooking, washing, he don't mind that at all'… And then you just ask little questions and like, you keep the answers stored in the back of your mind, sort of thing. And then you make up your mind for yourself one day, 'is it right for him to move in?'

Despite gathering all this information, Michelle was still slightly uncertain about the relationship because of the fear that he might change once living with her. So she made it clear to him that they would have to give it a trial run before agreeing to live together more formally:

> We even done a trial run for a couple of months… everything was fine, I thought great… he was lovely – I've been to work, he'll do tea.

For many women, the final commitment to a partner (short of marriage) was to share finances. This often meant either signing off benefit and becoming dependent on the new partner's earnings or signing on benefit together. For many women, this was a more significant hurdle to cross than allowing their new partner into their home. Rosa's new partner had given up renting his flat to move in with her formally. But she was still keen to maintain some independence. They shared housework but still kept their finances separate. She still received Income Support in her own right even though he went out to work and earned enough to float them outside the range of any means-tested benefits. From these earnings he paid her 'keep' of £50 a week. Legally, this woman was committing benefit fraud but, in her eyes, she was just maintaining a degree of independence from the man she was living with.

Some women were not officially declaring themselves as a couple because the relationship was still too uncertain. As Julie said:

> He's sort of on and off. At the moment, he's got nowhere to live so I'd say he is sort of living here at the moment but it's on and off. He's not signing on from here or anything like that but he is actually staying here... five nights a week... Actually he's got a room with his brother which he's got most of his stuff in. He's got some stuff here and some up his brother's, so I assume that's where he stays.

As well as a transition from informal to formal couple there was a further transition which sometimes occurred later. This was the transition from unofficial to official couple. Even when women had recognised that they were now part of a couple, they were sometimes reluctant to declare themselves as such to the social security authorities. This was often because they were reluctant to lose their financial independence even if they had accepted some degree of emotional dependence on a man. They were also concerned that, if the relationship were not to last, they would have to get in touch with the authorities again to de-register as a couple.

So the formal transition to coupledom involved a personal declaration about the nature of the relationship. The official transition involved an official declaration which gave it a quasi-marital status.

In Della's case, 'it just happened' that her new partner moved in with her. It then took a year before she felt prepared to sign on with him:

> I just thought he was staying for quite a while. It wasn't until he started bringing his furniture down from his dad's house that I thought, hold on a minute... Even though I've been dependent on the state, I've liked having my book. I've liked having my place. And I didn't think I'd ever give that up for anyone and having somebody cohabiting with you. We did it for a year [without telling the DSS]... because I thought, 'I'm not going to tell them and then if he sods off again, which a lot of them do...' so I had to make pretty sure that he was going to stick around.

Soon after signing on together, Della married her new partner. She said that it was only at this point that:

> To the whole world I then became no longer a single parent although I did have a partner that was living with me.

Although many couples were better off if they kept their finances separate, the financial disadvantage of becoming a couple was not the main reason why many women were reluctant to declare themselves officially as part of a couple. The main reason was that these women feared losing their emotional and economic independence and they were scared that the relationship would not last. Their sense of identity and independence therefore formed the major barrier to becoming a couple in the official as well as formal sense. Level of income was an issue but not the main one.

Living as a couple

Post-lone parent relationships were often very different from pre-lone parent relationships. Many of the women found that, in contrast to their earlier relationships, they were now in fairly egalitarian relationships where they could retain some of the independence they had developed as a lone parent. One difference was that the male partner was usually moving into the lone parent's territory which gave her a less submissive position from the very beginning. Penny's relationship with her ex-husband had been a very traditional one, with her looking after the home and children and him going out to work. She had been happy with this at first but had then changed and became disillusioned with the relationship. Her new relationship was:

> completely different. He knew what I was like when he met me. He knew that I liked to go out. Basically, we're very much alike... he didn't give me no ear-ache about anything. He didn't expect food on the table.

Her new partner was quite happy for her to go on holiday with her friends while he looked after the children.

Rosa's new relationship was also more egalitarian:

> I wouldn't say he 'looks after me', you know, we sort of rub along really. I mean, he does [look after me] if I'm ill but then I look after him if he's ill. But we're quite independent still.

Lisa was a single lone mother and, while living at home with her mother, had gone back to work when her baby was three weeks old. She was proud of being able to support her baby financially (with the help of Family Credit) and even though her new partner had a good job, she was keen to carry on working:

I'm quite independent and I don't like relying on people, even though he's absolutely brilliant... even before she was born I was quite independent, working.

Maria's new partner lived with her most of the time but still maintained a home of his own also. She wondered if she was 'too independent' in not accepting his financial support:

I'm probably too independent now. He wants to help financially and everything and I won't let him. And it's hard. It causes friction sometimes. He'll say, 'don't be so independent, let me help you'. And I say, 'no, when the time is right I'll let you, but not yet'.

Like many women, Lynne had an arrangement with her partner that he paid a weekly contribution to the household expenses, but the responsibility for the bills, and especially the rent, was hers. There was therefore a clear split between 'his money' and 'her money'. Penny had a similar view:

His money was his own money... as long as he gave me money towards the food then that was that... I never touched his money at all, I lived on mine.

Penny preferred this state of affairs because:

I felt I still had my independence. I didn't have to ask him for anything... I paid the bills, I bought the food, I paid the mortgage and as far as he was concerned he paid as a lodger would pay... he gave me so much a week – about £35 a week, which, according to the Social, Income Support book, I was entitled to have.

Heather felt strongly that she would retain what she saw as financial security until they got married:

Nothing's really changed – all the bills are in my name, the house is in my name. And it will be 'til we're married really. That's my security, the house.

Della also found it difficult to get used to sharing with someone:

After so many years of being completely independent you come to a different state of mind and you can do what you want and you know if the floor's a mess, the floor's a mess and you do it when you want to do it. And it is just completely different.

The difficulties of cohabiting after a spell as a lone parent were sometimes added to by the views of others. For example, the parents of Susan's new partner were not at all keen on their son getting involved with a divorced woman who had children. Their objection was:

> Why should they have to take to another man's children? [My new partner's] dad... came round to our house one night and... he turned round and says, 'you know them two upstairs [her children by her previous partner] I wouldn't give them nothing', he says, 'but this one here [his son's child], I'd give him everything'. And I just turned round and said, 'get out of my house'.

In a similar way, complications arose because the new partner was often an absent parent himself. Heather had difficulties with her new partner's daughter. She said that this was because his ex-partner was bitter and was undermining her to her daughter. Heather thought that this was strange given that it had been the ex-partner who had ended the relationship. There was also friction over money. Heather resented the fact that her new partner was paying £40 maintenance out of his £160 wages. She thought that this was too much, especially given that they looked after his daughter at the weekends and that her mother was now remarried. At Heather's insistence, her partner reduced the maintenance he paid to his ex-partner to £25 a week.

Throughout this report, we have talked only to the women involved in these relationships and the picture that they have painted of the men in their lives has often been an unflattering one. We only see a more sympathetic picture of men when these women talk about their current partners. For example, Heather recounts her new partner's version of his previous relationship:

> He met [his ex-partner] when he was 22 and... one thing led to another and she got pregnant straightaway... he thought, 'I'll stay with her and look after her'... and [his ex-partner] wasn't very good to him at all, she never loved him, she made it obvious. But he always thought it was his duty to stay with her and that. And the relationship broke down and he stayed with her for two years even though they never slept together... she knocked all the confidence out of him and when [his daughter] was about six, five or six, she said, 'I don't love you any more and I want you to go'... but she met somebody else and they got married a few weeks ago.

Rosa's partner was divorced and had a son and stepson with his previous partner. She said that their divorce had been 'messy' and that his ex-wife had deliberately turned his children against him.

As well as the difficulties faced by the adults in a new relationship, there were also sometimes difficulties for the children of the lone parent. From being in a family where it was just them and their mother, they had to get used to someone else whom their mother loved. Many women felt the tension between appearing to neglect their partner and appearing to neglect their children. Rosa's two sons reacted quite differently to the arrival of her new partner:

> The little one absolutely dotes on him, they're really close... he was only just over a year... when we got together... With [the older one] it was a bit harder because his dad poisoned him a lot against him. He had a lot of spiteful things to say... Also [the older one], even though he was only four, was kind of the man of the house, you know. He took that quite seriously so that was more difficult. But they get on really well now. It took a long time to iron out and it's been hard for me to keep out of it but I think that's the only way to let it happen really.

In some cases, women wanted to have another baby to cement their relationships with their new partners. This sometimes had the desired effect but not always. Heather had been a single lone parent when she met her new partner (who had a child by a previous partner). She described how they decided to have a child of their own:

> At first, I says, 'I fancy having a baby' and [my partner] said, 'oh, no, not yet' and we talked about it for a few months first and I forgot about the idea and he come back and said to me, 'well, shall we? We're getting on a bit now, we'll be too old'... I left it for a bit and kept saying, 'are you sure?' and he says, 'yes, yeah' and we went ahead and I got pregnant literally straightaway.

Susan had not planned to get pregnant with her new boyfriend and said that she had been 'absolutely devastated' when she found out she was pregnant because her two children were now seven and nine and she had started to feel more independent. She was wary of living with anyone again after her previous experience and her new partner's parents were not very keen on their only son moving in with an older woman who was a lone parent. But despite her doubts, the relationship bloomed and, three years later, Susan was happy in her new life. She maintained a degree of independence within her new relationship and her new partner was very much a 'new man', helping out with the housework and childcare.

Tessa had thought that a baby might cement the relationship between herself and her partner. She got pregnant 'accidentally' three times but her partner was not at all keen to become a father and she, reluctantly, had abortions on all three occasions:

> There's been a couple of times that I have fallen pregnant and he's been very unhappy, well not unhappy, sort of like not wanted them at all... they frighten the life out of him... whether it's because it's a big commitment or whether it's because it's going to be a big change – he's frightened of anything changing.

Tessa recalled that these pregnancies occurred when she was feeling broody and had been drinking and so 'forgot' to put her cap in. She said that she now used her cap 'religiously' because she had been terribly shaken by her last abortion:

> He took me to it and I went in one person and came out another.

Julie had got pregnant accidentally twice while living with her new partner. But on both occasions she had had abortions. On the first occasion, this was because she did not feel that she could cope with another baby but on the second occasion, it was her partner who felt uncomfortable with the idea of a new addition to the family.

Some couples decided to cement their relationships by getting married. In Laura's case, her partner was keen to marry but she was less so. Laura explained the nature of her doubts:

> I was a bit worried about getting married because I thought he might think he owns me now because I'm married – and tell me what to do... but he don't. It don't make that much difference. It's like, before, you know, if it hadn't worked out I could have walked away from it but because you're married, you can't walk away from it.

Although Julie's relationship was going well, she still felt confident that if anything happened to her new partner, she 'could go back to bringing the kids up and everything on my own again'.

In other cases, it was the new partner who was reluctant to marry. Tessa was keen to marry but:

He's very funny about marriage as well, ı must admit, because his parents broke up when he was 10 or 11 and it's affected him quite badly – very insecure.

Lynn wanted to get married so that they would be, and be seen to be, a 'proper family' but her new partner was not so keen. Like Tessa, she put this down to the fact that his parents' marriage broke down:

His parents divorced and that was quite messy and his mum walked out so they were left with their dad and he had quite a tough upbringing one way and another... it's his upbringing that's just made him very wary and it's like, 'Oh God, I'm not getting trapped thank you very much'.

Rosa and her partner would have considered marriage but they felt that this would definitely mean that they would have to declare their cohabitation to the authorities – which would, according to their calculations, make them £90 a week worse off. As well as any ongoing costs to marriage, the cost of a wedding was a further disincentive to tying the knot. A wedding is a social (as well as legal) declaration of the status of a relationship but if a couple, or their family, cannot afford to invite people, then the social side of the occasion will be diminished.

Penny did not really think there was much point in going through a legal ceremony, except, perhaps, for the sake of her children:

Father can't bear the expense of another wedding!... We probably would [get married] in the next two or three years... but it would be more so for the kids... because the oldest two have said that they want to change their name to his name... I'd be quite happy to change my name by deed poll and stick a gold band on my finger – it don't make no difference to me. But I think it would be nice for them, and have that stability.

Penny said that she could foresee no problems between her and her new partner and felt that this relationship was for life. Many others felt the same, but not all. Julie did not think that her relationship would last:

I don't think we'll stay [together]. Like it's wearing very thin and I'm trying to find him a place to live because it ain't working here... I really don't think it's going to last but who knows? Because we do actually love each other.

Julie's difficulties with her partner revolved around money. She said that she would be better off without him as he made virtually no financial contribution to the household, keeping his giro cheque to himself. Julie was scared to be on her own again but felt that the relationship was just not worth maintaining.

Moving in and out of lone motherhood

It is difficult, even in a qualitative study, to do justice to the complexities of people's lives. Some women had moved in and out of lone parenthood on more than one occasion. We saw above that some single lone mothers had had more children while still on their own. In this section, we consider the situations of two women who, at the time of the interview, were in a couple but who had both been lone parents when they had further children.

At 18, Laura had been single when she became a lone parent. About five years later she got pregnant again, this time by a different boyfriend whom she had been going out with for about two years. They were not living together and there was little chance that they would as, Laura said, he had other girlfriends at the same time. Her parents had supported her the first time but were now quite keen for her to consider giving up the new baby for adoption. She nevertheless went ahead with the pregnancy and kept the baby. Two years later, Laura was living with a third man when she got pregnant and had her third child. But this man was violent and he was arrested on one occasion for assaulting Laura. They split up. All three pregnancies had been 'accidental' as Laura had been on the mini-pill (which has a lower success rate than the combined pill and has to be taken at more precise times). She admitted to missing it sometimes and not knowing a great deal about how to take it. At the age of 26, with three children by three different fathers, Laura got sterilised. She did not expect to meet anyone else:

> I never thought anybody was going to take on three kids, especially after I was sterilised and knew that I couldn't have one of their own. So I'd always put it down to – I was going to be on my own.

A few years later, she met her current partner and although she was very wary of a new relationship, they moved in together. They were now living on his wages, supplemented by Family Credit. So Laura had not remained a single parent living on social security.

Rita had also had an eventful life. She had got married 25 years ago at the age of 22. In her late twenties she had two children. She then drifted apart from her husband and the marriage ended after 10 years. About five years later, she met a man who was a widower with two children. While on holiday with him, she got pregnant accidentally (she said she 'forgot' to use the cap). They split up before the baby was born because she did not think that he was a very good father to his two children and she did not want him to be heavily involved with her children. She received maintenance from both the fathers and managed to go back to work, employing an au pair to look after her children. At the age of 39, with three children by two different men, Rita met another man at a dinner party and married him within three months. She got pregnant fairly soon afterwards but then equally quickly realised that the relationship was a mistake. She felt that he had mainly been attracted to her because of her money. She left him but kept the baby (her fourth child). Some time later, Rita met another man, who was separated from a previous partner and already had four children of his own. Now, at the age of 47, with two young children still on her hands (the other two were now teenagers living with their father – her first husband), Rita was happy with her new partner but had no plans to get married.

KEY POINTS: THE DURATION OF LONE MOTHERHOOD

- The rise in lone parenthood is mainly due to increases in rates of entry by both routes: having a baby while single and separations of couples with children. There were also signs that single mothers remain in that state longer than they used to; but there has been no change in the duration of separated motherhood.
- Half of all lone parents will leave lone parenthood within six years. Half of all single lone parents will marry three years after having their first baby and half of all divorced lone parents will remarry five years after their divorce. The average (median) duration for separated lone mothers is higher – at eight years.
- Using survival modelling techniques, housing tenure was shown to have an effect on duration of lone parenthood: home-owners had shorter spells than women in other types of accommodation. The rate of local unemployment was also a factor – although it had a very complex relationship with the duration of lone parenthood.

- Women saw two main advantages to being a lone parent: general autonomy over their lives; and control of their finances. The disadvantages included loneliness, the burden of sole responsibility for decisions and lack of money.
- A few women who remained lone parents were adamant that they did not want to find a partner. A few were very keen to find someone. The majority were more open-minded – a happy relationship was their ideal but they preferred lone parenthood to an unhappy relationship. Women generally felt that they did not need a man but they would like one, if 'Mr Right' or 'Mr Almost-Right' came along.
- The ideal man for a successful relationship was considered to be someone with the following characteristics: kind; caring; non-violent; trustworthy; a good father; a breadwinner; willing to share the housework; and happy to allow their partner a degree of independence.
- Some single lone parents had had more children while still single but only one had deliberately planned to do so.
- Sixteen women were no longer lone parents at the time of the interview. Some of these had been very keen to find a partner because they felt that they needed a man. Others had been reluctant to leave lone parenthood but had, by chance, met a man they were very compatible with.
- For those who had cohabited prior to lone parenthood, their post-lone parent relationships were very different from their earlier experiences. The main difference was that their current relationships were more egalitarian and provided more independence than they had previously had. These relationships were sometimes complicated, however, when the new partner was also an absent parent with a ready-made extended family.
- Some women moved in and out of lone parenthood on different occasions. For example, they might originally become a lone parent by having a baby while single. They might then get together with a partner and have another baby before splitting up and so become a lone parent for a second time, albeit through a different route. There may even be a third and fourth entry into lone parenthood.

Chapter 5

Conclusions:
The growth of lone parenthood

There has been a dramatic increase in the incidence of lone parenthood over the last 20 or so years but little is known about why this has happened. In 1971 there were 570,000 lone parents (Haskey, 1994). By 1992 there were 1.4 million. In 1972, 6 per cent of children were living in a lone parent family. By 1994–5 this had risen to 20 per cent (Central Statistical Office, 1996). In the 1970s and early 1980s an increasing proportion of lone mothers were women who had separated or divorced from their partners. By contrast, in the late 1980s an increasing proportion were single women who had had babies while living without a partner. Widows and lone fathers account for a relatively small proportion of lone parents (Haskey, 1994).

This book sets out to investigate the growth of lone parenthood in Britain and these conclusions summarise our findings through a consideration of some of the key themes which we have highlighted. These are: dynamics and diversity; economic and social change; and changes in family structures and relationships.

DIVERSITY AND DYNAMICS

Two themes have dominated this book: diversity and dynamics. There is diversity in terms of the ways in which women become lone parents. Some (usually young) single women have a baby while they are living without a partner and so become lone parents in this way. Other women are married and have children and only become lone parents when their marriage ends. The growth of cohabitation has added a new category of women who have children within a cohabiting relationship which then ends. These women may have never been married and therefore be single in terms of their marital status but their experiences may be similar to women who have separated from a husband.

As mentioned above, the majority of lone parents have separated or divorced from a husband but in recent years, the number of single, never-married lone parents has increased. Our analysis suggests that the number of 'truly' single lone parents (that is, single women who have babies outside a cohabiting relationship) was low and fairly stable in the 1940s and 1950s, increased quite quickly in the 'swinging' sixties but then *declined* in the 1970s. This decline was probably due partly to the introduction of legal abortions during this time as well as to a general reduction in fertility rates. Evidence suggests that the 1980s saw another increase in the number of single lone parents. By contrast to this fluctuating picture, the number of separated lone parents has increased continuously since the Second World War and has not been reversed in any particular decade.

Our research suggests that there are different reasons for the growth of single lone motherhood compared with separated lone motherhood. For example, socio-economic background is linked to the growth of inflow to single lone motherhood but not to the growth of inflow to separated lone motherhood. Single women are more likely to become lone mothers if they come from poor socio-economic backgrounds, but this is not the case when we look at separated lone parents. The social class background of women in couples with children makes no difference to the likelihood of their becoming a separated lone mother, once other factors have been taken into account

Although there is diversity in terms of the way in which women become lone mothers, there is some similarity in their experiences after this point, with the majority experiencing similar problems of poverty. But despite these shared experiences, there is relatively little solidarity among lone parents as a group. Lone mothers make a clear distinction between those who, like themselves, became lone parents by accident or through no fault of their own and those (others) whom they believe had deliberately set out to become lone parents.

The rise in lone parenthood is due to increasing numbers of women becoming lone parents rather than an increase in the duration of lone parenthood. There are signs, however, that single mothers remain in that state longer than they used to; but there has been no change in the duration of separated motherhood.

Using survival model techniques, housing tenure was shown to have an effect on duration of lone parenthood: those in owner-occupied accommodation had shorter spells than those in rented accommodation, particularly council accommodation. Age and length of time as a lone parent also affected a woman's chances of leaving lone parenthood but few other variables, such as family background and economic activity of the lone parent, appeared to make a difference.

Some women moved in and out of lone parenthood on different occasions. For example, they might originally become a lone parent by having a baby while single. They might then get together with a partner and have another baby before they split up and so become a lone parent for a second time, albeit through a different route. There may even be a third and fourth entry into lone parenthood.

ECONOMIC AND SOCIAL CHANGE

Employment prospects of men and women

The evidence among our single lone parents supports the hypothesis that the employment prospects of men and women have affected the growth of lone parenthood, but the relationship between employment prospects and family change is not a simple one. Single women did not plan to get pregnant, but once they had conceived, some felt that the prospect of life as a single mother provided them with a role and an identity which was preferable to their current life in low-paid, unrewarding jobs. These women were from poor socio-economic backgrounds and often in work but in fairly low-paid, low-status work such as unskilled manual work in factories, shop assistant work, office clerk work etc. The prospect of becoming a mother was not a very negative one and life on benefit would not be too much of a drop in income. The quantitative analysis also showed a clear link between social disadvantage and the probability of becoming a single parent. Those who were not in full-time education or in paid work had particularly high chances of becoming a single lone parent.

The prospect of becoming a single lone parent was not only seen as preferable to their current life, it was also seen as preferable to the available future alternatives. This was because some of these women felt that the men who had fathered their children were not suitable to become husbands or regular partners. These men were either unemployed or in irregular employment or, in some cases, in regular employment but seen as 'irresponsible' either financially or personally.

Despite all of these findings, single women were not completely rejecting the traditional nuclear family – most single pregnant women said that they would have preferred to have married before having a baby and our research shows that, on average, single lone parents got married within three years of becoming a single mother.

The only woman who had planned to become a single lone parent was in her thirties and was in a professional job at the time she got pregnant. She felt that she would be able to support her child herself, if not in the short term while the child was a baby, certainly in the medium and long term.

If we turn now to separated lone parents, the immediate causes of lone parenthood are different. As we have shown, the quantitative analysis does not show a link between the social class background of the women or the level of local unemployment and separations among couples with children. Nor is the employment situation of the woman relevant. But the employment situation of the husband was very important – couples were three times more likely to separate if the man was unemployed rather than in paid work. Loss of employment and lack of money caused clear tensions between couples. Our evidence from the qualitative research also showed that the women who separated from partners had been in jobs at some point in the past. In some cases, women's difficulties in combining employment with domestic responsibilities led to conflict within the couple. More commonly, however, conflict occurred when the woman gave up her job to look after a newly-arrived child. In these situations, although women expected to take on the bulk of domestic responsibilities, they resented what they saw as their partner's reversion to more traditional roles. The partners apparently expected the woman to carry out all domestic chores and the women felt that they were now subordinate to their partner. The women also disliked the fact that they were now dependent on their partners for money and sometimes felt that their partners were being irresponsible and selfish with their earnings. So in many cases, it was women's experience of employment which caused problems, with problems occurring after they gave up jobs rather than while they were in them. Male unemployment did lead to tension within couples but conflict surrounded lack of equal access to money, not just lack of money itself.

Turning to the duration of lone parenthood, the quantitative research showed that housing tenure, which can be taken as a sign of social disadvantage, had an effect on duration, with owner-occupiers experiencing shorter spells of lone parenthood compared with renters. The qualitative research suggested that having become a lone parent, economic issues were of some importance in determining the duration. Women had very little money but they did not generally feel particularly worse off compared with their previous situation. They were now in control of the purse strings, even if there was little money to go round, so there was little economic incentive to find a partner. Moreover, some women found themselves able to work and support their families, particularly if they had help from their relatives (in the form of childcare) and help from the state (in the form of Family Credit). These women felt little need to find a male partner/breadwinner. Other lone parents, who were reliant on Income Support, would have liked to find a male breadwinner but few seemed to be around. Generally, the lone parents interviewed felt that they no longer needed a man to support them. They were happy to live with one if a suitable candidate appeared but, even though they were often on very low incomes, they were reassured by the fact that they were in control of those incomes.

The availability of social security and housing

Evidence from our study suggests that single women knew that social security would be available if they became lone parents but the prospect of financial and emotional support from parents was also very important to them – making the difference between mere survival and being able to live. But money was not uppermost in these women's minds at the time they were pregnant as they were facing the prospect of a life-changing event – becoming a mother. Such an event has far more than economic consequences. Many of these women had worked in low-paid jobs, so life on benefit would not necessarily have entailed a drastic reduction in standard of living. The prospective fathers were also in fairly low-paid, irregular work (if they were in work at all) and there was some evidence that these women preferred to receive benefit in their own right rather than be dependent on income from a man.

As far as the separated lone parents are concerned, these women also knew that social security would enable them to survive financially but they placed greater hope in being able to work. So it may be that the reduction in qualifying hours for Family Credit to 16 in 1992 is also significant for this group. Of course, in some cases it was the man who left the woman, so the existence of social security would not have provided an incentive or disincentive for the woman to become a lone parent. It may, however, enable men to feel more comfortable leaving their partners in the knowledge that they will be able to survive. And in the days before the Child Support Agency some fathers may have felt able to leave their partners without, themselves, having to contribute financially to their former family. It would be interesting to know whether the Child Support Agency has any effect on men's attitudes and behaviour with regard to lone parenthood: will single men take more precautions against becoming fathers? And will men in couples think twice about leaving their partners?

There was still a great deal of stigma attached to being a lone parent on benefit but lone parents distanced themselves from this by arguing that they had not deliberately planned to become lone parents and therefore could not be blamed for their current situation. Some went out to work in an effort to prove that they were not 'scroungers'. The support of their parents and friends also enabled them to survive the moral sanctions of the wider community.

Having become a lone parent, many women were wary of giving up their direct access to the benefit system which they assumed they would have to do if they signed on as a couple or became reliant on a man's earnings. Once again, it was control of money, rather than the source or level of money, which was a key factor to them.

Turning to housing, there were no single women in the qualitative interviews who appeared to have become pregnant deliberately in order to secure a council flat or house. Many were living at home and were happy to continue doing so in order to benefit from the support of their parents (especially their mothers). Once they had had their babies, however, many single mothers eventually applied for and were allocated council accommodation which they then moved into. The availability of council accommodation cannot, therefore, be said to directly increase entry into lone parenthood.

The separated lone mothers generally stayed in their own homes and so did not transfer into council accommodation. Some, however, left their homes and stayed with their parents or, in two cases, moved to refuges, so that they could escape their violent husbands. A few separated lone parents had difficulty gaining access to council accommodation after being labelled 'intentionally homeless' because they had left their partners. So, for them the prospect of council accommodation was certainly not an incentive to separate from a partner.

In the quantitative research, living arrangements and housing tenure did affect entry to lone parenthood and duration. Couples in owner-occupation were less likely to split up than couples who rented. Once they had become lone parents, women in owner-occupied accommodation were more likely than others to find a partner and leave lone parenthood. Single women were more likely to become lone parents if they had been brought up in council housing or if they were council tenants in their own right at the time they got pregnant.

Divorce law

Our evidence suggests that people did not consider divorce until they felt that the marriage was completely over. And little was known about divorce law until the decision to seek a divorce had been made. Some women did feel that it was too easy to divorce but they only came to this conclusion after the process had finished and this implied that they had originally thought that it might be a difficult process. So there is no evidence from our study that lone parenthood is caused or encouraged by weak divorce laws. However, it could be argued that the state's sanctioning of divorce could encourage a climate in which attitudes to separation become more relaxed. The relationship between legislation, social attitudes and social behaviour is a complex one – in countries where divorce is illegal, attitudes towards divorce are generally less permissive than in other countries, but it is difficult to know whether attitudes are affected by the legal situation or whether the legal situation is conditional on general attitudes. The evidence suggests that divorce laws (and perhaps other types of laws) only change after there have already been changes in social attitudes and social behaviour rather than before. There may be a feedback mechanism, however, whereby legal changes then lead to a further changing of attitudes. There may also be some kind of cohort effect whereby people see many other people getting divorced and so become more likely, themselves, to consider ending their marriage.

Sexual attitudes and behaviour

Evidence from official data suggests that the increase in single lone parenthood is mainly due to significant increases in extramarital conceptions over the last 20 years rather than to an increase in the proportion of such conceptions which result in the creation of a lone parent family.

Most of the single lone parents in our study said that they did not plan to become pregnant even though they either used no form of contraception or misused contraception in some way. Their reasons for not using contraception were partly related to risk-taking – they did not think that the risks of conception were high and were outweighed by the risks of appearing to be promiscuous by suggesting the use of contraception. Single women were leaving the responsibility for contraception to their male partners and these men perhaps either assumed that the women were on the pill or did not particularly care about contraception.

Whereas attitudes to premarital sex have become more tolerant, attitudes to extramarital sex have not (Wellings and others, 1994). Among separated lone parents, extramarital sex was generally condemned and while its discovery was rarely the sole cause of a separation, it certainly contributed to several break-ups. There was some evidence that men and (to a much lesser extent) women were searching for 'fun' through sexual relationships with people other than their partners. A premium was placed on individual happiness above any feeling of duty to the traditional ideal of monogamy. This was particularly true within couples who had joined together at early ages. Partners felt that they had missed out on youthful exploits. This links in to our quantitative findings that couples who had married at early ages were more likely to separate.

Having become a lone parent, greater sexual freedom could have two effects on duration of lone parenthood. Some lone parents might be more likely to find someone to live with through having relationships which began fairly casually. This would therefore lead to a reduction in duration. However, greater sexual freedom may also enable women to remain lone parents while also having more casual relationships. Our evidence is mixed. Many lone parents had had boyfriends while they were lone parents and in some cases these relationships led to cohabitation and marriage. In other cases, lone parents preferred 'the best of both worlds' – the autonomy of lone parenthood combined with the adult company of a boyfriend.

Attitudes to 'the family' and individual happiness

Among potential lone parents

Findings from our qualitative study suggest that women wanted a greater degree of autonomy in a relationship than would have been considered acceptable to their partners in the past. Women still believed that the ideal family was a 'traditional' two-parent family but they now wanted (and perhaps demanded) a more egalitarian relationship with a greater degree of shared responsibility. It is difficult to know exactly how such attitudes have developed but the women's movement of the 1970s, along with the increasing success of women in education and greater participation in the labour force have probably all contributed to women's changing expectations and demands.

Some men, too, wanted greater independence. In the 1960s and 1970s couples were getting married at lower and lower ages. There is some evidence from our study that some of these couples, particularly the men in them, regretted this and felt that they had missed out on youthful exploits. As far as single lone parents are concerned, their boyfriends rarely offered to marry the woman whom they had made pregnant – not that these women necessarily expected or wanted these men to marry them. They felt able to survive without men by relying on social security and support from their families. And some preferred to do this than to be dependent on a man – especially when the man was unlikely to be a stable breadwinner.

The growth of individualism should not be exaggerated, however. Many couples remained together long after their initial problems began because they did not wish to abandon the ideal of the nuclear family. And single women did not plan to become lone mothers – they would have preferred to have married before having children. The autonomy and independence gained during lone parenthood had their downside in terms of loneliness and the burden of sole responsibility for decisions. Women ideally wanted to be in a couple, but not at any price.

Among parents and friends of lone parents

One of the most striking findings in the study is the degree of support given to lone mothers by their own parents (especially their mothers). Some of these parents had experienced separation and lone parenthood themselves and so could sympathise with their daughters. Others had stayed in unhappy relationships and now advised their daughters not to make the same mistake. Parents told their daughters to consider their own happiness above any duty they might feel to their partners and even, in some cases, to their children.

Given the apparent breakdown in the 'traditional' two-parent family, it is interesting that single women, in particular, relied so heavily on parental support. Some women, particularly single women, may not have become lone parents without the support of their mothers. And as well as the initial moral support, practical support was often provided in the form of help with childcare and the lending/giving of money. In some ways, therefore, the growth of lone parenthood may have led to a revival in the extended family at the expense of the two-parent nuclear family or, perhaps, to a strengthening of the matriarchal family at the expense of the patriarchal family.

In society at large

Lone parents in the study felt that general attitudes to lone parenthood were more positive than they had been in the past – but that they were still fairly negative. Whereas lone parenthood had previously been unacceptable and a disgrace on the individual and her family, lone parenthood has become a generally acceptable but certainly not ideal situation.

Single lone parents were thought to be considered in a particularly negative light as having got pregnant deliberately in order to secure council accommodation and social security. The views of the general public may have been one reason why single women felt that they needed the support of their families. Separated lone parents developed strategies to distance themselves from the stigma which surrounded lone parenthood, for example by stressing that they had not been to blame for the separation. Stigma about lone parenthood was mainly focused on benefit dependence rather than the mere fact that a single woman was bringing up a child on her own. Hence women could reduce the amount of stigma they faced or felt by going out to work.

So although there may be some evidence that stigma against lone parenthood has declined, it still exists and may reduce the numbers of women who would otherwise become lone parents. It is particularly aimed at the group of lone parents who have increased most recently – single lone parents, suggesting that this growth has occurred despite the existence of stigma rather than as a result of a reduction in stigma.

CHANGES IN FAMILY STRUCTURES AND RELATIONSHIPS

Since the late 1960s we have seen a continual breakdown in the traditional two-parent family based on a married couple which includes a male breadwinner, a female housewife and their children. This has manifested itself in a number of ways, including the increase in lone parent families. The roots of this breakdown lie in economic and social change which has affected the attitudes, expectations and opportunities of both men and women. Although the traditional nuclear family has received a battering, it has not been completely demolished. Only a quarter of families with children are lone parent families at any one time: more over a period. And even those who appear to reject the two-parent family by becoming lone parents would, ideally, wish to live in a couple. But they prefer lone parenthood to the reality of living in a poor relationship or, in some cases, they do not have any choice about becoming a lone parent because their partner leaves them or they get pregnant while single and their boyfriend will not live with them.

The growth of lone parenthood signals a decline in the patriarchal, nuclear family structure, in favour of a more matriarchal family structure. Without a man around, women are in charge in lone parent families. And they often rely heavily on their own mothers and other women friends and family for support. The end of the twentieth century is therefore witnessing a growth, albeit limited, in the (extended) matriarchal family.

We are also witnessing changes in social norms – cohabitation is no longer seen as 'living in sin' and there is much less shame in illegitimacy than there was a generation ago. Shotgun weddings are a thing of the past. Once again, these changes should not be exaggerated. For example, couples are still reluctant to separate because of the stigma surrounding 'failed' marriages. And although there has been a trend in the law towards 'no fault' divorce, people still find divorce easier to justify to others and cope with themselves if they can blame the other partner for causing the break-up.

Although there is less stigma surrounding lone parenthood, women do feel uncomfortable about being seen as dependent on the state. From their own point of view, direct dependence on the state is preferable to dependence on a man, who might himself be dependent on the state. But women are aware that the rest of society takes a different view.

To sum up, the growth of lone parenthood has occurred partly because of two sets of circumstances. For single women from poor backgrounds who get pregnant, lone motherhood is a relatively attractive option beside the alternatives of living with a poor man or staying as a single woman in a poor job. For women in couples with children, a different situation applies. These women are no longer so constrained, by economic necessity and social norms, to remain 'for better or worse' in a traditional two-parent family.

Appendix 1

Event history analysis

The quantitative methods in this book are a part of 'event history analysis'. This is a series of techniques that are used to look at the length of time it takes for something to happen. This could be the length of time before a machine fails, or the length of time that a person lives. This book is concerned with how long people spend in one family type or another, before moving into another family type.

One of the assumptions used, although it is a simplification, is that people are in well-defined family types, that can be distinguished from all other relevant family types. This assumption is being explored in the qualitative work within this overall research project.

The general approach is to consider all the points of time at which people are 'at risk' of an event occurring, and for how many that event does then occur. This is a largely descriptive approach. If we take the 3,414 women in the sample, then all of them are 'at risk' of getting married from the age of 16 onwards. But only a small number did, in fact, marry at that age. There is then a smaller number at risk of marriage at age 17, and so on. This can be illustrated in the form of a so-called 'survivor curve'. To start with, all of the women are 'at risk' of marriage. But at older ages, the proportion who have not married (and hence are still at risk of marrying) falls quite quickly. Those not married at the time of interview, and in the younger age groups, are progressively removed from the analysis.

A complementary approach is to analyse the chances of getting married in any given year, if not married before then. This is known as the 'hazard rate', and may be treated as a type of probability (see Figure 2.5 in Chapter 2 for an example). The smoothed hazard rate line shows that the likelihood of becoming a single mother increases during the teens but then falls as women move through their twenties.

The next step in such exploratory analysis is to compare survival or hazard graphs by some characteristic of interest. An example is provided in Figure 4.1 in Chapter 4 which shows that the patterns of exit from lone parenthood varied considerably by type of lone parent.

It is possible to move beyond these descriptions to take account of different information about the people concerned, and the date of particular events. A range of 'modelling' or 'multivariate' approaches are available, which associate the chance of an event taking place, with characteristics of the individual and their circumstances. For example, how is the length of marriage affected by, say, the age at marriage, whether the husband becomes unemployed and the type of housing lived in. In the main sections of this book, we use powerful modelling techniques, which are designed to look separately at the effects of different factors. Using the example of marriage: do later age groups marry later because they are more likely to have jobs, or more likely to have higher qualifications – or is it just something that results from when they were born?

Some technical issues

There are a number of technical issues that need to be addressed in the analysis. The key feature of our data is that they concern life and work events. We use a number of items of information about each woman who had not (yet) had a baby or separated from a partner to predict the probability of her doing so in any particular month. Each woman is therefore considered to be 'at risk' of lone parenthood during each month. One difficulty with this approach, however, is that we do not have information on completed spells; there is a problem of 'censorship' where people are at risk of an event, but this has not occurred before the date of interview. The range of techniques known as event history analysis make the best use of this type of data.

Another important feature of the quantitative analysis is that it employs both 'fixed' and 'time-varying' variables. Fixed variables stay constant over time and include the woman's ethnic background and the occupation of her father when she was 14; but most other variables would not have remained constant throughout her life – clearly her age would change over time and so would her living arrangements and her economic activity. Our modelling therefore includes a range of time-varying variables so that we can assess the impact of different factors at the point when the woman was 'at risk' of lone parenthood. The inclusion of such variables adds to the complexity of the modelling and it is fairly rare to see so many time-varying variables in modelling of this kind.

One of the additional issues about using time-varying models is that we need to decide the exact point when a woman is 'at risk'. In our model, the crucial point for single women who became lone mothers was nine months prior to the birth of their baby. So we know the details of their situation at the approximate time of conception. It could be argued, however, that the crucial point is some time during the pregnancy when the woman might be making decisions about abortion and/or marriage, but then it would be difficult to know which month to take for analysis – the second? the third? the fourth?

Further details of the analysis are given in each chapter where relevant and the reader should also consult other texts for further information (see, for example, Allison, 1984; Dex, 1991).

Appendix 2

The Social Change and Economic Life Initiative dataset

The data being analysed in this book are from the Social Change and Economic Life Initiative. This is a unique dataset. A key feature is that questions were asked about all major events in a person's life. These included dates of marriage, having children, and changes of living arrangements. As a result, the data can be used to analyse flows into and out of different family types, including lone parenthood. The study was based in six areas, defined by Travel-To-Work Areas.[16] This means that information about the local labour market can be included in the analysis; in other words, to consider what effect the state of the labour market might have on the decision to have children, get married, or split from a partner. This has been identified as the key factor in American academic work. The survey also collected information about employment and jobs, enabling the effect of individual job status on family formation decisions to be examined.

The survey interviewed a total of 6,110 people, as shown in Table A2.1. At the time of interview, all were between 20 and 60 years of age. More women than men were included in the study (56 per cent were women), and the average age was around 38 years.

Table A2.1 Basic details about the survey

	Number	Percentage	Average age
Men	2,696	44.1	37.9 years
Women	3,414	55.9	38.3 years
Total	6,110	100	38.1 years

The analysis in this book will look only at the women in the dataset: women form at least 90 per cent of lone parents at any given time. All the sample were born between 1926 and 1966; the largest groups are those born in the 1940s and the 1950s. These cohorts would have participated in the rising labour force participation rates of women.

The main disadvantage of this dataset, and this is an important limitation, is its age. The data are now almost 10 years old, although reports based on it have only starting appearing in the last few years. This is a strong limitation on what can be said about the recent increase in single women having children. It is less of an issue in looking at the longer-term increase in divorce and separation that has been documented.

Appendix 3

Qualitative fieldwork

THE SAMPLE

We aimed to interview women in a number of different categories, including: single and separated lone mothers; and recent, long-term and former lone mothers.

By *single*, we meant women who had become lone parents by having their first baby while single. By *separated*, we meant women who had become lone parents by separating from a partner with whom they had been living with a child(ren).

By *recent*, we meant women who had been lone parents for less than a year (or less than two years if we are being generous). By *long-term*, we meant women who had been lone parents for more than two years. By *former*, we meant women who had been lone parents in the past but had become part of a couple in the last two years.

There was no overall sampling frame of names and addresses which we could use for this study and so we had to use a variety of methods to find the interviewees we needed. Fieldwork took place in the Midlands, London and the South West.

In the Midlands and London, we did have some names and addresses of women who had been lone parents in November 1994 as they had all been interviewed as part of a quantitative survey carried out by PSI (and published as Marsh and others, 1997). Some of these women were still lone mothers (that is long-term lone mothers) at the time of our fieldwork in the spring of 1996. Some were now with a partner (former lone mothers). We also knew from the PSI survey whether they were single lone mothers or separated lone mothers. A sample of these women were sent out letters from PSI to explain the study and to allow them to opt out at an early stage. We managed to find most of our long-term and former lone mothers from this sample.

In the South West, we had no names and addresses and so had to concentrate on finding more recent lone mothers. We got in touch with the National Council for One Parent Families who gave us access to their database of childcare groups but, unfortunately, this did not prove a very successful way of finding lone mothers. We also wrote to local childcare groups in the Midlands and South West to enlist cooperation but, again, few interviewees were forthcoming from this source. The main way of finding recent lone mothers was through more direct methods of contact. Interviewers went along to childcare groups, lone parent support groups and knocked on doors to find recent lone parents for interview. They then used snowballing techniques to increase the sample. But we allowed only one extra lone mother to be recruited per interviewee, otherwise we might have found that the situations of friends/acquaintances would be fairly similar.

FIELDWORK

Pilot interviews were carried out towards the end of April. The interviewers were then personally briefed on 30 April 1996 and fieldwork took place throughout May and June 1996. Respondents were interviewed in their own homes and paid a £10 payment as a thank you for their time.

All interviews were tape-recorded and other information was taken down in note form, for example, the arrival and departure of other people from the room, the demeanour and body language of the informant and his or her emotional reactions to the questions.

The following number of interviews were achieved in each of the relevant categories:

	Single	Separated	All
Recent	6	6	12
Long-term	9	7	16
Former	7	9	16
All	22	22	44

THE TOPIC GUIDE

The topic guide was in various sections and had been revised following initial piloting. It was fairly detailed and structured but less so than it was before piloting. Interviewers were briefed not to let the structure of the topic guide constrain them too much. The main focus of the interview was the movement in and out of different family types and the extent to which this is affected by:

- attitudes of interviewee, 'partners', family, friends;
- economic situation of interviewee and 'partner';
- housing situation of interviewee and 'partner'.

The topic guide was divided into the following sections, but there is quite a lot of routing depending on which one of the six groups of lone parents was being interviewed. It worked as follows:

Background information
All interviewees

Becoming a single mother   *Becoming a separated mother*
All single lone mothers   All separated lone mothers

Life as a lone parent
All interviewees

Still a lone parent   *Leaving lone parenthood*
All recent and long-term lone mothers   All former lone mothers

Final question
All interviewees

Topic guide

- **Current situation**

- **Background**
  Family background
      Parents' ages, marital status/relationship, occupations
      Brothers/sisters – ages, marital status/relationships
  Education – age left school, qualifications
  Age left home
  Employment since left school

Ask all who are/were single mothers

BECOMING A SINGLE MOTHER

- **Situation before getting pregnant**
  Living arrangements – relationships with family
  Economic status – at school/in work/unemployed
      Source and level of income
  Happy/unhappy with situation
  Hopes/expectations for the future
      Jobs/relationships/children

- **Relationships with men**
  Number of boyfriends, if any and nature of relationships
      Type of people – age? In work/unemployed?
  Nature of relationship with baby's father
      Type of person – age? In work/unemployed?

- **Getting pregnant**
  Was this first experience of sex? – when was first experience?
      Previous pregnancies?

Attitudes to sex
Use/failure of contraception and reasons
  Planned/unplanned

- **Responses to pregnancy**
  When found out
  How felt at first and then later
    Expectations about the future
  Feelings/attitudes of baby's father/family/friends
    Level of support from others

- **Possibility of getting together with the father**
  Father's response to news about pregnancy
  Was possibility of getting together discussed?
    Attitudes of interviewee's parents/his parents

- **Possibility of abortion/adoption (discuss each separately)**
  How far and in what way were these considered – why/why not?
  Level of knowledge about abortion/adoption
  Advice from others – sought/offered/used
  Attitudes of others (even if didn't give advice)
  Pros and cons of each possibility
  Feelings about decision made
    How much personal 'choice'?

- **Being pregnant**
  Coming to terms with becoming a mother
  Level of support from others
  Expectations of life after baby born
    Living arrangements/level and source of income

- **The period immediately after the birth**
  Feelings
    Interviewee/family/baby's father/friends
  Living arrangements
  Financial support – level and source of income
    How managed financially
  Coping with a baby/young child

- **Views about becoming a lone parent (with hindsight)**
  Would respondent have done anything differently?
  Advice to other young girls in similar situations?

How acceptable/unacceptable is it nowadays to have a baby while single?

What do other people think about this?

Would it have been different in the old days – when respondent's mother was young?

How would respondent have acted in the old days? How would others have acted?

Ask all who are/were separated mothers

BECOMING A SEPARATED MOTHER

- **Beginning and development of relationship with ex-partner**
  Date relationship began
  Situation of interviewee and ex-partner at that time
  (living arrangements and economic activity)
  Nature of relationship
    How quickly did it develop?
  Deciding to live together
    When/how/why was this decision made?
    Attitude of interviewee and partner
    Consideration of pros and cons/hopes and fears
  Changes in economic situation – sharing of finances?
  Attitude/discussion of marriage?
  If decided to marry: When and why? Change surname?
  If decided not to marry: Why not?
  Changes in nature of the relationship

- **Life with a partner and children**
  Amount of time spent with partner
  Nature of the relationship – similar roles or breadwinner/housewife?
    Living arrangements, level of commitment
    Sharing finances, sharing responsibility for children
  Arrival of children – when? (before marriage or living together?)
    Degree of planning
    Reaction of interviewee and partner
    Effect on relationship
    Father's involvement in childcare

Changes in living arrangements and economic situation
Likes/dislikes about relationship/partner

- **Events leading up to separation**
  Instantaneous or gradual?
    Early signs?
    Stages of separation
  Sources of conflict – superficial and underlying
  Attempts to resolve conflict

- **The decision to separate**
  Time when first thought about separation
  Taking the decision
  Joint or one-sided decision – partner's views/feelings
  Involvement/attitudes of family/friends
    Other experiences of separation (eg parents)
  Weighing up the pros and cons of separation
  Feelings about the decision to separate
  Age of children – concern about children
  Summarise the reasons for separation/relationship breakdown
    Underlying reasons?

- **Expectations about separation**
  Preparing and planning for separation – practical arrangements
  Hopes/fears about separating
  Expectations of living arrangements/employment/level and source
  of income

- **Immediately after the separation**
  Changes in living and financial arrangements (surname)
    How managed financially
  Feelings about separation/partner's feelings
  Reactions of the children
  Reactions/support from others

- **(If married) Consideration of divorce**
  Attitudes to divorce at time of separation and now
    Why divorce/why not?
  Knowledge of divorce law prior to separation
  Experience of divorce
    Explore the process at each stage
  Change surname?

- **Views about becoming a lone parent (with hindsight)**
  Advice to someone in same situation before separation
  How acceptable/unacceptable is it nowadays to separate/ divorce?
      What do other people think about this?
  Would it have been different in the old days – when respondent's
  mother was young?
      How would respondent have acted in the old days? How would
  others have acted?

Ask all

LIFE AS A LONE PARENT

- **Changes in income and employment**
  Employment/education/training since becoming a lone parent
  Source and level of income – how managing?
  Attitude to employment/training
  Barriers to employment/training

- **Changes in relationships with child's father and other people**
  Support from child's father/family/friends
      Moral support
      Practical support with looking after the baby/children
      Financial support
  Attitudes of people to lone parenthood in general
      Family/friends/general public

- **Child's/children's experiences**
  How has it been for the children?
      Contact with/absence of father

- **Comparison of life as a lone parent**
  – with previous expectations
  – with life previous to lone parenthood
      Changes for the better and changes for the worse
  – with what life might be like now if not a lone parent
      Employment/living arrangements/income

- **Likes and dislikes about being a lone parent**
  How happy/unhappy overall – why?
  Pros and cons of being a lone parent

Ask all recent and long-term lone parents

STILL A LONE PARENT

- **Personal relationships with men after becoming a lone parent**
  Relationship with child's/children's father
  > Does he have a girlfriend/wife?
  > Chances of getting (back) together?

  Number, nature, development, duration of other relationships
  > Personal and economic characteristics of the men
  > Likes/dislikes about these people

  Reason why relationships ended/didn't progress to cohabitation
  If none: Why not? Lack of time/energy/suitable men/prefer women/solitude
  > *Probe fully*

- **Attitudes to relationships/men**
  Do you need/want a man in your life? What for?
  Describe the ideal relationship for you
  > Living arrangements, level of commitment
  > Sharing finances/sharing responsibility for children?
  > Similar roles or breadwinner/housewife?

  Would interviewee like a 'partner'? Why/Why not?
  Describe the ideal partner for you
  > Personal and economic characteristics – looking for a breadwinner?
  > *If ideal partner is male:* How far do men around here fit this description?

  How far would interviewee compromise?
  How would things be different next time?
  Attitudes of prospective partners to interviewee as a lone parent

- **Why still a lone parent?**
  Positive choice/prefer women/independence
  Lack of opportunity/energy/time/suitable men
  Under what circumstances would interviewee get together with a male partner?
  How might children react to a new father figure?
  Do women generally these days need a man in their lives?
  What for?

- **Hopes and expectations about the future**
  Relationships
  Income/employment/training
  Children

Ask all former lone mothers

BECOMING PART OF A COUPLE AGAIN

- **Personal relationships (with men) after becoming a lone parent**
  Number, nature, development, duration
    Personal and economic characteristics of the men (women)
    Likes/dislikes about these people
  Reason why some relationships ended/didn't progress to cohabitation

- **Relationship with new partner**
  Date when relationship began
  Situation of interviewee and new partner at that time
    Living arrangements and education/work/unemployed
  How relationship developed
  When/how/why decided to live together
    Attitude of interviewee and partner
    Consideration of pros and cons/hopes and fears
    Was money a factor – need a breadwinner?
    Thoughts about the children
  When did start living together
    Immediate or gradual (eg staying over some nights)
  Attitude of others (family/friends/children)
  Attitudes/decision to marry?
  If decided to marry: When and why?
  If decided not to marry: Why not?

- **Life with a partner and children**
  Nature of the relationship – (different from previous relationship/s?)
    Living arrangements, level of commitment
    Sharing finances, sharing responsibility for children
    Similar roles or breadwinner/housewife?
  Arrival of any more children – when? degree of planning

Reaction of interviewee and partner
Effect on relationship
Father's involvement in childcare
Likes/dislikes about relationship/partner
Do women generally these days need a man in their lives?

- **Hopes/expectations about the future**
Relationships/employment/training/children

FINAL QUESTION

Q The interview has covered many issues about what it is like to be a lone parent in the 1990s. Would you like to add anything else?

Thank respondent

Give £10 postal order

Give information about the study with your name on it

Notes

CHAPTER 1

1 See reports from the General Household Survey for definitions of household and family.
2 Walker (1994) discusses this point in relation to measures of poverty.
3 These were Aberdeen, Coventry, Kirkcaldy, Northampton, Rochdale and Swindon.
4 All names used in the report are pseudonyms.

CHAPTER 2

5 Median age was used because the mean would be lowered if respondents who had not (yet) had sex were included. The median was unaffected by such bias.
6 About 10 per cent of women born in the 1940s did not have children and about 20 per cent of those born in the 1960s will probably not have children.
7 SCELI recorded only cohabitations lasting around a year. Since we are really interested in cases where the mother lived with the father of her child, the loss of shorter-term cohabitations is probably not too serious.
8 Only two women became single mothers after the age of 30, and that age has been assumed to be the end of the period at risk for the remainder of the analysis. The number of events analysed therefore falls to 223.
9 The unemployment data relate to the place where the woman was eventually interviewed – up to 15 years after the date under analysis. Some of the women will have moved from other areas, and the unemployment data are not a reliable indicator of economic conditions in the previous location. For periods to 1970, the national unemployment rate was used.

CHAPTER 3

10 The survey did not collect data directly indicative of the date of conception. The category consists of couples whose babay was born less than nine months after the wedding. Nor do we know whether the marriage was a response to the pregnancy or whether the pregnancy occurred after they had agreed to marry.

11 For example, the average age at which the respondent had married was 20.6 if her father had been in a semi-or unskilled manual occupation; 22.3 if he had been in a professional occupation.

12 As reported by the mother. Those partners who had separated from the respondent were not, of coursel available to report their own situation.

CHAPTER 4

13 The survey did not distinguish clearly between the date of separation and the date of a subsequent divorce. This means that for women who went through both stages, we cannot be certain when the period of lone parenthood started. To the extent that some women dated the start from their divorce, the survey will understate the true duration of the period she spent on her own.

14 The median duration is calculated on the assumption that the average monthly exit rate continues unchanged until half the sample have left (the Markov assumption). For this calculation only, children growing up are counted as one form of exit.

15 All this analysis is confined to women over the age of 16.

APPENDIX 2

16 These were: Aberdeen, Coventry, Kirkcaldy, Northampton, Rochdale and Swindon.

References

Allison, P (1984) *Event History Analysis: regression for longitudinal event data.* Beverly Hills, California: Sage Publications

Bartholomew, R, Hibbet, A and Sidaway, J (1992) Lone parents and the labour market: evidence from the Labour Force Survey *Employment Gazette.* London: Employment Department, November

Bennett, N, Blanc, A and Bloom, D (1988) Commitment and the Modern Union: assessing the link between premarital cohabitation and subsequent marital stability, *American Sociological Review*, 53, 127–138

Berthoud, R and Ford, R (1996) *Relative Needs: variations in the living standards of different types of households.* London: PSI

Blake, J and DasGupta, P (1975) Reproductive motivation versus contraceptive technology: is recent American experience an exception? *Population and Development Review*, 1, 229–249

Bradshaw, J (1989) *Lone Parents: policy in the doldrums.* London: Family Policy Studies Centre

Bradshaw, J and Millar, J (1991) *Lone Parent Families in the UK.* Department of Social Security Research Report No. 6, London: HMSO,

Bradshaw, J, Stimson, C, Williams, J and Skinner, C (1997) *Non-resident Fathers in Britain.* Paper to the ESRC Programme on Population and Household Change Seminar

Brannen, J (ed) (1992) *Mixing Methods: qualitative and quantitative research.* Aldershot: Avebury

Brown, J (1988) *In Search of a Policy.* London: National Council for One Parent Families

Bryson, A, Ford, R and White, M (1997) *Making Work Pay: lone parents, employment and well-being.* York: JRF

Burghes, L (1994) *Lone Parenthood and Family Disruption: the outcomes for children.* London: Family Policy Studies Centre

Burgoyne, J and Clark, D (1984) *Making a Go of It: a study of step-families in Sheffield.* London: Routledge and Kegan Paul

Burgoyne, J, Ormrod, R and Richards, M (1987) *Divorce Matters.* Harmondsworth: Pelican Books

Central Statistical Office (1996) *Social Trends,* 26. London: HMSO

Cherlin, A (1992) *Marriage, Divorce, Remarriage.* Cambridge MA: Harvard University Press

Child Poverty Action Group (1997) Child Support Handbook. London: CPAG

Cockett, M and Tripp, J (1994) *The Exeter Family Study: family breakdown and its impact on children.* Exeter: University of Exeter Press

Crow, G and Hardey, M (1992) Diversity and ambiguity among lone parent households in modern Britain, in C Marsh and S Arber, *Families and Households: Divisions and Change.* British Sociological Association. London: Macmillan

Dex, S (1991) *Life and Work History Analyses.* London: Routledge

Dormor, D (1992) *The Relationship Revolution: cohabitation, marriage and divorce in contemporary Europe.* London: One plus One

Ebaugh, H (1988) *Becoming an Ex: the process of role exit.* Chicago: University of Chicago Press

Ermisch, J (1983) *The Political Economy of Demographic Change.* London: PSI

Ermisch, J (1991) *Lone Parenthood: an economic analysis.* Cambridge: Cambridge University Press.

Ermisch, J (1995) *Pre-marital Cohabitation, Childbearing and the Creation of One Parent Families.* Colchester: University of Essex

Ermisch, J and Wright R (1993) *The Economic Environment and Entry to Single Parenthood in Great Britain.* Discussion Papers in Economics No. 9305. Glasgow: University of Glasgow

Finer, M (1974) *Report of the Committee on One-Parent Families.* Cmnd 5629. London: HMSO

Ford, R (1996) *Childcare in the Balance: how lone parents make decisions about work.* London: PSI

Ford, R, Marsh, A and McKay, S (1995) *Changes in Lone Parenthood.* London: HMSO

Ford, R, Marsh, A and Finlayson, L (1998 forthcoming) *What Happens to Lone Parents?* London: PSI

Furstenberg, F (1976) *Unplanned Parenthood: the social consequences of teenage childbearing.* New York: The Free Press

Garfinkel, I and McLanahan, S (1986) *Single Mothers and Their Children: a new American dilemma.* Washington DC: The Urban Institute Press

George, V (1975) Why one-parent families remain poor *Poverty,* 31, 6–12

Gillis, J (1985) *For Better, for Worse: British marriages, 1600 to the present.* Oxford: Oxford University Press

Guttentag, M and Secord, P (1983) *Too Many Women? the sex ratio question.* Beverly Hills CA: Sage Publications

Hart, N (1976) When Marriage Ends: a study in status passage. London: Tavistock Publications

Haskey, J (1987) Social class differentials in remarriage after divorce: results from a forward linkage study *Population Trends,* 47, Spring, 34–42

Haskey, J (1994) Estimated numbers of one-parent families and their prevalence in Great Britain in 1991 *Population Trends*, 78, Winter, 5–19

Hoynes, H (1996) *Work, Welfare and Family Structure: a review of the evidence.* Institute for Research on Poverty Discussion Paper, No 1, University of Wisconsin, Madison, 103–196

Illsley, R and Gill, D (1968) Changing trends in illegitimacy *Social Science and Medicine*, 2, 415–433

Kiernan, K (1989) The family: formation and fusion, in H Joshi, (ed) *The Changing Population of Britain*. Oxford: Blackwell

Kiernan, K (1992) Men and women at work and at home, in R Jowell, L Brook, G Prior and B Taylor, *British Social Attitudes: the 9th report*. London: SCPR

Kiernan, K and Estaugh, V (1993) *Cohabitation: extra-marital childbearing and social policy*. London: FPSC

Lampard, R (1993) An examination of the relationship between marital dissolution and unemployment, in D Gallie, C Marsh and C Vogler, *Social Change and the Experience of Unemployment*. Oxford: Oxford University Press

Lawson, A (1988) *Adultery: an analysis of love and betrayal*. New York: Basic Books

Leibenstein, H (1974) An interpretation of the economic theory of fertility: promising path or blind alley *Journal of Economic Literature*, 457–479

Macintyre, S (1977) *Single and Pregnant*. London: Croom Helm

McKay, S and Marsh, A (1994) *Lone Parents and Work*. London: HMSO

McKendrick, J (1995) *Lone Parenthood in Strathclyde Region: implications for housing policy*. Spatial policy analysis working paper 30, School of Geography, University of Manchester

McRae, S (1993) *Cohabiting Mothers: changing marriage and motherhood?* London: PSI

McRae, S (1998 forthcoming) *Changing Families*. Oxford: Oxford University Press

Marsden, D (1969) *Mothers Alone: poverty and the fatherless family*. Harmondsworth: Allen Lane, Penguin Press

Marsh, A, Ford, R and Finlayson, L (1997) *Lone Parents, Work and Benefits*. London: PSI

Marsh, A and McKay, S (1993) *Families, Work and Benefits*. London: PSI

Martin, T and Bumpass, L (1989) Recent trends in marital disruption *Demography*, 26, 37–51

Millar, J (1984) *Poor Mothers and Absent Fathers: support for lone parents in comparative perspective*. Paper presented to the Annual Conference of the Social Policy Association, London

Millar, J (1987) Lone mothers, in C Glendinning and J Millar (eds) *Women and Poverty in Britain*. Hemel Hempstead: Harvester Wheatsheaf, 159–177

Millar, J (1989) *Poverty and the Lone Parent Family: the challenge to policy*. Aldershot: Avebury

Millar, J (1997) Family Policy, in P Alcock and others (eds) *Students' Companion to Social Policy.* London: Blackwell/Social Policy Association

Modood, T, Berthoud, R, Lakey, Nazroo, J, Smith, P, Virdee, S and Beishon, S (1997) *Ethnic Minorities in Britain: diversity and disadvantage.* London: PSI

Morgan, S. Lye, D and Condran, G (1988) Sons, daughters, and the risk of marital disruption *American Journal of Sociology,* 90, 1055–1077

Mors-Rains, P (1971) *Becoming an Unwed Mother.* Chicago: Aldine Atherton

Murphy, M (1995) Are cohabiting unions more likely to break down than marriages? *Changing Britain: the official newsletter for the ESRC Population and Household Change Research Programme,* Issue Two, April

OPCS (1996) *Living in Britain.* London: HMSO

Price, S and McKenry, P (1988) *Divorce.* London: Sage Publications

Ratcliffe, P (ed) (1996) Ethnicity in the Census, in *Social Geography and Ethnicity in Britain.* London: The Stationery Office

Renvoize, J (1985) *Going Solo: single mothers by choice.* London: Routledge and Kegan Paul

Scott, J, Braun, M and Alwin, D (1993) The family way, in R Jowell, L Brook and L Dowds (eds) *International Social Attitudes: the 10th BSA report.* London: SCPR

Seccombe, K and Lee, G (1987) Female status, wives' autonomy and divorce: a cross-cultural study *Family Perspective,* 20, 241–249

Smith, R (1981) Fertility, economy and household formation in England over three centuries *Population and Development Review,* 7, No 4

Straus, M and Gelles, R (1986) Societal change and change in family violence from 1975 to 1985 as revealed by two national surveys *Journal of Marriage and the Family,* 48, 465–479

Straus, M, Gelles, S and Steinmetz, S (1981) *Behind Closed Doors: violence in the American family.* New York: Anchor Books

Thompson, B (1956) Social study of illegitimate maternities British *Journal of Preventive and Social Medicine,* 10, 75–87

Thornton, A (1985) Changing attitudes towards separation and divorce: causes and consequences *American Journal of Sociology,* 90, 856–872

Vincent, C (1954) The unwed mother and sampling bias *American Sociological Review,* 19, 5, 562–567

Walker, R (1994) *Poverty Dynamics: issues and examples.* Aldershot: Avebury

Wall, R, Robin, J and Laslett, P (eds) (1983) *Family Forms in Historic Europe.* Cambridge: Cambridge University Press

Weir, S (1970) *A Study of Unmarried Mothers and their Children.* Scottish Health Service Studies, No 13. Edinburgh: SHHD

Wellings, K, Field, J and Wadsworth, J (1994) *Sexual Behaviour in Britain: the national survey of sexual attitudes and lifestyle.* Harmondsworth: Penguin Books

White, L (1990) Determinants of divorce: a review of research in the eighties *Journal of Marriage and the Family,* 52, 904–912

Whiteford, P and Bradshaw, J (1994) Benefits and incentives for lone parents: a comparative analysis *International Social Security Review.* ISSA

Wilson, W (1994) *Lone Parents and Housing.* House of Commons Research Paper 94/11. London: House of Commons Library

Wright, G and Stetson, D (1978) The impact of no-fault divorce law reform on divorce in American states *Journal of Marriage and the Family*, 40, 575–580

Yelloly, M (1965) Factors relating to adoption decisions by the mothers of illegitimate children *Sociological Review,* 13, 1, 5–13